Titanic Town

Mary Costello was born in West Belfast in 1955 into a Catholic, working-class family. She grew up in Andersonstown, an IRA stronghold, and experienced at first hand the outbreak of the Troubles. She now lives in Australia. *Titanic Town* is her first novel.

MARY COSTELLO

Titanic Town

A Novel

Methuen

A Methuen Paperback

First published in the United Kingdom
by Methuen London 1992

This edition published in the United Kingdom in 1998 by
Methuen Publishing Limited
20 Vauxhall Bridge Road, London SW1V 2SA

Random House Australia (Pty) Limited
20 Alfred Street, Milsons Point, Sydney,
New South Wales 2061, Australia

Random House New Zealand Limited
18 Poland Road, Glenfield, Auckland 10, New Zealand

Random House South Africa (Pty) Limited
Endulini, 5a Jubilee Road, Parktown 2193, South Africa

1 3 5 7 9 10 8 6 4 2

First published in paperback
in the United Kingdom by Mandarin 1993

Copyright © Mary Costello 1992, 1998

The right of the author to be identified as the author
of this work has been asserted by her in accordance
with the Copyright, Designs and Patents Act, 1988

Methuen Publishing Limited Reg. No. 3543167

A CIP catalogue record for this book
is available from the British Library

ISBN 0 413 77210 1

Printed and bound in Great Britain by
Cox & Wyman Ltd, Reading, Berkshire

Papers used by Methuen Publishing Limited
are natural, recyclable products made from wood grown in
sustainable forests. The manufacturing processes conform to
the environmental regulations of the country of origin

Contents

Author's Note

The incidents depicted in *Titanic Town* are based on events which took place in Belfast in the sixties and seventies, when the extraordinary was commonplace and the bizarre was the norm. Along with thousands of my fellow citizens I was witness to the absurd as well as the despicable and this account is drawn partly from memory and partly from imagination.

I don't pretend that *Titanic Town* contains all the facts of my life and times, but Annie McPhelimy is certainly part of me. The people in the book are not intended to be portraits of people I used to know and watch. Certain traits and quirks and bletherings have indeed been borrowed from family, friends and enemies, but the story imposed its own form on character, events and circumstances, and shaped out the truth and untruths, misunderstandings, myths and rumours which, in Belfast, ferment into history. This dismembrance of things past accommodates the natural and necessary exaggeration attendant upon the recounting of any Irish story, and seems to me to be a creative way of dealing with the trials of a youth troubled by the Troubles. But the spirit of the book is true, the tone authentic. *Titanic Town* is a tribute to the people of Belfast – on both sides of the Peace Line.

P.S. Needless to say, names have been changed to protect the guilty, as well as the innocent.

The Valium Talking

For years we slept with only a withered mattress between us and the floor. It was not an orthopaedic thing, posture was not a consideration. Father had dismantled the beds as a security measure, in case we'd get a bullet through the window. Maybe people all over Belfast were sleeping on mattresses in the early seventies, I wouldn't know, but none of our friends were. It's not that we were a particularly fearful family, but we were extreme in our outlook, and we lived in Bunbeg Gardens where bullets had, from time to time, perforated windows. During the course of Irish history such occurrences had not infrequently proved fatal.

Once, in the middle of a nocturnal riot, a non-directional, random brick came through glass. Grim panic.

'Aw Jaysus no!' Unholy yells from my brother Thomas; 'Christ! look what the bastards have done!'

There was a thunderous stampede within the parental chamber. Havoc-ridden bodies burst out on to the landing.

'Oh holy Jesus Christ!' Mother shrieks, routinely, knickers clipped to the head to keep the perm under control. Father stumbles behind her, one leg struggling into his trousers. He flourishes a sword of Toledo steel in his right hand, a souvenir of my trip to the ancient Spanish capital. El Cid McPhelimy. *Excalibur Na H'Eireann*.

'Oh Christ Jesus, son,' Mother is now screaming. 'Is Brendan shot?' It's the Valium talking.

'No,' an impatient response from Thomas, contemptuously dismissing the younger brother who still sleeps fatly under a shower of glass shards.

'He's all right.' Thomas emerges from the boxroom, finger holes for ease of scratching worn into the sagging crotch of his pyjama bottoms. He is waving his Spanish guitar in one hand, slightly damaged, and in the other the culprit brick: 'But look what the bastards have done to my G-string!'

'Oh thank God and His Holy Mother!' Grateful, motherly ejaculation. The Valium talking.

If Thomas or Brendan were late in coming home from school Mother would ring the Incident Centre to see if they'd been shot or arrested. She knew that I would have more sense. But she suspected, and quite rightly, that I spent many nights sitting up at the window, wrapped in the patchwork quilt that was Granny's wedding present, watching the local battalion on urban manoeuvres – the Belfast Brigade – or the British soldiers on foot patrol, the frequent riots, the women battering the bin-lids to let the 'boys' know that the soldiers were on the estate.

I held nightly vigils, while the news that would be misreported in the media the following day happened under the window, or over the road.

'Annie, are you out of bed?' Mother would yell up the stairs. A quiet, practised scuffle across the room. The creep in the dark.

'No, I'm almost asleep. Why?' Effective use of the simulated drowsy slur.

'There's shooting outside, stay away from the window.'

'OK. Ni-night.'

'Ni-night, love.'

I lie still for a good thirty seconds and then, with elaborate care, slip from under the forty blankets, and in less than four slow steps I'm on the other bed, lowering my weight gently, silently, between the window and Sinead's feet. She never moves, except to grind her teeth. A sound sleeper.

I pull back the curtain and rub the mist off the window. There's a soldier in the garden, a Gordon Highlander – I can see his pom-pom – lying on his stomach behind the shallow concrete wall. Stupid cow. The street-lamp is directly overhead, one of the few in the street not shot out by the boys, for safety's sake. A rifle cracks in the dark. The soldier raises his head and looks around. Someone in Murray's garden next door snaps an order at him. His head goes down. It's starting to rain. The boys will go in now. Let the Brits lie out in it and get saturated. A man's army. It's spoiled the garden, all this running in and out through it with guns and army-issue boots. There's only the young flowering cherry left in the middle, its spindly, bald branches tied down with cords. To make it droop.

Once, just after we'd moved to Bunbeg, Aunt Kay's husband Jack arrived with armfuls of marigolds. He didn't call at the house first. We just looked out of the window when we heard the thuds, and there he was, stamping the marigolds into the soft earth around the cherry tree with his big boots.

'They'll make a magnificent display this spring coming,' he swore. Not one of them came up.

'They say marigolds will only grow where blood has been spilt,' my father, ever anecdotal, mentioned at the time.

Now they would thrive.

Violence alone enlivened my girlhood, for I was allowed out only to go to school and mass. But from my bedroom window, under a ceiling black with night and creeping mould I could see the goings-on. The boys and the Brits, and the RUC. The dim, indistinguishable figures crawling damply through the neglected gardens, or running in cautious relays across the roads. And the sky above all of it, clear and brittle with stars, though more often clouded and changeful, fitfully illuminated by a dangerous moon. The moon could be a killer: a black balaclava an essential accessory. The black balaclavas of the IRA. The charge of the armalite brigade.

The army began to use helicopters with searchlights. Powerful. They would light up my room like broad daylight as I crouched below the window, not wishing to be mistaken for a sniper. One night a helicopter tracked a sniper all over the street. He ran up our path and took cover in the porch. The helicopter moved in and hovered just above the glory hole. We were all standing half-dressed on the landing, Mother feeling particularly nervous as Father was in hospital with his detached retina at the time. We heard the sniper fire up at the helicopter.

'It's only an oul' Ml carbine,' sneered Brendan.

'Might as well be farting into a cannon,' Thomas agreed.

The soldiers returned fire from the helicopter. The bullets could be heard zinging off the concrete path.

'Should we let him in?' Thomas wondered.

'Jesus no! You'll all be lifted.' Mother was getting angry. She was halfway down the stairs, her dressing gown tripping her. Her dressing gowns were always too long. She insisted she was five feet tall, but we didn't believe it. She was smaller than all her children by this time, and we called her the wee woman.

'Mammy, for Christ's sake wise up, you'll get shot.'

'I don't care. I'm not having them shooting at this house.'

She had opened the front door. The helicopter had gone for the moment; it was circling the block. The sniper was no longer on the porch, he was crouching in the shadow of the gable further up the path. He would have been about seventeen, skinny, with long ginger hair parted like a curtain in the middle. It was a wonder he could see through it to shoot at all. The four of us followed Mother out onto the little porch and stood in a bunch looking up the path. The helicopter sounded farther away now. The ginger sniper looked at us, disconcerted.

'Get in, missus,' he said, not unpolitely, 'you'll get hurt.'

Mother bristled belligerently. 'If I do it'll be your fault.

What the hell do you think you're doing shooting from this house? You'll get us all killed. Now get the hell off this path and go and shoot at your own door.'

'You haven't a hope in hell of hitting a helicopter with that,' added Thomas.

The sniper paused, undecided, then determined to take a hard line. 'Get the fuck inside, missus, or I'll blow your fucking head off.' He had spoken with conviction, but now watched uncertainly as Mother edged out the lower lip and really lost the temper.

'The insignificant wee bastard!' she yelled with unaccustomed profanity.

Her two fine sons, helpless with laughter, were restraining her for her own protection. But she broke away and charged up the path, her dressing gown flapping candlewick, the pink knickers bobbing on her head. The sniper rose, somewhat shakily, and half raised the gun. Mother made to lay hands . . . He backed away.

'Don't make me shoot, missus.'

'You get off this bloody path now or I'll shove that fucking gun up your arse,' she yelled, now entirely out of control. She had always been bad with her nerves.

The sniper turned and edged down the path.

'Over the gate on your right, through the garden and you'll be in Carnan Gardens.' Thomas gave helpful directions.

The sniper leapt over the gate and disappeared behind the coal-hole. We had taken the Mother in hand and now led her forcibly back into the house. She took two more Doriden and four more Valium, but they were no use to her. She sat up all night reading *The Walk of a Queen*, by Annie M. P. Smithson.

I never learned to fall asleep easily. I blame my granny, Maryanne Mohan. She shared a room with Thomas and me until she died. When I was almost five my mother told me

I was a girl and moved me out of my brother's bed. The matter came up one day when I went with my mother to collect Thomas from St Comgall's Primary. I was admiring his teacher, Mrs Minogue, his first crush. He said she had big muscles on her chest.

'Will she be my teacher too?' I asked.

'But you'll not be going to this school,' responded Mother, 'you're a girl. You'll be going to St Vincent's down the road.'

I was disappointed, I felt cheated. For what seemed like a long time I had wanted to go to St Comgall's and have a school bag that smelled good, and play games with the priests in long black dresses, and climb the see-through stairs. But I didn't seek a clearer explanation. I was used to being different from Thomas: he was five and I was four, he was big and I was small, he wore trousers and I wore skirts, he was obedient and I was bold, he had big blue eyes – frog eyes – and I had a red nose. So why shouldn't he be a boy and I a girl?

So I moved in with Granny. She had begun to dote at that stage and didn't concern herself with the proper distinction between night and day. We used to lie awake well after Thomas had gone to sleep – he was such a biddable child – and she would tell me about her girlhood in Crossmaglen, Murder Triangle, in the county Armagh.

'From Carrickmacross to Crossmaglen, where there are more rogues than honest men,' she would recite, chortling in her mildly deranged way. 'Don't be kicking my shins.'

'What's shins?'

'And did you treat your Maryanne to dulse and yellow-man, at the oul' Lammas Fair in Ballycastle O!' Sometimes she would sing for me all night.

Her parents left her with her Uncle Peter and went off to Belfast to find work. That was in 1885 and she was three years old at the time. But ancient, senile, and close to death she remembered it clearly. Under the blankets in the middle of the night she would whisper how she watched her mother and father load their few sticks of furniture and their other eight children onto a cart. She charged after them as they set off that morning, crying for them to take her too. She lay down in the dirt of the road as they disappeared from sight, and cried and sobbed, and couldn't be comforted.

And the old woman lying with her head on the pillow beside me could still cry at the thought of it. I would watch the slow tears falling across the deep lines of her face, trickling into the thinning grey hair. I must have been a ridiculously sentimental child, for I would get her to tell me all about it again and again.

'And was your Uncle Peter bad to you?' I would ask. I suppose I also had sadistic tendencies.

The uncle had lost an arm in the Canadian Mounties and so he came home lopsided, but with a good pension, and bought a farm. He was also the matchmaker for the district and young Maryanne would hear him striking deals between the local farmers as she lay in the bed above the kitchen. She was not keen to become the price of a field or a few cows.

We have no reason to believe that the uncle molested her sexually or any other way. Indeed she had all her orders and a servant to look after her. But at the age of sixteen she stole two of her uncle's chickens, sold them at the market and bought a train ticket to Belfast. When she made her final confession at the age of eighty five she was still telling the priest about the theft of the two chickens.

I did not follow her example of pure truthfulness as a child. From my first to my last confession I trembled on every occasion, while at the same time trying to vary the fortnightly catalogue of vice, presumably in an effort to entertain the priest. There were some sins I would not tell, although I was happy to admit to lying, fighting and general disobedience. I suppose I never had much to confess to. But then I could not have sinned more opulently, considering the tyrannical regime in power on the domestic front.

There was, however, one crime of innocence in my early youth.

I would have been almost three when my mother walked me up to Pud Logan's shop at the top of the street. She was pregnant with Brendan at the time and was trying to teach me the independent skills so essential to a child about to be usurped as the baby of the family. Logan's was an old-fashioned corner shop – cold meats, cheese, tins, bundles of sticks, sacks of potatoes and dolls' teasets all piled together on the counter, the floor and in the window. When she had bought Father's tea, a daily choosing ritual of holy moment, she said to Logan, 'Give her a pennyworth of sweets, Pud.'

He waved me down to the end of the counter where it seemed that the riches of Solomon had been spread at my small, deformed feet. For there, laid out on three low-set shelves, were boxes upon boxes of caramels, chews, gob-stoppers, fizzers, gum-boils, toffees, sherbert dabs, parma violets, squirrel's lips, acid drops and sweety lollies. The heavens had indeed opened and showered rich abundance upon me. I put out my hand and fixed my fingers around chews in red and white wrappers.

'Here,' said Logan, helping me to some more, 'four for a happenny.' And he filled my other hand with desirable objects bound in blue and yellow cellophane.

I toddled out behind my mother, unable to believe my luck. So this was where sweets came from; Pud Logan's shop. Now that I knew where they were I could get them whenever I liked. And so I did, three or four times that same morning. I would simply go into the shop and there would be no one around. Logan would be in the back. I was too small for him to see me over the half-door of his living room, and so I would walk up to the sweet shelves, take my time about choosing and leave with fistfuls of every-thing. After a couple of raids I began to wonder if I should be doing this. But that was mostly because I had already noticed that the enjoyment of any activity was directly proportionate to the level of prohibition surrounding that activity.

Logan caught me with a fistful of jujubes, trying to decide between a chocolate mouse and a toffee drumstick. He grabbed me by the wrists and squeezed, and the sweets went all over the floor. Then he trailed me outside by the arm and skelped my arse in front of the whole street. The hot humiliation of exposed knickers. I suppose he was making an example of me, which was grossly unfair considering my ignorance of commercial realities. The thing is I encountered sweets before I encountered money, and had no notion that the possession of one might depend upon the exchange of the other. Anyway, Logan was a mean oul' bastard, and I'm pleased to say went bald and died before his time.

But if my moral rectitude was in question my grasp of church dogma was tenacious. I knew I was an Irish Catholic and thus one of the new chosen people. The Jews stopped being 'chosen' apparently when they failed to become Catholics themselves and let the old Romans murder baby Jesus.

At the time we lived just round the corner from what was to become, comically enough, the Peace Line – a half-hearted and in places permeable Berlin Wall, thrown up in the seventies to prevent impoverished Protestants and oppressed and impoverished Catholics from knocking the shite out of each other.

One day I was coming along the street dressed in my new navy and royal blue school uniform, which sported the emblem of the miraculous medal on the tunic, the beret, and the blazer pocket. Fearing that this mere trinity of icons would prove inadequate to my protection in time of danger, my mother had sewn a lovely silver and blue enamelled medal onto the front of my tunic. This holy bauble now drew the attention of a rough-looking child who was playing not far from my front door. She marched up to me and took my medal in her dirty little Protestant paw. 'You're a Roman Catholic, aren't you?' she demanded – there was no use talking to Protestants, they have always insisted on calling us Roman Catholics – and she began twisting the medal round and round on its loops of navy blue thread.

She was my first Protestant, in the flesh. I didn't know how to react. I'd heard Protestants didn't like Our Lady. I sensed a vulgar hostility, but it may have been merely curiosity. I wondered if I should run over home. Certainly I was forbidden to hit people.

'You're far too ready with your hand, wee girl,' my mother would warn me, edging out the dreaded lower lip and slapping me across legs and arse – whichever was handy.

Still I sensed that the medal-twister wasn't one to be reasoned with. I glanced over the road and saw old chicken-faced Mrs Drain eyeing us from the watchtower of her front hall. She would stand there blocking the doorway until the day she died, mournful and scrawny in her printed apron and black suede bootees. She had noticed the sacrilege in progress. I wanted to do the right thing.

I chose the fairer portion; I grabbed at the medal, slapped away the child's grubby little hand, pushed her out of my road and charged away home.

'That's the girl,' said Mrs Drain approvingly; 'go on into your mammy now.'

My assailant was standing at the corner picking her nose. It was to be many years before I would meet and be manhandled by another Protestant.

2

The Glamour of Evil

For days my parents had been warning me not to go round to Cooper Street. It was just around the corner, off Lucknow Street. I didn't mind. Cooper Street was wide, dull and quiet, with no shops and no children. It didn't interest me. But the prohibition did. I cornered Mother when she was counting stitches.

'Why can I not go round to Cooper Street?'

'Forty-one, forty-two . . . get off the wool . . . because the Orangemen will be marching for the twelfth.'

'Orange men? Are they really orange?'

'No. They wear orange sashes. They're Protestants, but they think they're British. Now look, you've put me off my count. I'll have to start all over again.' She started again at the bottom of the knitting needle. But I couldn't let it drop at that.

'Why are they marching?'

She made a threatening face and went on counting. Father looked out from behind the *Irish News*.

'They're marching to commemorate the Battle of the Boyne – when King William defeated King James and the Catholics. Now leave your mother alone. Don't you see she's counting her stitches?'

'Who's King William?'

'He was a Dutchman – from a country called Holland. And he became the King of England. It was a long, long time ago, 1690.'

'How long ago is that?'

'Nearly three hundred years.'

'Before I was born?'

'Before even your mother was born.'

I gave up. It was beyond conception.

But that Saturday morning I was out in the yard at the toilet when I heard music. It seemed to upset Dan Mooney's pigeons perched on the back yard wall. It was loud and jaunty, a battering rhythm. I could hear the drum above the rest. It came from up the street. I would have to go and see. I reached up with difficulty to the big sink in the kitchen and washed my hands like a good girl and dried them on my dress. It had a sticky-out petticoat and a big bow. And now it was a bit wet. I pulled up my knickers and socks and slipped out the front door. I was halfway up the street when Mary Scullion came running after me.

'Are you going to see the parade?'

'I'm going to see the music.'

'Come on. It's the Prods in Cooper Street. They're having a parade.'

I stopped, hesitated. 'I'm not allowed to go round to Cooper Street.'

'Just for a wee minute?' she proposed. That seemed reasonable.

'All right. Just for a wee minute.'

We turned the corner, went down to the end of Lucknow and halted in astonishment at the spectacle before us. The dull, grimy street was livid with movement and colour. Hundreds of smartly dressed men with bright orange sashes round their necks stepped up the road, six abreast, their arms and legs swinging in time to the thumping music. They all wore round black hats and bright white gloves like clowns, and had tassles and writing and pictures on their lovely orange sashes.

'God!' said Mary, 'it's gorgeous.'

The music was wonderful, but deafening. It made me want to dance. The marchers were singing as they swung along, so proud and jolly. They carried huge banners that spanned the width of the road, beautiful banners, all orange with red and gold embroidery. Just like Our Lady's banners at the May procession, only those were all blue. These were brighter. There was a handful of people watching from the bottom of Lucknow Street. But they weren't enjoying it as much as we were.

'Annie, what are you doing here?'

It was my cousin Terry. He was a big boy and he lived up the street. He was standing behind me with a few of his mates.

'I'm just watching,' I said defensively.

'Wait til yer da hears you've been round here watching the Prods,' he teased.

'Well you're watching them,' I countered. He only laughed. He wouldn't tell on me. He was a corner boy.

'You see those big pikes they're carrying?' He pointed out the long, spear-like poles carried by many of the marchers. 'You know what they're for?'

'No. What?'

'They're for sticking in Catholics who try to cross the road when the Orangemen are marching.'

This was disturbing. Up until then I'd forgotten the Orangemen were Protestants.

'Can we not cross the road?'

'Not while they're here.'

'Why not?'

'They want to show us who's boss.'

'Oh. But I didn't want to cross.'

'You see that banner? You know who that is?' He pointed to an enormous banner floating across the centre of the road; a man in a lovely red coat on a superb white horse rearing up on its hind legs. The man had magnificent, long, curly hair and above his head waved a great hat with a long feather.

'Jesus?' I ventured. I knew Jesus had long hair.

Terry roared with laughter. 'Jesus! Christ that's a good one. No, dopey! It's oul' King Billy. King William the Third. Their hero.'

I remembered something about him. The bottle of the boing.

Just then a band in black and purple kilts drew level with us. Out in front a young man beat a horrendous tattoo on the most enormous drum imaginable. I jumped in fright, covered my ears.

'Don't,' hissed Terry, 'that's the Lambeg drum. They only beat it to frighten the Catholics. Don't let them see you're afraid.'

I dutifully uncovered my ears, put on my cheeky face and stared brazenly at the men in the dark skirts. They had little badges and ribbons on their kneesocks. They had big, furry bags hanging in front between their thighs. But they didn't look at all stupid. The band passed on, still banging the Lambeg drum and whistling on their tinny wee pipes. Then came more men in suits and sashes. Above them flew two flags. I recognised them both. The red hand of Ulster and the Union Jack. At the sight of the English flag a loud, derisive cry went up behind me: 'Butcher's apron! Take it down!'

Terry and his friends hissed and booed. The Orangemen momentarily broke ranks, but one of their marshals moved up quickly, waved an imperious white hand and ordered them back into formation. As he stepped back into line a shower of glass bottles rose into the air from the ranks of the marchers on the far side and crashed down around Terry and company. I heard the Orangemen cheering, I saw the corner boys scattering. I scattered with them, laughing with the excitement of it, all the way up Lucknow Street. We stopped at the relative safety of Benares Street corner. I turned to Terry and saw the blood streaming out of his head and down over his face.

'Christ!' gasped Paul Morgan, 'the bastards got you. Your head's split open.'

'Aye,' said Terry, 'but it's just a wee cut. It doesn't hurt.' He was trying to stop the blood with a dubious oil-spotted hanky.

'They'll have to shave your head,' another companion reassured him. 'You'll probably have a bald patch now.'

'You better go in and get that fixed. Yer ma'll kill ye.'

'I didn't do nothing!' Terry remonstrated. 'The friggers attacked me.'

'Your Terry said a bad word,' whispered Mary Scullion.

'So?' I snapped. 'He's allowed. He's got a cut head.'

We followed the boys down to Aunt Minnie's house. She was standing at the door talking to Chrissie McCann. When she saw Terry she shrieked, stuffed her apron into her mouth and started crying.

'Jimmy!' she screamed out for my uncle, 'Terry's hurt. His head's split open. Come here, son. Who did it on you?'

'It was the Protestants, Mrs McVeigh.'

She was wiping his cut with one hand but now thumped him across the shoulders with the other. 'What did I tell you, Terry? You stupid get. Didn't I say not to be going near that parade? Wait till your father hears.'

'You'll have to get that head stitched up, Minnie,' advised Mrs McCann. 'He could get tetanus or anything. Was it a bottle, son?'

'Aye, an oul' beer bottle.'

'The bad oul' bastes! You could take polio or anything out of that.'

'Annie,' said Aunt Minnie, spying me in the little crowd that had gathered around Terry's bleeding head, 'go and ask your daddy if he'd borrow Logan's car and take us to the hospital.'

I went down home and delivered the message. I could hear Terry halfway down the street asking if he'd have a bald patch.

'What exactly happened to Terry?' Mother inquired as Father set out to get the car.

'Somebody cut his head with a bottle.' It struck me at that moment, it must have been the bottle of the boing.

'Was he round at the march?'

'I don't know.' Bland innocence.

'Were you, Annie?'

'No,' I replied calmly. 'I was playing wee houses with Mary Scullion.'

'That's a good girl.'

'I'll say one thing for the Protestants,' Mother commented that night.

'What?' Father looked up over the *Belfast Telegraph*.

'They fairly know how to dress.' Father rolled his eyes in good-humoured disgust. 'No, but they do, Aidan,' she continued. 'They always look immaculate on parade. With their bowler hats and all. Not a speck on their white gloves, their very shoes gleaming. You have to hand it to them, they do know how to dress.'

Father grunted non-committally behind the paper.

'Not like our boys,' she went on, 'they were pathetic at the Easter parade. Half of them hadn't even bothered to run a comb through their hair. No suits, no ties . . .

'No jobs,' Father interrupted. And he didn't want to hear any more about it.

I had severe trouble with the Catholic dogmas. Sin, for example. There were two varieties, the mortal and the venial. Venial was manageable. A quick confession, at the appropriate age, and all the little black spots of veniality would be sponged off. Mortal sin was an entirely different matter. One great black blot on the eternal soul. What I couldn't understand . . . if a person committed enough venials, didn't the dots begin to join up so that the whole thing would become one mortal smudge? Mrs O'Callaghan, primary one, assured me that that would never be the case. An Act of Contrition would fix all but the gravest transgressions. I simply had to make sure that some convenient priest would whisper it into my ear as I lay dying. Oh my God I am very sorry for having sinned against you, because you are so good. And with the help of your grace I will never sin again; amen. That was all it required, promised Mrs O'Callaghan, and maybe a few Hail Marys for penance. After all, there was more rejoicing in heaven over one sinner who repented than over any God's amount of just men, which, when you thought about it, was very unfair. I was not persuaded by her arguments.

I had religious tendencies from an early age. Particularly once acquainted with Clonard Monastery, round the corner and up the Kashmir Road. The Redemptorist stronghold. Cluin Ard. The high meadow. No faint relic now to be seen of the original. But at the top of Clonard Street it rose, a Gothic imposition, the interior gleaming, candlelight reflecting off gold. Notre Dame paled.

The place was like a great, opulent palace. The house of God. I particularly liked the side and rear altars, saintly apartments done in marble, mosaic, gold embroidered cloths. The heaven's embroidered cloths. I made my daily rounds. St Gerard, patron saint of pregnant women, St Alphonsus, who accused him of abominations, the Great St Theresa, the Little St Theresa, St Anthony of the well-rubbed foot, St Maria Goretti, virgin martyr and my favourite, a life-sized doll in blue and white, with an armful of daggers and Easter lilies. Easter Rising Lilies. A Republican saint.

I enjoyed the lives of the saints and the blesseds, they had more than a touch of Hitchcock. I liked to see Oliver Plunket's head whenever we went through Drogheda, and I liked to hear about St Rose who stuck a hat-pin in her forehead when she went to a party to remind her of Christ's crown of thorns – crown of hat-pins – and to stop herself committing sin. Particular sins. Impure acts.

It was impure acts that Alexander wanted Maria Goretti to commit when he called her into his bedroom. I was unclear as to the precise nature of those acts, but I believed it had something to do with looking up her skirt. Anyway she wouldn't let him and he stabbed her fourteen times as she crawled, bleeding, down the stairs out into the wheat fields in the middle of the harvest. She made her first communion on her death bed and died on the feast of the Blessed Sacrament. Alexander repented and became a monk. It was a wonderful story, I almost wanted to be a martyr myself. But for the time being I would come and stare at the blond statue – not typically Italian – and rub my fingers over her naked plaster feet. The special blessing of the bare-footed virgin, victim of a bare-arsed rapist.

When the church was almost empty I would rearrange the altar settings, polish the tabernacles with the sleeve of my jumper, ensure a fairer distribution of flowers among the vases, scatter real rose petals among those made of plaster at the feet of the Little St Theresa. With every rose there comes a thorn, but aren't the roses sweet? I was never once caught by old Brother Bernard. At the first creak of the vestry door and his arthritic hip I would assume the praying posture. A devout child, yet not without Satanic tendencies. I have never quite been able to reject the glamour of evil.

It started with the painting of the devil that Uncle Stoker the lunatic brought for Father to frame. It was a big painting, about four by four. It stood in the corner against the wall for weeks. While not a Satanist in the strict sense, I took a fancy to the painting. It was a lovely thing to look at. The devil sat on a red velvet scroll-couch and behind him a heavily pleated crimson curtain hung the width of the picture, from ceiling to floor. Lucifer – I preferred that name to Satan – looked remarkably at ease for a creature damned to eternal torments. He sat on the couch, slightly inclined, his left elbow resting on the scrolled end, his hand supporting his head. His legs were crossed, the right over the left, ending in highly polished cloven hooves, and in his right hand he swung his long sleek tail. He was naturally all in black, a body-hugging ensemble that revealed the muscles of his chest and calves. I was fascinated. I had never seen a beautiful man before, and he seemed very agreeable. I wished he had an altar in Clonard. He would fit in very well between the confession boxes and the oratory.

But this early leaning towards devil worship did not deter me from my devotions at the chapel. The place drew me like a magnet every lunch-hour as I set out from school for home and a plate of stew. I loved the smell of incense. I liked to chew the varnish off the glossy brown pews. I enjoyed turning on all the electric candles at the altar of our Mother of Perpetual Succour. Now there was an altar if ever there was one. Behind a trellised façade of gold railings, white marble steps carpeted in red and gold, a lace-draped marble altar and a large gold tabernacle. Genuinely jewel-encrusted. My mother's engagement ring formed part of that crust; she had offered it up to Our Lady when I was two years old. Father's ulcer had burst.

'I blamed his doctor, Devenish, he was a drunken oul' cow,' recounted Mother, 'although it was your granny's fault too. Brigid never once cooked your father a meal, she just let him eat all the oul' gutters out of their shop. She wouldn't put her arse in a cramp.'

So by way of exchange Mother offered her engagement ring for Father's life. It was a deal. He's still eating all the oul' gutters of the day. That ring is one of the pieces of jewellery I will not be inheriting. Among the other pieces are my father's mother's amber earrings. My mother refused them for want of pierced ears. Pierced ears are known to skip a generation, for mine are pierced and would look well hung with amber. I would like to have had something belonging to Brigid.

Brigid McPhelimy, that is. A woman of wit and vigour, not entirely of her generation. No cook, unskilled in the womanly arts, unlike the nimble-fingered Maryanne of the Crossmaglen lacemakers. Yet she bore eleven children, counting Kevin who died at birth following a raid on the house by the RUC. They had come to seek out Grandfather. Needless to say he had not waited to be collected.

Brigid would tell outrageous stories, like the one about her hysterectomy. She was well up in years at the time, living on her own. She got up from the fire one day to put on a shovel of coal. As she walked across the kitchen she suddenly felt something drop beneath her skirt onto the oilcloth. Splat. Something organic. She inspected it briefly. She said it looked like liver. Unperturbed she scraped it up on the shovel and threw it into the back of the fire. Smoky sizzles would have arisen.

She mentioned it to her doctor a week or so later while visiting about some minor ailment, corns or some such. The good doctor Devenish, himself a little drink-sodden, felt obliged to examine.

'That would have been your womb, Mrs McPhelimy. It must have dropped right down over the years. The muscles would have gone.'

'Well,' sez she, 'it did me my day.'

No fuss, no nonsense, presumably no knickers. Which may be why my father, her youngest, and I suppose the scrapings of the very womb in question, was impelled to marry a woman who wore knickers twice over. One pair on the head at nights. Nocturnal plumage in polycotton.

I take after Brigid. She had a weak chest and died of bronchitis. Of course, she was eighty-five at the time. I doubt at this moment that I will live to see my well-worn womb drop liverishly to the floor, in the family tradition. I'll be buried in Milltown cemetery. Maybe not far from the Republican plot where there's always plenty going on. Comrade, tread lightly, you're near a hero's grave. But even up by the plague ground would do.

My father has remarked that his children will not dispute over the worldly goods that he will leave behind. But he has six good graves in Milltown and I intend to lie in one of them. I have no wish to be burned, urned and scattered, not even on the waters of the North Atlantic. I intend to crumble back into the earth. I want to feel the clay soil wrap damply around my brown satin shroud. Naturally I am entitiled to wear blue, as an ex-president of the Children of Mary. But brown seems more appropriately earthy.

My cousin Bernadette was President of the Children of Mary before me, at the same school. Another of Brigid's grandchildren, we had much in common. The only one in the entire connection who looks like me – except for her ears. Aunt Marie has always maintained that my ears are my best feature. Bernadette was less fortunate in that area; the amber earrings would have been wasted on her. There is a photograph hanging over the stairs in our school of Bernadette's upper sixth class dressed for a dinner dance, she with her hair knotted on the top of her head. A pea on top of a mountain. And *enormous* ears. Protruding, winged, opera-house ears. I have never seen ears like them. It may have been the ears which did the damage.

She went to America, and one day came down with a terrible headache. The next day she was dead. A brain tumour. I don't know if there was any significance in the unusual ear dimension. She was thirty-two when she died and I am now thirty-two years old. I will know when my time comes, I will look for the warning. I will listen for the knock on the door.

They heard the knock when Granny Brigid died. I was five at the time and was taken down to Albert Street to say goodbye to her. The house full of family and neighbours. We knelt with tortured knees on the kitchen floor, around the bed. For years now she had slept in the kitchen. The rooms upstairs were full of the second-hand clothes she sold at the market on a Friday morning, full to overflowing. The stairs were covered in stuffed pillowcases and piles of garments.

'What's them clothes on the stairs, Granny?'

'That's Joe Big-Toe's sock.'

'Who's Joe Big-Toe?'

'He's the giant who lives up the stairs.'

I peer up the stairwell, trying to see around the corner of the bedroom door. I dare not put my foot even on the first stair.

'Which room is the giant in, Granny?'

'In the back room. Now come away out of that, love, or Joe Big-Toe will get you.' And she would give me the wireless or clock off the mantelpiece to play with.

But today she lay wheezing faintly, feebly passing her rosary beads through her big hands. She still wore her gold-rimmed spectacles, her brown-grey hair still in plaits. But she could not speak. Later she lost consciousness. The parish priest had arrived, grim with authority. We said the decades of the rosary.

'The first Sorrowful Mystery, The Agony in the Garden.'

The grown-ups mumbled purposefully. Kneeling back on our heels now, we grew bored.

'Incline unto my aid, oh Lord . . .'

'Oh God make haste to help me.'

The priest finally rose to go. I was removed from the scene under only faint protest; with my mother it was never wise to insist.

That night the clan gathered again. I was not among them, having been sent to bed as usual in broad daylight, so that I would lie listening to my friends playing skips in the street below. It was important that my brain should be alert for school the next day. I was therefore not witness to the strange events that were said to have occurred that night.

Apparently the mourners-to-be were seated round the fire and the death bed just before midnight, drinking tea. The talk had died down for the moment when suddenly a loud, sharp rap was heard at the front door. For some reason no one got up to answer it. One might have supposed that it was a deserted child in search of its mother, or some man from up the street wanting his supper made. But it seems that rationality wasn't a consideration. A cold sense of alarm had pervaded the room. Uncle Jack, the marigold planter, who drove a taxi, had a foul tongue and no imagination, finally got up to open the door. A bitter wind gushed through the house. There was no one there. He looked up and down the street.

'Not a sinner about,' he reported matter-of-factly.

'It's the death knock of the McPhelimys,' Aunt Roisin, a woman drenched in melancholy – she being married to a genuine lunatic – is accused of having said.

'There'll be a death in this house tonight,' declared her sister Maggie. There were no prizes for guessing who it would be. My father, judiciously, held his tongue.

'We have always had the knock,' said Aunt Bee, 'we had it with my father and with oul' Maggie. The Cassidys have a pigeon coming down the chimney when they have a death.'

'There must be soot everywhere,' said Kieran lightly. He had married Bee's eldest daughter and came from a very low connection.

'I've heard from Minnie Moore that they have frogs in the house.' A titter arose from the men.

Brigid died that night. There wasn't another peep out of her.

But a strange thing happened the next day when we went down to see the corpse. On the meter box near the fire she had kept a little statue of an old woman sitting saying her rosary. It had been a present from Thomas and me; we saw it in a shop window in Omeath and it reminded us of Brigid. She used to sit, her brown rosary beads in one hand and a novel in the other, her mind probably more often on the book than on the sacred mysteries. She kept her hair in plaits and wore ankle boots and an apron, like the statue.

'This is you, Granny,' Thomas said when we gave it to her. She had kept it on the meter box ever since.

Granny had been laid out on the bed, on fine Irish linen, candles smoking at her head. There was a bottle of holy water in the shape of Our Lady of Lourdes on the little table. She had turned a yellow colour. She wasn't wearing

her glasses, but still had her brown rosary beads in her
hands – they matched her dress – and her hair was still in
little plaits. There were brown and blue and green scapulas
around her neck. Dozens of cards had been placed around
the body.

Suddenly there was a crash – plaster on oilcloth. It was
the statue of the old woman. It lay in pieces beside the
meter box. There seemed to be nobody near it.

'I didn't touch it, Mammy,' declared Thomas in a routine
denial of guilt.

'I know you didn't, love.'

The fate of the statue was also ascribed to the supernat-
ural. Indeed the thing was very odd.

As the coffin left the house for St Peter's Cathedral,
round the corner, it began to rain heavily. The man from
Curran's the undertakers discreetly approached my father,
the patriarch.

'Sir, would it be best if we put the coffin in the hearse
now?'

But Uncle Jack intervened, outraged; 'Certainly not,' he
admonished the neat little undertaker. 'We carry our dead!'

Father's face twisted into a big smile. Kay looked at her
husband in disgust.

'You'd think we were a tribe of bloody Indians,' Father
commented later. But they carried the corpse.

3

Calvary

Australia was the only continent my grandfather Paddy Mohan did not visit. He pottered around the world for twenty-two years before coming home and marrying Maryanne. Of course he went into exile at an early age. He had a bad relationship with his father, who, according to his descendants, was a thorough reprobate. Indeed all the men in that connection left much to be desired. It started with Great-great-grandfather James Mohan the eleventh.

James was a wealthy Catholic landowner, rare bird, from Carlingford. He owned half the town and a great house on Carlingford Lo: gh, grazing ground for the brown bull of Cooley. Queen Maeve's bull. There is no reason to think that bestiality was involved there. She did not, as far as we know, give the animal the warm welcome of her white thighs.

The Mohan house still stands, but no longer in the family. James is to blame. For some reason, perhaps an excess of saintliness or stupidity, he donated the house to the Catholic Church, sold up his holdings in the county Louth and moved to Belfast. Christ knows why. We will not soon forgive him. The oul' eejit.

Belfast. The town that gave the world the Titanic. The ship would have been the highlight of our achievement. We did it arseways. Belfast holds the real secret of the sinking of the Titanic. It was the serial number on the ship; they say that if you held it up to a mirror it read: NO POPE HERE.

Paddy Mohan worked on the Titanic, but only briefly.

When his co-workers discovered that his name was not truly Victor or George or Robert they threw him into Belfast Lough, and a clatter of spanners after him. But the bold Paddy escaped, lived to fight another day. So they were bound to have no luck of the ship. Ill-fated. Like the city itself. It's a hard town to look at, into the bargain.

And yet Belfast is beautifully situated. Surrounded by a rim of soft, glaciated hills – the Black Mountain, Carrick Hill, Divis – opening out onto the lough, it lies like a puddle of cold tea in a saucer. Much of the town was built on marsh and bog. Like my secondary school, St Catherine's Girls Convent School. The Sisters of Charity. The Brown Bombers. It rose out of the bog meadows, with the cemetery on one side and the Protestants just over the Peace Line to the east. For years we held fast to the hope that the school was sinking into the bog. But even at an inch a year it wouldn't be fast enough.

Among its other charms Belfast is a gathering place for damp mists and bad vapours, which make it perilous to the weak-chested. Nor is it the spot for the weak-minded. Like James Mohan, like the Titanic, like the buildings at the boggy heart of the place, the Mohans sank in Belfast. Prosperity dwindled from one generation to the next. Great-granda devoted his life to drink and, less typically, to women. It was when Grandfather Paddy objected to his father's third marriage that he ended up in the street with only the clothes he stood up in. He was fourteen at the time, in 1883. He lied about his age and joined the British army. My own father, quaintly, appears to hold my mother responsible for this gross act of treachery on her father's part. Maybe because she's not properly contrite.

'He took the Queen's shilling.'

'What else could he do? He was only fourteen for God's sake. His father had just thrown him out of the house.'

'He did the Brits' dirty work for them.'

'No he didn't. He never fired a gun.'

'Then what was he doing in the bloody army?'

'He was the priest's batman. He didn't believe in violence. He only joined the army to get work. There was no boru those days you know.'

This was a low blow on Mother's part. Father had been unemployed for weeks and had just turned down a job at the Royal Belfast Hospital because it entailed taking an oath of allegiance to the Queen. Still there was no need to bring up the matter of the boru.

We don't know what Granda saw and experienced during his travels with the militant clergy in Asia and Africa, but I do know that he would never let a banana on the table. He also grew averse to the British and to their foreign policy. But he never recovered the family fortunes and he never managed to buy back the great house in Carlingford. He was a disappointment to his sons. Certainly Uncle Jim never forgave him.

I must have been ten when Uncle Jim first reappeared. It was a very wet Saturday morning and my parents had gone down town to do the shopping. Thomas was blowing the guts out of thrushes' eggs, while Brendan and Sinead and I were playing wagon train. Brendan had a bandage on his head and we pretended it was from an arrow wound. Actually he had fallen out of the car the week before. It had been moving at the time. Fortunately the road fell away into a ditch at the spot where the door swung open, and Brendan rolled down the slope in his good beige camelhair coat getting it all covered in blood and muck. He recovered after a night in hospital, but the coat had to be put down. The wee woman had been in a terrible state all that week, worrying that the cuts and dents on Brendan's skull would result in brain damage. So we were being extra nice to him, and wagon trains was his favourite game.

It was a magnificent game, requiring that the three-piece suite be dragged into the centre of the living room and set end to end, to form the wagon and the team. Then we would load up the provisions for the journey. This involved emptying every cupboard in the house and piling up the contents on the wagon. There was tinned food, cooking utensils, crockery, bedclothes, buckets, brushes, books, garden tools – for the first crop in the west – stools, sponges, towels, medicine, toys, and of course guns, for we travelled in constant danger of Indian attack.

'My ma's going to murder you when she gets back,' said Thomas ominously.

'We'll put it all away in time,' I assured him.

'Whip crack away!' yelled Brendan, lashing the belt of Father's good trousers over the back of one armchair to get the horses going. Sinead, who was two at the time, sat bewildered on top of the hill of blankets, bound for Californy. I mounted up, presumably on the buckboard, and gave the order:

'Wagons Rrrrrrroll!'

There was a distinctly loud knock at the door.

'Oh God! It's Mammy and Daddy.' I dismounted in panic and ran to the window. But there was no sign of the car in the street.

'No,' said Thomas, 'it's too early.'

He went out to the hall, the three of us after him, and opened the front door just a crack.

There was a neat, middle-aged man standing there, leaning into the porch for shelter from the heavy rain. He wore a white shirt, dark tie neatly knotted and grey suit. The collar of his jacket was turned up against the rain, his bright white cuffs were already damp. There was a brown leather suitcase at his feet, spotted with rain.

'Yes?' Thomas challenged.

'Does Bernie Mohan live here?'

We looked at each other and then at the strange man, suspiciously. He had used our mother's maiden name.

'Why? Who are you?'

'I'm her brother. I'm your Uncle Jim.' He paused, anticipating an Irish welcome.

We stared hard and failed to find a family resemblance. At that stage we had not grown accustomed to identifying the Mohan nose.

'I've been living in England. Jim Mohan?' He was a good deal wetter already.

Thomas thought for a minute. 'Never heard of you,' he said. Then turning to me, 'Did you ever hear of him?'

I shook my head. I thought of the wagon train, the things all over the sofa. We couldn't let visitors in with the house like that.

'Brendan, have you ever heard of Uncle Jim?'

'No, but I heard of Jimminy Cricket.' He was only seven at the time and knew no better, but Thomas slapped him across the head anyway, behind the door.

'No, we never heard of you. We only have an Uncle Jimmy McVeigh.'

The stranger was becoming exasperated. The rain was dripping off his thin hair and onto his horn-rimmed spectacles.

'But she does live here?'

Thomas considered briefly. 'I'm not saying. We're not supposed to talk to strangers. I shouldn't even be *talking* to you.'

'But I'm your Uncle Jim.'

'How do I know that? You could be anybody.' Thomas scowled ruthlessly. 'What do you want her for anyway?'

'I just came to see her,' the man replied limply.

'Well, she's not here.'

'Do you know where she is?'

'I can't say.'

'When is she expected back?'

Thomas shrugged indifferently. 'Dunno.'

The man shivered. The wind had changed direction and was now whipping into his face. He had trouble keeping his jacket closed. The good leather case had turned black with rain.

'Look,' he said in desperation, 'can I at least come in and wait until she comes back?'

'No, we're not allowed to let strangers into the house.'

'Well can I at least leave my case here for the time being?' he pleaded.

'No. There might be a bomb in it or anything.' Thomas was quite clear on that score.

The stranger relented. It would be easier to confront the naked elements. He hoisted his case and turned to leave.

'Look, tell your mother I called. Tell her I went down to Minnie's in Benares Street. OK?'

Thomas nodded begrudgingly.

The man went off down the path and set his face towards the wind. He looked back forlornly, hoping we would take pity. Thomas slammed the door shut and we watched him from the living-room window, his slim figure leaning uncomfortably into the wind.

'Do you think he had a nose like Mammy's?' wondered Thomas as we climbed back onto the wagon.

Later that afternoon Mother burst in, burdened with shopping bags, string bags and assorted parcels.

'Who turned my brother away in the rain?' she demanded as we rushed to dismantle the wagon train.

The stranger came in behind her, eyeing us uncertainly. He stayed for almost a year. It was during that year that he first saw the ancestral home at Carlingford.

We travelled the road to Calvary in a jaunting car, donkey drawn. From Omeath. Omeath of the shingly beach and cups of williks, its shop windows full of plaster and delph leprechauns. We bumped along in the valley of the potholes, dipping and rising past the hedgerows heavy with hawthorn blossom, the jarvey calling out: 'Ah you'll be all right now. Just hold on there.'

'Long-nosed gits,' muttered Uncle Jim. 'Bloody ridiculous the roads here. I tell you what, they wouldn't put up with it in England.'

He was forever denigrating the place of his birth,

although he also left England on the worst of terms with the country and its people.

'A great Irishman in England,' said Father, 'and a great Englishman in Ireland.'

We didn't care, he made us laugh. He called everybody a long-nosed git.

We alighted shakily at the gates and entered the gardens. The Twelve Stations of the Cross rose from among the flower beds and hedges, life-sized sculptures bright on the land. We began the short tour. We children ran ahead of Mother, Father and Jim, stopped to stare at the first shrine; Jesus takes up his cross. The statues eight feet tall, women in cloaks, soldiers with gilt breast-plates, and the stooping figure of Jesus struggling with the large wooden cross. Tear-shaped gouts of plaster dripped from the crown of thorns, plaited briars.

'The shrine was part of the original estate. The priests keep it up,' Mother was saying. 'Aren't the stations magnificent?'

Jim muttered vague assent as he eyed the monuments in plaster and stone. Jesus falls the first time. Father held Sinead over the low railings surrounding the second shrine, let her touch the poor baby Jesus. I was disappointed that there were no candles to light before each gruesome tableau.

'Where's the candles, Mammy?'

'There's no candles here, love. The wind would only blow them out. You only have candles inside.'

Jesus falls the second and third time. Increasingly prostrate. The Roman soldiers raise leather whips, barbed at the end. Brendan is climbing over the railings, trying to look up a soldier's stone skirts.

'Get down out of that, Brendan, for God's sake!' Mother commands. 'Those spikes'll go right through you.'

Father retrieved him by the seat of the pants. Brendan had to be watched. He was always falling off things or having things fall on him.

'He's a terrible handful, Jim,' she apologised.

'He's all right, girl. He's just a cheeky little kid,' said Jim
with his odd English accent.

'He always says "little",' Thomas whispered, 'he never
says "wee".'

'He's a very mischievous child. It was massacre when he
had his tonsils out last year. The nurses put all the kids
down for their afternoon nap this time, but the bold
Brendan refused to sleep in the middle of the day. So he
waits 'til he gets them all asleep, nips out of bed and goes
round all the other kids' lockers drinking their orange
juice. They got him in the end, in the next ward, doing the
same thing. The sister said he must have drunk about
fifteen pints of juice. It's a wonder he didn't burst. But he's
full of divilment all right. He has my heart broke.'

As we turned the corner where Simon of Cyrene helps
Jesus, Carlingford Lough lay before us, brilliantly blue with
a rare clear sky above it.

'God but it's magnificent!' exclaimed Jim, suddenly
carried away. 'Did you ever see the like of it, girl?'

'I know, it's gorgeous. They say James Mohan used to
row across the lough in a wee boat. From the back of the
house all the way over to Moneymore. And he used to
shout at the children who came down to swim. They say
you could hear the yells of him all around the lough and
all the way into Carlingford.' Mother paused, stared out
over the water. 'Our family has always had great lungs.'

A little further on Jesus met his afflicted mother, then
had his face wiped by St Veronica.

'What happened to the towel?' I wondered.

'Why was she carrying a towel in the first place?' Thomas
wanted to know.

'I couldn't tell you,' said Father looking over the lough
through his new binoculars.

'They must have lost it, or it would be like the shroud of
Turin.'

'So they must.'

'I still don't see what she was doing with a towel in the street.'

Jesus and the women of Jerusalem, and just beyond that the family crypt of the Mohans. O'Golgotha. The place of the Mohanesque skulls. Black marble on three sides, black railings trimmed in gold for the fourth wall.

'This is where your ancestors are buried,' says Mother calling us over.

Jim holds on to the railings, his head thrust between them. But the place is locked against him. A big, rusting padlock secures a chain threaded round the entrance gate. Jim would not have the opportunity to moulder with the bones of his ancestors. He would be more likely to end up with Karl Marx. We joined him at the railings. Inside there are four or five biers; stone, coffin-like constructions with brass name plates. James Brendan Mohan, Thomas James Mohan, Anne Mary Mohan, James Francis Mohan, Bernadette Mary Mohan.

'There's you, Mammy! There's your grave. And yours too, Uncle Jim. See? James Francis. That's you isn't it?'

'Yes.' Jim seemed more annoyed than usual.

'Where's the bones?' demanded Brendan, 'I can't see any bones.'

'Can we go in, Daddy?'

'You're not allowed. That's why it's locked.'

'They're our bleeding graves!' said Jim with sudden spirit.

'God I hate graves and graveyards, Jim,' Mother interceded. 'I don't know what anybody sees in them. They're always awful cold.'

'What do you want?' said Father. 'Central heating? Now come on, leave the dead in peace. They're doing nobody any harm.'

Jesus is stripped of his garments, in the modest, Irish fashion.

'So that's what happened to Veronica's towel.'

We rounded another bend and found ourselves at the top

of the gardens. Jesus is nailed to the cross. Behind the tableau a hedge and a ha-ha separating the shrine gardens from the main grounds, beyond that a patchwork of small fields and through the bare places in the hedgerow we could see in the distance a great house. It rose with the curve of the land, hovered between field and sky, swept down to the edge of the lough. The ancestral seat of the Mohans. Jim held his breath, stared unbelieving, one hand shielding his eyes from the sun's glare. In the ditch in front of us two water-rats scuttered up the bank, detected our presence, chose to ignore us.

'Is that it, Bernie?'

'It is. It's a private school for boys now.'

Jim was silent for a moment. He stood shaking his head bitterly from side to side. 'To think that I could have been living there and I end up in a bloody council house in Ilford.'

Father was finding it difficult to keep his face straight.

'But, it's been over a hundred years, Jim, and there are so many Mohans ... the chances are you wouldn't be living here anyway.' Mother struggled to reason with him.

'Course I would. I'm the second son, in the direct line. This should have been ours by rights, girl.'

Father continued to hide behind his binoculars.

'All this bloody land for miles around ... if it wasn't for that old bugger.'

'Who?'

'James Mohan. Just bloody gave it away! And to the bloody Catholic Church!'

'But it was his, Jim, to do what he wanted with. He had every right.'

We arrived back at the entrance gate. The jarvey came forward with the donkey and jaunting car. 'Wasn't that grand now?' he inquired as he lifted us up onto the strange and precarious cart.

Jim seemed reluctant to leave. He stood for a few moments looking over at the house and the lough.

'Up you go now, sir!' urged the jarvey as he helped Jim up and set off with a jolt for Omeath.

As we pulled away from Calvary Jim raised himself off the hard wooden bench and strained for one final glimpse of the house beyond the hawthorns.

'Long-nosed git,' he mumbled as he bumped back onto his seat. 'Long-nosed bloody git.'

The following night he was on the Liverpool boat on his way back to England. He wrote regularly for years, complaining about the overcrowding, the English mentality and the unavailability of potato bread.

The Troubles were always with us. Even to the consummation. In the Easter parades, in remembering 1690, in the music and the comeallyez, the poems and the novels, and in men like Oisin. Living in the shadow of the 1916 Rising. He first appeared when I was three years old.

It was a Sunday afternoon. My mother was in bed and my father was reading in front of the fire, about Michael Collins, the big fellow. He looked like a fairy prince on the front cover. A green jacket and the lovely bright green, white and orange flag behind him.

'Daddy, tell me a story.'

He looked up from the book and spat into the back of the fire, sending soot balls down on the flames.

'I'll tell you a story of Crock McCrory,' he began, 'a hole in the wall, and that's it all.' He stopped, smiling. I was waiting for him to go on.

'Tell me the rest.'

'That's it, there is no rest. A hole in the wall and that's it all.'

I thought of the wee hole between the bricks out at the back door, maybe that was the hole in the story.

'I don't like that story. Tell me another one.'

'What?'

'Tell me the one about my granda and the bear.'

'Well, your grandfather used to go all over Ireland entertaining the people in the streets. People had damn all to do in those days. He had a great big bear that would go round with him. Now – '

'You didn't say what colour was the bear.'

'Brown, it was a big brown bear. Now your grandfather used to play the flute and the bear would dance, and all the people would gather round to watch and they'd throw money into your granda's cap. But then one day a rag-cart ran over the bear's foot and he couldn't dance, so instead the bear played the flute and your grandfather danced.'

'And what happened when Granda died?'

'Well, you see, the bear got old and died and your granda didn't have anybody to dance for him. So he started a new trick to entertain the people. He would get a tin bucket and put a big sponge at the bottom of it and put it in the street. And then he would go upstairs and jump out of the front window, head first, and land in the bucket. But then one day when your granda went upstairs somebody moved the bucket and your granda jumped and landed on the pavement and got killed.'

'Did his head get split open?'

'It did, aye. Now I'm gonna have a wee sleep so be a good girl and keep quiet.'

A minute later he was dozing, his head thrown back, breathing noisily through his broken nose. I was trying not to make a sound. A figure appeared in the little hall outside the glass kitchen door. It was Oisin. He didn't knock, just called through the glass: 'Aidan? Aidan?'

My father shook his head and sat up immediately. 'Yes?'

'There's a man at the door, Daddy.'

'Oisin? Holy God! Is it you? Come on in. I don't believe it. Where in God's name have you been these last few years?'

Oisin came in, removing his cloth cap, so that his loose black curls fell over his gold-rimmed spectacles. He wore a long overcoat, full of pockets. He had a thin, craggy face, and somehow looked wild and thoughtful at the same time. He and Father stood there studying each other, filling up the dim room.

'I've brought this for the wee girl,' said Oisin taking something out of a polythene bag and handing it to me without ceremony.

It was a huge furry rabbit, white and pink and leggy. I held out my arms for the unexpected gift. I thought it astonishingly beautiful. When the two men sat down in front of the fire I took the rabbit off into the kitchen to examine it closely. It had black lips and nose, and yellow eyes, like boiled sweets. It had a pom-pom on its bum like the one on my red snood which made my ears hot and itchy. Its front was pink and its back white. I pulled away the fur where the two colours joined. There was a line of stitching. I pulled harder and a little hole appeared. I poked my finger inside and wiggled it around. There was something in there. I tugged and pulled a small chip of stuffing through the hole. Remarkable! It looked like yellowman candy. Only soft, and tasteless. There was more, so I made a bigger hole and gradually, piece by piece, took all the lovely yellow stuffing out of the rabbit's body and limbs. It was amazing. All that inside the rabbit. I pulled at the boiled sweets to see if they would come off. They did. I popped them in my mouth and began to suck.

I went back to show Father and Oisin, the limp body of the rabbit in one hand, the other holding a pile of stuffing foam against my chest.

'Look, Daddy, look what I did.' Just wait till they saw this.

My father took me under his notice, frowned absent-mindedly. Oisin surveyed me briefly, unperturbed.

'Give me that, love,' said Father, rescuing the rabbit. 'What have you got in your mouth?'

I stuck out my tongue, beads and all.

'Spit them out now, like a good girl.'

I spat them out onto his big, brown hand. 'Look.' I held out the handful of foam.

'It's OK. Your mammy'll fix it when she gets up. Now be a good girl and be quiet. Go and play over there.'

Fortunately they were both tolerant men. I can't remember if Mother ever got the stuffing in again.

Oisin didn't appear for years after that. There was a postcard one year. He was travelling with continental gypsies somewhere in the South of France. Among other things Oisin was an accomplished linguist. And then one day he just turned up at the door.

'I'm back,' he said. 'Is your father in?'

It was as if he'd just gone down to the shop for a loaf and a bottle of milk. As always my father was delighted to see him.

'Come in out of that, Oisin, for God's sake. What are you doing standing there at the door?'

We brought him in and sat him down by the fire. He was carrying a large shoulder bag, stuffed to the zipper. He put it between his knees and sat back to examine us all.

'They've all fairly grown, Aidan,' he pronounced.

'Aye, they have indeed. So where have you come from this time?'

There was a pause, intended to be dramatic. 'I was over the border.'

There was something about the way he said it. We visited the Free State half-a-dozen times every year, but this seemed more significant. Father seemed to think so too.

'Were you indeed?' he asked, his voice loaded.

'Aye, down in Dublin. I had a wee job to take care of.' He was smiling broadly.

'Yesterday was it?' asked Father knowingly, 'about three o'clock in the morning maybe?'

Oisin burst out laughing. 'Three five precisely. I set the charge myself.'

Father shook his head in delight. 'Christ, you left a hell

of a mess for the Gardai to clean up! It must have been one
hell of an explosion. I'd have given anything to be there!'

'It wasn't a bad oul' bang now. It seems to have got
enough publicity anyway.'

'What explosion?' Mother demanded, coming in with a
pot of tea and setting it down in the hearth.

'Nelson's Pillar,' said Father gleefully.

'Nelson's Pillar?' Mother seemed alarmed. She turned to
Oisin. 'It wasn't you . . . surely to God?'

Oisin only laughed. 'It's about time somebody blew the
bloody thing off the face of the earth.'

'But, Aidan, Nelson's Pillar has sentimental associations
for us,' she said.

'Has it? What do you mean "sentimental associations"?'

'What do I mean?' she was becoming outraged. 'You
proposed to me up Nelson's Pillar! Christ! Do you not even
remember?'

'Oh aye, so I did.' But it only made him laugh the harder.

'I didn't know that, Bernie, or we'd have blown up
something else,' said Oisin with mock contrition. 'Look
I've brought you a souvenir anyway.'

He opened the bag. It was full of grey, speckled chunks
of rock. The smithereens of Lord Nelson's Pillar, late of
O'Connell Street, Dublin. My mother picked over the rock
samples, chose three small pieces and went up the stairs
with them. She still keeps them in a little cardboard box
displayed on her dressing table.

'So how did it go?' Father wanted to know when Mother
was out of the way.

'Not a bother,' said Oisin. 'It went like a bomb.' He
smiled apologetically. An unintended pun.

'So was it just yourselves involved?'

'I had some assistance from our European neighbours.
1798 revisited.'

'Did they get away all right?'

'They were out of the country within half-an-hour.'

'Not too bad. The Gardai'll be up to their arse in it,' said Father referring to the Free State police.

'They will surely,' replied Oisin with satisfaction. 'But sure they'll be wasting their time.'

'So the French got their own back on oul' Nelson.'

'They did indeed, and not before time.'

Thomas and I had been playing behind the sofa, but at this point we were put out into the back yard to play. Oisin was gone when we came in for dinner. We never discovered where he got to that time.

4

The Informer

Until, after twelve years on the waiting list, the Housing Trust managed to find my parents a house in Bunbeg Gardens, my mother's sister Nora was the only one we knew with a garden. She was one of the first residents of Andersonstown. She lived at 13 Mullagh Gardens. A good name for a street. 'There is great beauty in the Irish names, that fall like music on the listening ear, and breed a deep-felt love that never wanes in hearts of exiles gone for many a year.'

It was an estate like a hundred others at the time. Cul-de-sacs miles from anywhere, no transport, the beginnings of pebbledash. But a damn sight better than Benares Street where the pokey little houses had been flung up around the great linen mills a hundred years before, arseways, and the streets named to commemorate Britain's colonial triumphs. Benares Street and Clonard were 'down the Falls' while Andersonstown was 'up the Falls' – the Falls Road being the central spine, thoroughfare and, according to the media, 'nationalist heartland' of Catholic Belfast, bound by mountains on one side and bogs on the other.

Apart from the consolation of the pebbledash and the picture window, Aunt Nora had a hard oul' life. She had made an unfortunate marriage; Uncle Des McGlinchy took a drink. In fact he was an alcoholic from a family of alcoholics. Of course he had taken the pledge on their engagement, but it lasted no longer than his first post-nuptial visit to the maternal home. His mother mocked him. His brother Felix mocked him. Felix was that very rare commodity, a Catholic policeman, soon to be dishonourably discharged from the force for being drunk and disorderly on duty. The RUC should have had more sense. Uncle Des must have been overcome with a grave sense of shame after abandoning the family tradition, for he took to drink again with the dedication of the prodigal returned.

Des led Nora a damnable life. He drank his pay religiously every weekend, disappearing on Saturday morning before the house was awake and rolling home in the middle of the night to demand a bowl of chicken soup and his 'conjugular rights'. They had seven children. We considered that our cousins were rarely privileged: they had a garden with a swing and a rabbit, and a father who let them do whatever they liked. They had the run of the kitchen and would make lovely margarine sandwiches whenever they felt like it. The margarine eaters were adventurous at play and would wander out of the street without asking permission, or steal a ride on the back of the milk float or climb up the monkey puzzle in Mrs Coogan's garden next door. They suffered interminably from broken limbs and split heads. We, severely disciplined, were warned not to go mad when we went to visit the McGlinchys.

There was a whole crowd of interesting people living in Nora's street: a family of simpletons; a man who beat his wife; another with a missing ear. And the Currans. It was on Easter Sunday that I first saw Barry Curran. I was sitting with Mother and Aunt Nora in the living room, listening with great attention to their talk of Uncle Frank and his third 'wife'. I was supposed to be looking at the Freeman's catalogue. I wasn't allowed out in case I tore my new blue chiffon dress.

'You tear something every time we go up to your Aunt Nora's,' Mother lamented, 'and look at those scabs on your knees! They'll go lovely with your new socks and sandals.'

She had bound an oversized green bow about my closely shorn head, to make me look festive.

'You look like an Easter egg,' remarked Mary Scullion

after mass, not purposefully unkind. 'I mean your head's all smooth and round, with a big bow. Like an Easter egg.' Perhaps she thought the effect was intended.

After lunch my cousin Tim appeared in the doorway. There was only three days' difference in our ages but Tim was tall, lanky and ginger. It was a great relief to Thomas and Brendan and me that we hadn't inherited Granda Mohan's ginger streak. But the McGlinchys were pitiously blighted – freckles, ginger eyelashes, red hair. The ginger head entered, smiling affably.

'Mammy, can me and Barry go down to see the parade?'

'No Tim,' said Nora quickly. 'They're expecting trouble.'

It wasn't an Easter Parade of the Judy Garland variety, even though it was before the Troubles started again. More a reminder that the people would rise once more, 1916 could be revisited; the swing of manly arms and saffron kilts; lines of die-hards, ex-internees, old Republicans armed with the symbolic hurley stick, the tricolour and the starry plough. The first Battalion of the Belfast Brigade, celebrating all that delirium . . . The marchers would make their way to Milltown cemetery. The spectacle would culminate in the oration over the Republican plot. A quotation from Pearse, the man himself, was traditional. His oration over the grave of O'Donovan Rossa:

'The fools, the fools, the fools. They have left us our Fenian dead. And while Ireland holds these graves, Ireland unfree will never be at peace.'

It's handy when a country's revolutionaries are also its poets. It makes them eminently quotable.

'Who says there's gonna be trouble?' The McGlinchys had the cheek to talk back.

'That's what I heard. Ask Felix.'

'Ach, Mammy, we won't go near any trouble, I swear to God. Just for a wee while?'

She wavered fatally. 'Is Barry there?'

'Aye, he's in the hall. Barry?'

A small, darkly handsome boy came shyly into the room. 'Hello, Mrs McGlinchy.'

'Hello, love. Did your mother say you could go down to watch the parade?'

'Yes, Mrs McGlinchy, so long as we were back by five and didn't go near the police.'

'Where were yous going to watch it from?'

'Milltown. We wanted to hear the oration at the Republican plot.'

'OK then, Tim, but I'm warning you, any trouble starts and you head home. All right?'

'Yes.' He was already out the door.

'Or you don't set foot across this door for the rest of the year,' she yelled after him. But they were halfway up the street.

My mother was smiling agreeably, but we would have gone to the parade only over her dead body.

'Do you know who that is, Bernie? Did you not think that wee fella looked like anybody?'

'He didn't put me in mind of anybody,' said Mother doubtfully.

'Barry Curran?'

'Holy God! You're kiddin'! Is he one of the Currans?'

'He is. Young Barry's wee boy, Una's nephew.'

'So he's oul' Barry's grandson? Would you credit it?'

'You would not.'

They paused to reflect. They'd forgotten I was there.

'And does the wee lad know?'

'About his granda? Oh aye, they wouldn't let them forget it around here. Even now.'

'God love him. And they were all great Republicans too.'

'They were indeed. So's his father, a real die-hard.'

'He's a lovely lookin' wee boy. He must take after his Aunt Una.'

'They were always a very good lookin' family. Even that bad-hearted oul' bugger.'

'So they were. I often think about Una.' Mother turned

to include me. 'Your Uncle Jim was mad about her for years. She had the most magnificent complexion you ever saw, hadn't she, Nora? And do you know she never washed her face, she'd hardly give it a lick on a Saturday night before she went out to the dance.'

'And she never had a pimple, girl.'

My mother and her sisters, for some reason which they couldn't explain, called each other 'girl'.

'No, she never had, Bernie. The Yanks went mad about her.'

'So they did. She married a Yank and went to live in America,' Mother added for my benefit.

For some reason I assumed the Yank was a millionaire.

Later as we walked the mile and a half to the bus-stop I asked why people teased Barry Curran.

'What did his granda do?'

Mother, who could generally be depended on to take me into her confidence, responded enigmatically: 'Well, there was a terrible scandal at the time, even now there's still talk.'

'But what did he *do*?'

Mother glanced about her. An automatic check. There wasn't a sinner for miles and there wasn't going to be a bus for another half-hour. 'He was an informer . . . He informed on the IRA.'

Aha! An informer! Most despicable of life forms. He turned on his own. Like Victor McLaglen in the film. Took the Queen's shilling in a big way. Still, he was a bit simple in the film. I cried when they shot him at the end, but could see the necessity of it. An informer. It had a ring to it. Nowadays they just call them touts.

It seems there was nothing simple about Barry Curran. He was a bit of a businessman, with fruit shops in Cawnpore Street and down the Falls Road. A good Catholic, lived in the shadow of the monastery, had a clatter of kids. He was in the IRA. It was a reasonably active period in the history of the organisation, just before the Second

World War. England's difficulty soon to be Ireland's opportunity – again.

At the time the IRA – the boys – were souls of military
discretion. Organised on a cellular structure, each volunteer had only the few contacts. The family wouldn't
necessarily know that he was involved. Mrs Curran certainly didn't. Nor was she aware that he was even more
involved with sloe-eyed Ita Donnelly, spinster and
homewrecker.

Ita was a delicate little woman, a fancy embroiderer at
the Blackstaff Mill, and Barry's fancy woman in her spare
time. They had been seeing each other for almost four
years when the RUC found out. It was valuable information, for they suspected Barry of being in the IRA and
now he could be blackmailed.

No doubt there would have been a clandestine approach,
vigorous denials, assertions and threats, and at last a
fearful agreement to cooperate. Barry finally gave them
what they wanted. A number of men were arrested in the
Clonard area, and a small cache of arms was discovered
down a manhole in an entry off Leoville Street. At first it
wasn't clear whether all this was the result of the astute
detective work of the officers of the Springfield Road
barracks or of a paid informant. But the question was soon
settled.

An operation had been planned for Easter week, to
commemorate the Easter Rising; the birth of a terrible
beauty. There was to be an attack on the barracks in
Cooper Street, at three in the morning on Spy Wednesday.
There would only be the desk sergeant and one constable
in the building. Four men were to force their way in, tie up
the officers and raid the armoury. A token attack only. No
one would get hurt.

Barry was one of the men chosen to go on the raid.
Instead he passed the information on to his contact, and on
the evening before, he sent word to the commandant of his
unit that he was sick and would not be fit for action. He

got a message back: no problem, another volunteer would go in his place.

He heard the news on the wireless the next day. There had been an attempted raid on the Cooper Street barracks which had been foiled by the large number of policemen and B-Specials in the street at the time. Two of the perpetrators had been shot dead, three others were being held in custody. One of the dead men was Paul Curran, Barry's eldest son, who, unknown to his father, had recently joined up to do his bit for the cause. Although inexperienced, Paul had volunteered at the last minute when his father called in sick. Barry's wife took it very badly, but he handled it well, and still didn't give himself away. The IRA might never have discovered the identity of the traitor but for Sean Crolly's boots.

Sean was a navvy; he was also in the IRA. At the time he was working on a building site near the centre of Belfast. One Monday lunchtime he went to collect his boots from the cobbler's in King Street; he had left them there on the Friday to be re-soled. But the cobbler's was closed. 'Back in fifteen minutes,' said a cardboard sign in the window. Sean crossed over the road to the Horseshoe bar for a quick drink while he was waiting.

The place was dim and almost empty. He ordered a Guinness and sat down at a corner table near the window where he could see the cobbler's shop. There was only one other man there, wearing a dark suit and a bowler hat, a businessman type. He was sitting at one end of the bar, his back to Sean, bending over his drink. After a while another man came in, glanced quickly round the room and sat down at the bar. Sean knew him to see; it was Barry Curran. Sean remembered him from his son's funeral. God help him, Sean was thinking, is it any wonder he needs a drink in the middle of the day? Curran ordered a short one but strange to say he didn't lip it. He sat with his head down, his hands round the glass. The publican was out the back taking delivery of some crates of stout. Sean kept one eye on the cobbler's shop. No joy yet.

Then he noticed that Curran was talking, in a low, barely audible voice. He was talking to the dapper little man at the end of the bar. It was very bloody odd, but sure enough the little fella was talking back, his eyes on the wood of the counter in front of him. Neither of them so much as turned their head. When Curran stopped talking he got up suddenly and walked straight out of the bar. He hadn't touched his drink. Later Sean used to say that that was when he realised what was going on, but that he just wanted to be sure.

When, a few minutes later, the little man left the bar, Sean went after him, with no more thought of his working boots. He followed the slim figure for about half a mile until he saw him turn into York Street police station. That was all he wanted to know.

Some months after that my mother and her friend Una Curran were coming home from school up Clonard Street. They were both eleven years old and already Una was a smasher, taking after her comely father. They went into the monastery to have a rest and to say a prayer for their exams. When they came out again they turned up towards the Kashmir Road. Kashmir, former princely state, former British colony. Doubtless a trouble spot. There was a crowd gathered there now and they could see Father Toner running out of the presbytery.

'Come on,' said Una, 'let's see what's goin' on.'

'I'm supposed to go straight home,' said Mother.

'Ah come on, sure we'll only be a wee minute.'

They ran up the street and followed the crowd into the entry off the Kashmir.

'What is it?'

'There's a man dead up the entry.'

They pushed through the men and women and emerged at the little clearing round the corpse. Little clearings invariably form themselves around corpses. People want to see, but they aren't keen to get too close.

The body of a man was lying face-down on the grey concrete. His hands had been tied behind his back. He had been shot in the head and one of the first women on the scene had thrown her apron over his head, for the sake of decency. There was a hardboard placard hung round his neck by a hairy cord, with the word 'TOUT' inscribed in white paint. A rough illuminated manuscript, it accurately chronicled the event.

'What does "tout" mean?' Una wanted to know.

'I dunno,' said Bernie. 'Maybe it's his name.'

'He was an informer,' said a man standing behind them. 'They had no choice but to shoot him.'

Mother and Una made their way home. Later that evening Una learned that the body up the entry had been her father's.

'I'll never forget that oul' piece of hairy cord round his neck,' said Mother as the bus rumbled up the road. 'I can see it to this day. It's funny the things that stick in your mind.'

'And this will be your fourth child ... is it, Mrs McPhelimy?' asked the sour woman from the Housing Trust.

'Yes, there's the two boys and Annie here.' I sat immobile on the edge of my mother's chair while we were inspected.

'That's not a large family, by any means.' The woman was smiling the whole time.

'But it's too large for this house, and we have my mother living with us, as we said on the form. She's an invalid and it's very hard for her to get to the toilet outside.'

The woman studied the papers on her clipboard. 'What are the sleeping arrangements exactly?'

'My husband and the baby and I have the front room and

Thomas and Annie and Granny are in the back room. I
don't know what we'll do when the new baby comes.'

'Still, you're not what I'd call overcrowded. I could name
plenty of families with a dozen children in a two-bed-
roomed house and they're not complaining.'

'We have no bath, and only the geyser for hot water.'

'But the house is very sound, Mrs McPhelimy, I mean
there's nothing I can see that would make you a high-
priority case for rehousing.'

'But we've had our name down these twelve years.'

'You and thousands of others.' She rose to go. 'I'm sorry
but you'll just have to wait your turn.' When she had gone
my mother started crying, silently, hanky over her mouth.
I hung around the hearth watching her face get red and
puffy.

'Was that woman a Protestant, Mammy?'

'I don't know, love.'

'Mrs Scullion said the Protestants get all the houses.'

She said nothing.

'Do they?'

'What?'

'*Do* the Protestants get all the houses?'

'I don't know, love. I'm sure they don't.'

'Who gets the houses then?'

'There's not enough houses, love. There's too many
people.'

'Why don't they make more houses?'

'There's not enough money. You need money to make
houses.'

'Why don't they get more money?'

'I don't know, love. Now go on out and play.'

I turned with one hand on the doorknob. I had a good
idea. 'We could live in the chapel. There's plenty of room
in the chapel. It's lovely there.'

'You can't live in the chapel, love, God lives there.'

'But we're his children . . .'

'Annie, go out and play.'

'Well,' I said from the safety of the hall, 'Protestants pick their noses,' and I made off up the street before she could lay hands on me.

We first heard about Ian Paisley when Sinead was born. It had been a bad birth. Mother stayed in hospital for almost three weeks afterwards.

'Who's Ian Paisley?' she wanted to know when she came home.

Father was surprised: 'Where did you hear of him?'

'From that wee woman in the next bed. She seemed to think he was a great man.'

'He's a bad-hearted oul' bigot, that's what he is.'

'She said he was a minister or vicar or whatever they have.'

'He's got some bloody church of his own, up the Beersbridge Road. He's a fanatic, he hates Catholics. I hear the men in work talking about him.'

'Well this woman thought he was a saint. She gives him money every week of her life, and God help her she hadn't twopence to rub together. She had to wear one of the hospital dressing gowns and I had to give her one of my flannels. I felt sorry for her.'

'But she'd enough to give Paisley every week. He only takes up paper money in his church. Silent collections.'

'She seemed to think there was nobody like him.'

'There hasn't been a cursed troublemaker like him these years.'

It wasn't long before we would hear of Paisley again.

5

The Mothers

Either through an inexplicable quirk of destiny, or simple clerical error, we were allocated a brand new house in the new part of Andersonstown just after Sinead was born. Bunbeg Gardens. Not far from the mountains, it was free from all conveniences and civilising influences such as schools, churches, pubs, shops, public offices, transport, cinemas, and industry, light and heavy. Even the social security office, the 'boru', was irritatingly distant.

Bunbeg formed a meeting of the ways. A long street running from Carnan Gardens at the top end, down past two lines of semi-detached houses, round the bend and on past our house, right down to the Shaw's Road which ran right through the centre of Andersonstown. We were number one hundred and thirty-nine, right in the middle of the road junction which occurred one third of the way down the street. At this point, opposite our house, the street formed a great open-topped triangle, Bunbeg proper being on the hypotenuse and on one side, with Macroom Gardens opening away at the top, a wedge-shaped street with houses at the lower end and ugly, two-storey maison-ettes further up.

There was an immense green opposite our front window and another sizeable patch facing the door. The road broadened here and a side-road ran up through Macroom, forming another convenient exit onto the Shaw's Road. An expanse of tarmac and grass filled up the ground between the widely spaced rows of houses. Further down the street two other streets ran off the main spine of Bunbeg. On our side a cul-de-sac, further on down, opposite, was Bunbeg Court, which also led to Shaw's Road. A big, broad gathering place where roads converged within a length of five hundred yards. The space, the distance, were a revelation after the brown brick and tarmac confinement of Benares Street. I liked it. It was the middle of everywhere. People passed the house all day to go down to the shop on the next block, to get onto the Glen or Shaw's Roads. I liked to be in the thick of it. I was not at an age to value privacy.

And the house seemed grand. We had three bedrooms, a bathroom inside the house, and a kitchen well able to accommodate two people at once. The front door was at the side of the house, but an enormous 'picture' window in the living room faced onto the street. There was a garden front and back, and an extra little strip of garden that ran along the side gable, past the front door. A low concrete-clinker wall separated our strip from the Frenches' front lawn and in time became an essential demarcation line.

The Frenches were our next-door neighbours, a houseful of hard cases. The mother was the worst, repulsive to the point of fascination. A shapeless figure, hefty, unkempt and unwashed, she invariably wore a stained floral pinafore – although she avoided housework of any description – and men's grey socks, which hung loosely around her fat ankles. Otherwise she would go bare-legged, even on the coldest winter's day. Her legs were permanently measled from the long hours spent with her chair pulled right up to the fire, front chair legs in the hearth, her feet resting on the mantelpiece.

Although no more than forty-five when we first encountered her she had already lost all her teeth and would never insert her falsies before lunch-hour. Her hair was dyed strawberry blond, but never recently, so that it would graduate in tangles round her big, bloated face and down over her shoulders changing in colour from grey at the crown, to mousey, the blond at the dried ends. She never put a comb through it, but she did scratch it a lot.

She told us that she had been a doffer in the Blackstaff Mill as a young girl and she was delighted when, the day after we moved into Bunbeg, my father sang to her as they chatted in the garden:

Oh you can always tell a doffer when she comes into town
With her long yellow hair and her ringlets hanging down,
With her picker slung before her and her scissors in her hand,
You can always tell a doffer 'cos she'll always get her man.

'That was me all right,' she said, well-tickled, as Father tried to keep his face straight, 'hair that long I was able to sit on it, like burnished gold, and every man on the Falls after me.'

To all appearances Mrs French was a dirty, throughother sloven, yet she had a remarkably positive self-image. She saw herself as Roisin Dubh, sloe-eyed symbol of young Mother Ireland, an inspiration to gallant patriots, a stalwart soldier in the fight for national freedom. She believed that she had pioneered urban guerrilla warfare in Ireland. A great seanachie, the traditional narrative bent, no respecter of chronologies, she would tell of an unspecified time in the past, 'When I was a commandant in the *Cumman na Mban*.'

'DeValera picked me out one time, he was inspectin' the troops, "You see that fine lookin' woman with the gold ringlets," he sez to the commandant of the Belfast Brigade, "she puts me in mind of the Countess Markievicz in her young day." Of course,' she would add, 'I was somethin' to look at in those days, I had the loveliest complexion ever you saw.'

'Were you still doffin' in those days?' Father would inquire politely. She was very fond of Father and certainly provided him with hours of entertainment.

She was the mother of four ignorant, obnoxious and stinking children. She neglected her kids, but for that at least no one would fault her. Michael, Danny, Bernadette and Niall — a catalogue of rogues feared and deplored throughout the estate. The lawless ensemble, a hazard to picture windows, the dread of the soignant gardener, the horror of the childish possessor of bike or guider. Mrs French's treatment of them was entirely justified.

Every evening about five o'clock Bernadette would go down the street to Brogan's new shop, still partially under construction, for a giant box of cornflakes and a bottle of milk. This was the evening meal, the staple diet of the French establishment, the woman of the house having scant interest in the lesser, domestic matters. Mrs French liked to talk politics, to sing along with ranting rebel ballads, to watch the comings and goings of the neighbourhood. But mostly she liked to drink. She also battered her husband.

Mr French was slight and ferrety-looking, but essentially pleasant and harmless. He was chronically unemployed even at a time when the unemployment rate in Andersonstown was as low as twenty per cent. For eleven months of every year Mickey French was on the boru. He didn't seem to mind. He enjoyed a relaxed, idle lifestyle. He would sit on the front porch for hours on a fine day watching the comings and goings of his more industrious neighbours. He rarely had anything to say, but he did take a drink, and most of his evenings were spent scrounging drinks in the pubs and sheebeens on the Glen or Shaw's Roads. The only dim patch on his otherwise agreeable existence was Mrs French. Theirs was a stormy relationship. Mr French was a battered husband. Admittedly when he got drunk he became moody, even a bit verbal. But his plaintive twitterings did not compare with the response they evoked from his wife. Although a drinking woman herself she objected when Mickey came home bluttered, and the whole street was privy to those objections.

She would be waiting for him when he rounded the corner; she would start before he set foot on the garden path. Her shrieks and curses would rend the night, his pitiful little voice would be raised in querulous retort, momentarily, only to be quieted by the rough slap of a meaty hand on mouth. She resorted to violence. She often left him black and blue. We were in Bunbeg hardly a fortnight before they had a major dispute. It was a Sunday morning. Their shouting disturbed people getting ready for mass, putting themselves in a state of grace. It seemed to go on forever.

'Maybe you should go in and check he's not beating her, Aidan? He might hurt her,' Mother suggested in a spirit of Christian responsibility.

'Listen to the yells of her!' laughed Father. 'It's not her I'd be worried about. It's poor oul' Mickey with that targe.'

Shortly afterwards, with a deal of thumping and breaking of glass, Father was proved to be right. We looked out of the boys' bedroom window which overlooked the Frenches' front path and door. Mr French was lying in the garden, a little dazed and bloody. His wife had thrown him through the large glass panel on the lower half of the door. She stood now, calling through the shattered portal, warning him not to try to set foot in the house ever again. He took a swift revenge. When he recovered enough to stand up he went off to seek consolation at the White Fort Inn, came back in the evening, emboldened by drink, and broke every window in the house. Somehow they made up their quarrel the next day.

'Is that the two of them away down the street arm in arm?' asked Mother in disbelief.

'It is,' said Father. 'He's taking her out to the pub. It just goes to show you . . .' He assumed the orator's stance and declaimed:

> There's the love between a man and his wife
> There's the love of a son for his mother,
> But there is no love that can compare
> With that of one drunken sod for another.

Mother smiled and sighed. 'Do you think, Aidan, the Housing Trust would give us a swop? Maybe somewhere quieter, maybe up on the Shaw's Road where Kitty and Alex are getting a house?'

'Maybe . . . If you apply now you might hear back from them in another twelve years.'

Our house was attached to the Murrays' on our left. The Housing Trust had decided on an interesting arrangement whereby their front door shared a wall with our picture window, and the path to their front door bordered our garden. We therefore got a great view of all their comings and goings. They seemed to be decent people, a couple with a car, three daughters and an early and lasting aversion to the French family.

Mother had worked at the stitching with Mrs Murray in her youth. She was a huge woman, tall, hefty, blond. Totally Wagnerian. A couple of years later she fell on the icy pavement outside the house and broke her hip. After that she got about very little, walked with a limp and put on another few stone.

The Murrays had moved into Bunbeg the week before us and as we traipsed in and out of the house with bundles and boxes the two matriarchs were soon gabbling in the garden.

'That was Nellie Doran,' said Mother when she finally came in for the first cup of Bunbeg tea.

Father got up to look out the window, suddenly interested. 'Nellie Doran? That was Michael Matthews' cousin?'

Mother gave out one of her dramatic gasps and hissed, 'Yes! But for God's sake say nothing! Never even mention it to her, Aidan. I'm sure she's never got over it.'

Michael Matthews was the last man ever to be hanged in Ulster. He was also Mrs Murray's cousin, and she was considered by many to be responsible for his capture by the RUC. It was during the war. Matthews was an IRA man

and with another volunteer he planned a traditional sniping attack on a police patrol. The police were to be attacked
while on foot patrol on the Kashmir Road. The snipers
would escape through the small streets and entries around
Clonard. Michael would run down Lucknow Street where
Nellie and her friend would be walking by. He would pass
the handgun to his cousin who would slip it into her
handbag, walk on and deliver it to a house down the Falls.
The RUC, in their panic, would not think to stop and
search two young girls, and if the men were detained or the
area searched the gun would not be found.

However, all did not go according to plan. Nellie panicked. When she heard the shots and saw the young men
running towards her holding out the gun, and the noise of
the police whistles erupted in the next street, she went
into a fit of hysterics and bolted. The yells of her immediately attracted the policemen. Michael had the presence of
mind to grab her, clap his hand over her mouth and bundle
her and the other girl into a nearby house. But once started
she could not be stopped. Her screams were unmerciful.

'God love her,' Mother would say when she told the
story, 'she couldn't help herself. Michael had to throw her
onto the sofa, cover her head with a cushion and sit on it
to try to keep her quiet. She says she'll never forget it to
this day. But the squeals of her brought the police right to
the house. They surrounded the whole place. The cousin
tried to shoot his way out, but sure he'd no chance. He was
tried and condemned to death. Nellie and the other girl got
off because they were so young – hardly sixteen – but
Michael Matthews would have been about twenty-one at
the time. They wrote a song about him and all.'

Sinead was such a quiet baby that Mother thought she was
retarded. It was bloody oul' Anna McIlhone who put the
idea into her head. McIlhone was a mournful, gossipy
woman, built like an elephant seal. When she was over

forty she had a daughter who had Down's syndrome. One time my mother mentioned that Sinead wouldn't eat. McIlhone's eyes kindled: 'That's just what our Siobhan was like at her age, she refused her bottle,' she said encouragingly. 'That's how the doctors knew she was a mongol. You'd better get her seen to.'

Mother got her seen to immediately. Two days later Sinead was examined by a coven of consultants, student doctors and nurses at the Royal Victoria Hospital. I sat politely on a hospital trolley looking out the window at the giant black statue of Queen Victoria. It was covered in pigeons and their droppings. I knew Queen Victoria was a bad oul' baste, but I was trying to remember what she had done. It was something about India and a Scottish gamekeeper.

The men in white coats were circling and surveying mother and child. A fat, sandy-haired doctor turned to the students: 'Now, lads, this infant has undergone a series of tests today and we find nothing wrong with her. Yet her mother says she's off her food.' He waddled across the room sucking the arm of his glasses. 'Now can any of you hazard a guess as to what might be the matter?'

The students looked at each other and at the fat baby lolling contentedly on the examination table, her two legs in the air. A pimply youth stepped forward and half raised his hand.

'Yes Mr . . . McAuley?'

'Sir . . . em . . . well . . . I think the baby might be overfed.'

His colleagues, encouraged, nodded in agreement. The specialist signalled terse approval. 'Exactly. This child is overfed. In fact, this baby is fat.' He turned sternly to Mother, 'Could I suggest that you take the child home and give its stomach a rest for the next few days?'

He motioned to the staff nurse and we were ushered ignominiously through the green plastic swing-doors. We took Sinead home and despite Mother's anxious attendance she managed to develop normally.

She was a very beautiful and serene baby and would lie for hours in the enormous Silver Cross pram, waving her legs in the air and eating Farley's rusks and poking the soggy crumbs down the side of the mattress. At the age of eighteen months she unwittingly provided an object lesson for Thomas, Brendan and myself.

It was the occasion of the last party ever to be held in the family home, in honour of Uncle Patrick's annual visit, over from London for the week. This time he came with his third wife, Lucy. We later discovered the relationship to be purely *de facto*. Drink was served that night. My parents generally did not approve of drink, but Uncle Patrick was rarely comfortable without it. He said he drank to be sociable. He led the singsong: 'The Green Glens of Antrim', 'The Mountains of Mourne', 'The Forty Shades of Green', odes to the sites and scenes he'd abandoned in company with his brother Jim thirty years before. Then Aunt Minnie did a mournful solo, 'Moya My Girl', and all the Mohans wept as Mother and Granny passed around the ham sandwiches and sausage rolls. Mother's sister Kathleen persuaded Mrs Murray to say a poem.

'Keep quiet everybody,' Kathleen hissed. 'Go on, Nellie.'

Mrs Murray sat up straight in her chair, took a deep breath, swelling her big, shapeless chest. Her normally pasty face flushed rose. She gave the slightest of coughs and began: 'A poem by Joseph Plunket,' she announced:

> I see his blood upon the rose
> And in the stars the glory of his eyes,
> His body gleams amid eternal snows,
> His tears fall from the skies.

Thomas was grinning behind her back, trying to make me laugh. But I was sitting beside Mother and kept my face straight. Brendan, however, tittered. Mother lowered her bottom lip revealing clenched teeth. He attempted to come to order. Uncle Patrick and Aunt Kathleen were listening with rapt attention. Mrs Murray's voice rose excitably for the last stanza. The crucifixion crescendo.

> All pathways by his feet are worn,
> His strong heart stirs the ever-beating sea,
> His crown of thorns is twined with every thorn,
> His cross is every tree.

There was an eruption of clapping.

'Yeoh,' cried the crowd. 'Aras Aris!'

'Brilliant, absolutely brilliant,' called Uncle Patrick. 'It's years since I've heard a poem said like that, girl.'

'Oh she's terrific,' agreed Kathleen. 'What about another wee one, Nellie?'

Mrs Murray took a dainty sip from the cup of tea Mother had handed her, mentally ran through her repertoire. 'What about this one?' she suggested.

Anything at all.'

'"The Mother", by Padraig Pearse.' famous poem

'Yeoh!' Another cheer went up. A popular selection.

> I do not grudge them: Lord, I do not grudge
> My two strong sons that I have seen go out
> To break their strength and die, they and a few,
> In bloody protest for a glorious thing,
> They shall be spoken of among their people,
> The generations shall remember them,
> And call them blessed.

[margin note: Irish mother losing sons in battle against British - battle for freedom]

She paused for breath. One or two dry sobs were stifled about the room.

'It'd take the tear out of a glass eye,' hissed Kathleen.

> But I will speak their names to my own heart
> In the long nights;
> The little names that were familiar once

Round my dead hearth.
Lord, thou art hard on mothers;

Mother nodded in vigorous agreement.

We suffer in their coming and their going;
And tho' I grudge them not, I weary, weary
Of the long sorrow.

I felt a little catch in my throat.

And yet I have my Joy:
My sons were faithful, and they fought.

Mrs Murray broke down as the guests broke out in cheers
and applause. She covered her puffy eyes with dimpled
hands, felt for the box of tissues Mother offered.

'God love her,' whispered Kathleen, 'she's thinking of
Michael Matthews. He too was faithful, and he fought.
Now what about our Colum?' she suggested next. 'He has
a quare voice.'

Colum, her son-in-law, was located in the dinette and
duly egged on. He pushed his way through chairs and
bodies using his drooping beer gut to clear a path. He came
up to the fireplace, turned to face the company and downed
the dregs of his glass.

'Right,' he proclaimed rubbing his hands in anticipation,
'What'll it be?'

'"Danny Boy",' ordered Kathleen.

'Oh not bloody "Danny Boy" again, Kathleen, everybody's sick of hearing it,' he declared derisively. 'Now
what do yez want?'

'Our Kathleen's hell for "Danny Boy",' muttered Mother
to Lucy by way of explanation.

'Sing a rebel song,' requested Terry.

'Aye, well spoken, sing a decent rebel song, Colum.'

'Right yez are.' He paused, looked down and pulled at his

mouth. 'Aye, here's a good one. "The Sniper's Promise".'
He drew in his stomach, the room stilled. It began like a
lullaby, measured and melodic, a reasonable baritone.

> The night was icy cold. I was alone,
> Waiting for an army foot patrol.
> At last the British soldiers came in sight,
> And I squeezed the trigger of my armalite.

The line was unexpected, it got a laugh. But Colum filled
his lungs again, raised the volume and picked up pace:

> Oh mama, oh mama, comfort me,
> I know these dreadful things have got to be.
> But when the war for freedom has been won,
> I promise you I'll put away my gun.

Colum sang rebel songs for half an hour. He sang of the
theft of the 'Four Green Fields', he sang of the battle in
'The Foggy Dew', he sang of the deaths of 'The Soldiers of
the Rearguard', Roddy McCorley, and of Kevin Barry. Aunt
Minnie grew restless.

'That's awful morbid, girl,' she whispered.

'I know,' Mother agreed, ' and it's hardly the sort of thing
you sing for the visitors.' Lucy was English. 'I hope he isn't
going to start on all those oul' comeallyez. Colum,' she
called out, 'what about "The Jug of Punch"? Nobody sings
that like you.'

Colum glowed, he loved Mother Ireland, but he also
liked a good drink. He knew how well he could put over
that song and he obliged.

'I hate that song,' Mother whispered to Minnie, 'but in
present company it's better than "The Rifles of the IRA".'

Among the other blood relatives present were Aunt Nora
and her eldest son Desy. At eighteen he had all the makings
of a hardline alcoholic. That night he arrived watery-eyed
and unsteady and he deteriorated noticeably as the evening

progressed. But then he was a quiet drunk and gave no offence as he sat in one corner under the budgie's cage, sipping and burping and occasionally swaying forward uncertainly on the straight-backed chair. Shortly before eleven he was seen disappearing upstairs in search of the bathroom. He never found it. At first we heard the bang and clatter of the bedroom door being pushed open and knocking against a piece of furniture. As the room hushed to listen there came the pained sound of a loud human belch followed by the howling of an agitated infant. Desy had encountered Sinead in the dark.

There was a rush for the stairs, Father at the head of it, ascending two steps at a time. I was detained by Granny. She caught me by the sash of my dress and slapped me around the legs for acting the goat. But I could hear my father yelling from the top of the stairs.

'Send up the children, I want them to see this.'

We obediently tore up the stairs and crowded into the doorway of my parents' room. And there was Sinead, sitting wailing and bewildered in her little blue cot, covered in vomit.

Father was incensed. He was cursing and abusing Desy and his father and the whole drunken crew of them. Mother was hissing for him to keep his voice down: 'Please, Aidan, there are people in the house,' she pleaded as she tearfully attempted to wipe the baby clean.

Poor shamefaced Aunt Nora came in with a bucket and floor-cloth, got down on her knees and began cleaning up her son's mess, well practised in mopping up human spillage. Meanwhile, for his own protection, Desy was escorted into the garden where he was sick again over a border of deadly nightshade and sweet-scented stock. Mrs French watched from her doorstep with kindly interest.

'I want you all to take a bloody good look at this,' Father threatened, 'and I don't want you ever to forget what drink has done in this house tonight. And I swear to God, if I ever see any of you as much as touching a glass of beer, I'll break your two arms.'

We nodded in ready assent and clattered downstairs for bowls of whiskey trifle.

6

Vigilantes

The Troubles really got underway for me up the Kashmir Road one Saturday morning while I was attempting to buy a sirloin roast for the Sunday dinner. It was the morning after the Protestants burned out Bombay Street. We went to see Aunt Minnie in Benares Street, which was just around the corner from the action. They were all safe. Happily we were in time for a bowl of Minnie's Irish stew. Magnificent stew, fine lumps of carrot and potato and lamb. We will not soon see its like again.

'That's a lovely coat, Annie. Salmon?'

'Aye it's a wee suit. Open your coat, love, and let your Aunt Minnie see the dress to match.'

Obediently I undid the cloth-covered buttons and opened the coat.

'That's lovely, girl,' said Minnie, who saw good in everything. 'You're fairly gettin' tall.'

'She's a terrible appetite,' lamented Mother, disgracing me. She was always telling people I had a terrible appetite.

'Sure she's at that age, Bernie, she'll be twelve in September. Do you want another bowl of stew, love?'

I politely declined, the beginnings of the young lady in me.

'Oh Christ, Aidan, there's one of them bloody cockroaches.'

'Where?' Mother arose in alarm.

'It just came out of the coal-hole.'

Cousin Terry – formerly of the split head – followed its swift progress along the floor.

'It ran under the settee, Aidan,' he advised unconcerned.

'Do yez think I'm a bloody spider or something?' Father muttered.

But the men were obliged to get up and pursue the black brute with shovel and brush. The incident happily diverted attention from my appetite.

'So is Jimmy's sister OK, Minnie?' asked Mother blowing on a lump of steaming carrot.

'Not too bad now, girl. Dr Giles gave her a sedative, God love her. She was in that house thirty years near.'

Minnie's sister-in-law had been burnt out of Bombay Street.

'Did she know the ones that did it?' Father was inclined to get to the point.

'She did, but it wasn't any of her own neighbours; a crowd came down off the Shankill Road.'

'And is there any Catholics left in the street?'

'No. The McGukians three doors up didn't get burned out but the Prods wrecked the house instead. A lot of people are staying in the monastery until they get fixed up,' said Terry, who had one ear to the TV, Hoof-Hearted was coming up the inside stretch, and the other to the conversation.

'How did it start anyway? That's what I'd like to know. Apart from the twelfth of July Bella's never had no trouble these years . . .'

'It's the oul' story, Ma. The bastards don't like it when the Catholics stand up for their civil rights. Look what happened at Burntollet last year. They beat the shite out of the civil rights marchers, just in case we didn't get the message – croppies lie down.'

'But why last night?'

'Wasn't it bloody oul' Paisley started it as usual? There was a tricolour in the window of a shop at the bottom of the Falls and Paisley came down from the Shankill Road with a mob to remove it. That's when it all started.'

'Were you over in Bombay Street since, Terry?'

'Aye, Paul and I went round early this mornin'.'

It was just a block beyond the bookie's.

'Was it bad?'

'Bloody awful, Aidan. There's nothin' left of it. Our side has thrown up a barricade across the bottom of the Kashmir. M'da's away up to Ardoyne with Bella. She's gonna stay with her daughter.'

'She'll not be much better off there. Weren't they shootin' into Ardoyne last night?'

'That's what I sez. Ardoyne'll be next.'

'I can't get over the peelers standin' by and lettin' them do it,' said Minnie.

'Wise up, Ma, sure they're a shower of bastards, every last one of them.' Terry was no longer a corner boy. Now he was a wee hard man.

'I know the B-Specials are bad bastes,' Minnie agreed.

'Sure half the police is in the B-Specials anyway.'

'And where was the bold IRA when we needed them?'

'For Christ's sake, Ma, the IRA haven't been active in the north these years.'

'They will be after this,' Father predicted.

'Too right they will.'

'Annie, run round like a good girl and get your daddy's roast for tomorrow.'

'Are you sendin' her to Meeley's, girl?'

'Oh aye.'

'For they have lovely meat.'

'So they do. Thon roast last week was magnificent. Here, love, tell Jackie I want a good, tender sirloin, and tell him it's for your father and that he has a bad stomach.'

Meeley heard about Father's stomach every week.

'All right.'

'And don't be goin' down to Bombay Street, do you hear me?'

'Yes.'

I went out and round the corner, up Lucknow Street where the kids all wore National Health specs and picked their noses and ate it. I turned into Kashmir Road. The butcher's was right on the corner, opposite the bookie's, but I stopped to watch the smoke rising from the ruins of Bombay Street at the bottom of the hill. The street was full of people coming and going, congregating in little groups, discussing the depredations of the night before. The place was alive with tension.

I went into Meeley's to get the roast, being careful to edge past the carcasses of beef hanging at the back of the shop. They were dripping blood onto the sawdust. I stood behind the high, glass counter waiting my turn, blocking my nostrils from the smell. The butcher was sawing at a leg of lamb, his bare arms raw red, like the meat he sold. I hated going to the butcher's.

'Yes, love?' he asked cheerfully when it was my turn.

'A big sirloin roast, please.'

'No sirloin left, love, I'm sorry. Give you a nice piece of topside.'

He might as well have asked me if I'd take a quarter of jelly babies. What was topside? I wondered.

'My mammy said sirloin, because my daddy has a bad stomach.'

'The topside's very tender.'

'I don't know . . .'

'Is your mammy round in Mrs McVeigh's?'

'Yes.'

'Well go on round and ask her would she take a nice topside instead.'

'OK.'

I went out of the shop and at that second half-a-dozen shots were fired up the Kashmir from the direction of Bombay Street. The place exploded. More in anger than in panic. The doors of the little terrace houses were flung open and men charged out and ran towards Bombay Street. A few of them were wielding hurley sticks, traditional weapon of the nationalist peoples in the absence of fire power.

'Down to the barricades! The fuckers have started again,'
someone yelled as he tore off into the thick of it.

Part of the crowd was running away from Bombay Street,
most were running towards it. All around me women were
dragging children in off the street, crying 'Snipers!', while
dogs ran round in circles barking mad with excitement. An
oul' fella with a donkey-drawn cart, decorated with bal-
loons and piled up with rags, was half pulling, half coaxing
the animal out of the line of fire. There were a few more
shots, no one was hit. A group of bold young men were
helping each other onto the roofs of the houses, trying to
spot the source of the gunfire. I was still standing outside
the butcher's, under the striped awning, enjoying the
drama.

The shooting seemed to stop. Even more people drifted
down towards Bombay Street. I drifted with them. As we
breasted the hill I could see the black skeletons of the
burnt-out houses, the smoke still rising from some of
them. And between us and them the improvised barricades,
made from old gates, beds, doors, chairs, tyres, anything at
all. Cars were a later development. Matching slogans
blazed from gable walls. 'Fuck the Queen', it said at the
bottom of Kashmir; 'Up King Billy with a red-hot poker'. I
went down to have a better look. But before I'd gone ten
yards the shooting started up again. The people in front of
me turned and charged back. I was caught up in the
stampede. Just before we drew level with the butcher's
shop they all stopped and looked back. Somehow we sensed
we were out of range. They were still shooting, entirely
without effect. It was as if they didn't really mean it.

Another lull, and we advanced a little more cautiously,
but no one seemed to be afraid. They fired again, and again
we turned to run up the hill. As I ran I noticed that I was
laughing at the same time. Great crack. Just then I felt my
feet lifting clear off the ground. For a second I was running
in mid-air. There was a hand on the back of my coat collar

and a big face bore down on me. It was Father. He lifted me off my feet and ran me out of the firing zone. I turned my head to ask him, 'Will you take topside, Daddy? Mr Meeley says there's no sirloin?'

'For Jesus sake!' he exclaimed in exasperation, 'to hell with the bloody roast. These fellas aren't joking, you know!'

He ran me all the way back to Benares Street unmindful of the condition of my coat collar, with no thought that my cloth-covered salmon buttons were straining the fibrous limits of my new coat. I was delivered without ceremony to the McVeigh residence where my mother told me off for not coming back sooner.

'The stupid cow! Running up and down the Kashmir in the middle of all the shooting!'

'God love her, girl,' said Aunt Minnie, who saw good in everyone, 'she wanted to get her daddy's dinner. She's not a bad wee girl.'

Later that afternoon my father went somewhere with Terry in the car and they sent me round to my cousin Kitty's house in Cawnpore Street. I sensed there was something going on, but I was happy to visit Kitty. She was Minnie's eldest daughter. Her husband Alex was a fascinating man; brilliant, gentle, an original thinker, he came from a family of assorted eccentrics. Yet he seemed normal. Although Father used to say that he couldn't be entirely normal as he had married a Mohan.

Alex was unlike most of the men I knew. He smoked a pipe instead of cigarettes. He spoke a dozen languages, played board games for diversion and dressed beautifully. He always had elbows in his jumpers, and there were no oil stains on his trousers. He was polite and soft-spoken. He taught for a living, reluctantly, for there were so many interesting things he could be doing. And he had a bad back, which was more interesting than anything. Strange

the things you couldn't do with a bad back. He had to get
an orthopaedic bed. Thomas adapted a Dylan song for the
occasion. 'Lay lady lay, lay across my orthopaedic bed.'

Kitty was sweet and good-hearted and, unlike Mother,
let us get away with murder. She even let us read comics,
which Mother feared would stunt the intellect, and she
made great teas. Cakes with icing and wee silver balls, jam
tarts, sandwiches in the shape of triangles with nice, soft
lettuce leaves. Kitty and Alex always had dessert. I loved
going round to their house. It was only one street away
from Clonard Chapel, and not far from a sweet shop full of
candy apples dipped in coconut and homemade raspberry
ice lollies. They had a son, Benedict. It was a funny name,
but Kitty said they called him Benedict because he was a
special blessing from God. I didn't like Benedict. He was
bad-tempered, and he cried all the time. And if he wasn't
crying he was eating. Kitty said he would grow out of it,
but Mother said that Aunt Minnie had spoiled him rotten
because he was her first grandchild. I didn't care about
hateful wee Benedict. I just ignored him.

'Alex is going up the road to see his brother Fergal, so
they'll give you a lift home. We'll not be too long. Don't
let the boys eat all them buns now,' said Mother. 'And for
God's sake stay away from Bombay Street.'

We spent the afternoon playing monopoly and later Kitty
and Alex drove me home. We had a bit of trouble getting
into Andersonstown. Crowds of men and kids were erect-
ing barricades at the entrance to the estate on the Glen
Road. In anticipation of Bombay Street Two. The
onslaught of the Protestant hordes. They had commandeered the bulk of their materials from the building site
nearby. Huge sheets of corrugated iron, plaster-board par-
titions, barbed wire, great concrete pipes, and even a
cement mixer and mechanical digger. Alex, the soul of
caution, edged the car up to the improvised barricade. A
group of young fellas bore down threateningly. Benedict,

who had been asleep in Kitty's arms, woke up and immediately began to wail.

'Can we get through?' asked Alex pleasantly. He had to shout to make himself heard over Benedict's bawls.

'No, it's a no-go area,' declared one long-haired lout.

'But I'm going to see my brother.'

'Oh yeah? Where does he live?'

'Just over there,' said Alex patiently, pointing to the house.

'Please, we have a young child in the car.'

The lout glanced distastefully at the screeching Benedict. 'You can't come in unless you have a pass.'

'But I live here,' I protested, sticking my head out of the car window. 'Ask Niall French over there, I live next door to him.'

'No pass, no entry,' he maintained. 'You might be Protestants.'

'You could make them say the Our Father in Irish,' suggested one resourceful lad wielding a rubber tube.

Alex, a fluent Irish speaker, considered this reasonable and was prepared to accept the challenge. 'Fine,' he said. '*Ar nAthair ata ar neamh, qo naofar d'ainm . . .*

'Na!' broke in the lout, 'that doesn't prove anything. He could be a Special Branch man.'

At that moment a middle-aged man emerged from the workmen's hut, which had been taken over to serve as vigilante headquarters. He had a cup of tea in one hand and a bacon sandwich in the other. He wandered over to the car. 'What's going on here?' he inquired mildly.

'We've been told we can't come into the estate.'

'Why the hell not?'

'This young lad says it's a no-go area.'

The man turned to survey the boy with tolerant pity and shook his head. 'Would you for Christ's sake stop acting the lig Maguire, and leave decent people alone?' He gave a signal to clear the road and they moved the cement mixer to one side.

'Go on now,' he said as he waved us through. He disappeared into the hut again and sat down at a glowing brazier. The keepers of the gate dragged the cement mixer back into place across the road.

It was just after three when Kitty and Alex dropped me off and within an hour my parents pulled up in front of the house. There were two young fellas in the back of the car. I'd never seen them before. One of them looked a bit on the scruffy side. Mother got out of the car and went straight into the house. As we came out to help bring in the shopping Father was opening the boot of the car. The two strangers were standing beside him as he lifted something out from between the bags of vegetables and bread and potatoes and passed it to them. It was two rifles, half-wrapped in an old rug.

'There yez are, boys,' said Father amiably as they uncovered the weapons.

'Thanks, mister.'

'Don't waste any ammo, there's little enough of it.'

'Can we not keep a rifle?' Thomas wanted to know.

'The men'll need them on the barricades, son. The Protestants could come in from Finaghy, very handy.'

We were warned to say nothing to anyone about the guns.

That night Father did his first stint on the barricades. Thomas and I had to do our homework and weren't allowed out.

'I should be up at the barricades,' Thomas declared, shortly after Father went out.

'No way,' said Mother, 'you're too young.'

'I'm fourteen. That's old enough. Anyway I saw Niall French up at the barricades and he's a year younger than me.'

'Oul' Ma French is a mad woman to be letting her sons run wild up on the road. She doesn't give a shit about those kids. But no son of mine's going out to be shot for Ireland or for any other cause. Now get that straight.'

Thomas punished her by withdrawing from her company for the rest of the evening.

While Mother believed that milieus such as dances and parties were ripe with danger for thirteen-year-old girls, she somehow imagined them to be less at risk than their brothers in a war situation. She had the gallant idea that men, even Protestants and B-Specials, would never harm the fairer sex, and that bullets and other missiles were by some law of physics more attracted to masculine tissue. So when I suggested later in the evening that I should bring Father up a cup of tea, she agreed.

'Aye maybe you should, love. His stomach will be at him if he doesn't get a bit of toast or something. Here, he likes these Marie biscuits. Bring him up the packet. I'll make him a flask.'

At that time a flask of tea was like a safe-conduct. I went up through Carnan Way on to the Glen Road and ambled leisurely down to the main entrance to the estate at Carnan Gardens. I was in no hurry to find Father. He would only make me go home again. A wide stretch of green separated the hedges bordering the road from the first row of houses on the estate. The area was black with men and boys. They milled about carrying hurley sticks and other impromptu weapons. I could see no guns. Dozens of them crowded around roaring braziers sipping tea and Guinness. Others scanned the Black Mountain opposite with inadequate binoculars.

'Sure you can't see a cursed thing in the dark there, Sean.'

'Not much, but you never know. You might see movement handy enough.'

'Why? Do ye think the Prods is going to come down over the mountain like a crowd of bucking Apaches?'

Good-hearted laughter.

'I wouldn't put it past the bastards. There could be snipers or anything up there.'

'Thinks he's in a John Wayne movie.' More relaxed chuckles.

But they looked uneasily to the hills behind the brewery and St Mary's Christian Brothers' school.

It started to rain heavily. I had neither hat nor umbrella and the water dripped in rivulets down my neck. I was soaking by the time I reached the main barricade. The men scorned to run for shelter. They stood about in wet groups behind the barricade, inviting rheumatism and other rain-induced aches, Father among them. He was standing entertaining a small bunch of men outside the workmen's hut. Alex was beside him, doing a double act.

'And do you think will the Free State intervene?' asked one man.

'It'd be a bit late if they did,' answered Father, 'fifty years too late.'

'But Lynch has announced he won't stand idly by . . .'

'Lynch doesn't know his arse from his elbow.'

I hovered on the perimeter for a few minutes, disinclined to butt in. Finally Alex spotted me.

'Is that you, Annie, standing there in the rain?' he asked with concern. Always a gentleman.

'I brought this tea.'

'You shouldn't be out on that night,' said Father coming over and taking the flask and biscuits. 'Your mother shouldn't have sent you up here. Now go right home.'

'It only started to rain after I came out.'

'It's not the rain I'm worried about. It's a bloody bullet in the head that concerns me.'

'Has anything happened?'

'Nothing yet,' he said as he crunched a biscuit. Then, with one of his twisted smiles, 'But we're hopeful.'

'Are there any women on the barricades?'

'Of course not. Christ! Wouldn't that be lovely!'

'Well there should be. I don't see why women can't man the barricades as well.'

'Would you talk sense, Annie, and get on home.'

'Can I not stay until you're coming?'

'Annie . . .'

I could see that he wouldn't be swayed. I reluctantly turned down Carnan and went home. Still, I considered recent developments as very promising. The Troubles would alleviate the boredom if nothing else.

Father came in about one o'clock in the morning, well saturated, his face grim.

'What is it, Aidan?' Mother in a flutter at the sight of him. 'Is your stomach bad?'

'No,' he said shaking his head bitterly. 'We were listening to the twelve o'clock news up in the hut. The army's moving in.'

'The Free State Army?' asked Mother astonished.

'No,' he growled, reaching for the baking soda. 'The bloody British!'

Kitty called the next day.

'I'm staying with Fergal and Aine for a few days,' she announced, 'I wouldn't risk bringing Benedict down home after last night.'

'Why, what happened?'

'Didn't you hear?'

'I haven't heard anything. Aidan's been in and out at the barricades all night. What was it?'

'You didn't hear about Paul Morgan?'

'Terry's friend? No, what?'

'He was shot dead.'

'Holy God! When? What happened?'

'Him and Terry were round at Clonard helping with the refugees and the Protestants started sniping from Bombay Street. Paul was behind the monastery moving camp beds or something and they shot him in the head.'

'God dekervus!' This was the wee woman's short-speak for 'God take care of us'. 'God help Mrs Morgan, she idolised him. They could never have another child. Is Terry all right?'

'He's badly shaken. They've been friends since they were wee toddlers. He went mad when he heard. He just wanted to kill somebody. Mammy's afraid he'll get a gun and go down to Bombay Street and shoot rings round him.'

'God help him. I'll have to go down and see your mammy. Maybe we'll bring Terry up here for a few days?'

'He wouldn't come, sure he could have stayed with Fergal. But he wants to be down there in the thick of it, especially now. He has m'mammy sick with worry. But as she says, at least he's alive. God love poor Mrs Morgan.'

'God love her. Her heart must be broke.'

7

The Pangs of Ulster

The smell of wet dexters still rose from the radiators. Skirted thighs had steamed all day, a familiar smell of comfortable boredom. A fit of yawning rippled around the classroom. We hung or slumped over the desks. A few dozed behind hands, others stared out the big windows, over the bogs, towards Milltown cemetery.

'Give yourselves a shake and sit up now,' commanded Miss Savage.

We attempted to rouse ourselves. Miss Savage was not the worst. She was still young. We were her first O-level class. She was unusually tall, and pear-shaped, a narrow top, broad beam and pole-like legs. She had a habit of sitting with her arms folded on the desk, hands cupping her small breasts. We would stare and titter when she assumed the groping position.

'Look, she's dropping the hand on herself,' Anne McCann would whisper and we'd crack up laughing. Miss Savage considered us giddy.

She came from Lisburn, which is a black hole, although she was of course a Catholic. Her people were very well to do. Her father owned a funeral parlour and the pub attached, a lucrative combination. If we managed to get her off the O-level syllabus she would tell us about her grandfather, who at seventy-six read books on self-improvement. Once he read Dale Carnegie's *How To Win Friends and Influence People*. He decided to try out a method of striking up a friendship with a stranger; he would find a stranger and admire some aspect of their

person. He practised on his son's customers in the pub.
There was a woman of middling years sitting alone, drink-
ing gin. She was wearing a hideous purple hat. Granda
Savage saw his chance.

He went straight up to her and said: 'Excuse me for
interrupting you, madam, but I just had to have a word
with you. I just had to tell you that that is by far and away
the most striking hat I have ever seen, and you wear it
wonderfully well.'

She blushed and stammered.

'Why, thank you. It's . . . very nice of you . . . I wasn't
sure about the hat, actually.'

'Well, it wouldn't be an easy hat to wear, I'll grant you
that, many's the woman would be overtaken entirely by it.
But you now, you have the face for it.' He had made a
friend for life.

We liked to hear stories about Miss Savage's family; it
was preferable to the Viceroyalty of Fitzwilliam or O'Connell's alliance with the Whigs. Happily she got bored often
enough to cooperate.

'OK, girls, you can put away your books now. I'm going
to read you another bit from *Women of Celtic Mythology*.'

Relieved, we eagerly shoved tatty copies of the history
book into bags. A depressing lesson, the Penal Code. The
ultimate battering into the ground of the native Irish. Not
relished last thing on a Friday afternoon, especially not
now that the English were back on the street with the
welcome turning sour on them. The friendly cups of tea
for the wee soldiers had vanished with the first house
searches, and the barriers which rose up in response to
fresh ethnic clashes, as the media called them, now
excluded Brits as well as nearer neighbours.

'*An Badhbh Catha*,' read Miss Savage, 'The Raven of
Battle, *Badhbh Catha* is one of three Celtic War Goddesses,
probably distant cousins of the Greek and Roman Furies.
Frances Blainey!'

'Yes, miss?'

'Do you know all about this?'

'No, miss.'

'Well then, would you like to shut up and let the class learn something?'

'Yes, miss.'

'And, Patricia Breen, take that chewing gum right out of your mouth. Now, "Ireland has many names, all feminine. The practice of personalising the country poetically by attaching a woman's name persisted into historical times, but we do not know how far back it reaches into prehistory. Nor which of these splendid females is the original 'Mother Ireland'. *Leabhar Gabhalam*, the Book of Invasions, tells of a Gaelic invader being welcomed by three queens, Banba, Fodhla, Eire. Some scholars suggest that this is the old chronicler's way of telescoping history by amalgamating three distinct invasions and conquests and asserting the finality of Gaelic dominance. *Cailleach Bhearra*, the Old Woman of Bearra . . ."'

'Miss?' Anne McCann raised her ruler in the air.

'What is it?'

'Miss, are there no love stories in that book?'

'Oh for heaven's sake!'

'Well, miss, that's awful boring. What about Deirdre? You said last time you were going to read us that one.'

'Oh, all right, but pay attention.' She found the right page and began again. Her pleasant voice droned into the afternoon, telling the old story. 'One day, in winter, Deirdriu's foster father was outside, flaying a weaned calf for her. She saw a raven drinking the blood on the snow, and she said to Lebarcham, "I could love a man with those three colours: hair like a raven, cheeks like blood and body like snow."'

'So could I,' added Anne McCann. We laughed, same here.

'That's enough, madam! "Then luck is with you," said Lebarcham, "for such a man is nearby. It is Noisiu, son of Uisliu." And Deirdriu replied, "I will be ill then, until I see him."'

I knew exactly what she meant. But men like Noisiu were thin on the ground. Men of any description were hard to come by. It was beginning to be a strain. So I invented a man: Hugh. I first encountered him in a history book, *Ferment and Change*. He was suggested by an old engraving of the Great Red Hugh O'Donnell. A bold and noble outline of one of the great rebels. He exuded a mythical manfulness, all beard, tunic and leather-laced legs. The brat, the traditional Irish cloak, was slung stylishly from shoulder to broad shoulder, secured by a vicious-looking tara brooch. The first day my eyes fell warmly on him he lifted off the page and took life, became indispensable. He developed into an even finer figure of a man. Six foot six and broad as a door. But no spare flesh on him, a stomach as flat as a table and big, well-rounded thighs, arms and chest. There was also a judicious amount of body hair, a manly coating, and he had a fine, healthy complexion. I imagined his hair to be of a copper tinge. His was a mellow, resonating voice, pleasing to the ear. His laugh was warm and musical, infectious and possibly throaty. I was thinking of Hugh while the teacher read.

'What caused the pangs of the men of Ulster? It is soon told.' She had finished with Deirdre, moved on to the *Tain Bo Cuailnge*, the Cattle Raid of Cooley, one of the great war myths, telling of earlier Ulster pangs.

'Five days and four nights, or five nights and four days, the pangs lasted. For nine generations any Ulsterman in those pangs had no more strength than a woman on the bed of labour. Only three classes of people were free from the pangs of Ulster: the young boys of Ulster, the women, and Cuchulainn. Ulster was thus afflicted from the time of Curir Ulad, son of Fiatach mac Urmi, until the time of Furc, the son of Dallan, son of Mainech mac Lugdach. It is from Curir Ulad that the province and people of Ulster – Ulad – have their name.'

Like Cuchulainn, Hugh would have escaped the pangs, his manhood would be unimpaired.

'"Do these heads belong to our people?" said Maebh. "They do, and to the very best among them."'

Hugh's fine head would not have counted among them.

'And Maebh said to Mac Roth,' Miss Savage soldiered on, '"Say to Daire that if he will lend me the brown Bull of Cuailnge for a year I will give him a portion of the fine Plain of Ai equal to his own lands, and a chariot worth thrice seven bondmaids, and say too that I will give him the warm welcome of my white thighs."'

A squeal went up around the room.

'The dirty bitch!' exclaimed Anne McCann.

'That will do now!' Miss Savage rapped on the desk. 'Now, if you're too immature to listen like civilised beings we can always go back to the Penal Code.' We groaned submissively.

I settled comfortably back on one elbow, stared out over the bogs, shut out the modified Lisburn accent. The warm welcome of my white thighs. Hugh was, needless to say, a being of immense charm. Intelligent but not an intellectual. Witty but not gay. Bold yet never foolhardy. Wise but not pompous. Communicative but not a blabbermouth. Cultured but neither a bore nor a sissy. The apotheosis of maledom. His circumstances too were pleasing. He was of the native landed gentry. He would have countless rich and productive acres in desirable spots such as Donegal and Tyrone. But he would keep a fine townhouse, up the Falls, on the front of the Andersonstown Road. He would force upon me handsome gifts and flowers and chocolates into the bargain, hard centres. Those chocolates would be free from calories and would not induce pimples. I thought of him often. Ours was an entirely satisfactory relationship.

'And Maebh led her army against Ulster, whose warriors of the *Craobh Rua* lay as helpless as pregnant women under the spell put on them by the dying Macha, wife of Crunnchu.' Miss Savage ended on a high note.

'Miss!' Theresa Fusco's hand shot up. 'When did you say that all happened, miss?'

Miss Savage lowered her head into her hands and muttered threateningly: 'I didn't say it actually happened, dear,
it's a myth.'

'Miss, miss!' Anne McCann was on her feet again,
waving her hand in the air.

'Well?'

'Miss, you know the way Maebh was fighting? Was she
like the *Cumman Na Mban*?'

'Pardon? What on earth is the *Cumman Na Mban*?'

Anne looked astounded. But Miss Savage, coming as she
did from Lisburn, was naturally ignorant.

'It's the women's section of the IRA, miss.'

'Oh Holy God!' Miss Savage threw up her hands. 'Look,
I don't want to hear about it, Anne . . . now don't start.'
The bell, mercifully, tolled.

The trouble with the Troubles was that it was impossible
to leave them at the front door. Especially in Bunbeg. And
it did not help that the area directly outside our house was
a great spot for a riot. There was a fine selection of escape
routes – places to run to that led to other places to hide,
and the greens, although exposed, were a great rallying
point; not a tree or a shrub on the huge, flat expanse of
them. No suggestion of a park or garden, but great scope
for rioters. They gave a crowd space, somewhere to retreat
and regroup, induced a feeling of freedom, even abandon.
Our house commanded a superb vantage point. As the
political situation disintegrated we monitored the activities of gunmen, soldiers, rioters by moving from window
to door to upstairs window. But the ugliness began to
encroach on the domestic front. The tension, the
aggression, the tendency towards sporadic outbursts of
violence. Like with Father and the wardrobe.

Actually it was Sinead's fault. She was five at the time.
She does not remember Belfast before the Troubles, but
she never got used to it. By the time she started school

Andersonstown had been a no-go area for some time. The shooting went on around the clock. Sinead would stand at the window every morning at seven when Mother was leaving for work. She would refuse to get dressed or to let me comb out her ringlets until she had a last view of Mother disappearing round the corner.

'Come on, Sinead, let me do your hair.'

'In a wee minute.'

'We're going to be late.'

'I want to see Mammy doesn't get shot,' she would insist as I arranged the huge tie around her little neck, or tried to force her stubborn feet into fur-lined boots.

When she was in primary one there was an explosion next to her school. She was blown out of her desk by the force of the blast. Mother, stitching pink tuxedos at a factory about three miles distant, abandoned her machine the instant after the blast and ran panic-stricken all the way to St Vincent's. The unruffled child was carried home intact, a blessed relief, while police collected the real victims in large plastic bags.

Later that afternoon Sinead climbed into an empty wardrobe in the back bedroom and closed the door behind her. It was never clear what she was doing in the wardrobe, certainly it was in her nature to seek dark, quiet places. But when she attempted to emerge, the door was stuck fast. When pushing and calling for her mammy proved useless she threw herself with all her slight weight against the door. But as it burst open the whole mahogany structure heaved, leaned forward and came crashing down onto the floor with Sinead inside.

The screams were unmerciful, the panic universal. Father threw us all out of his way, righted the wardrobe and retrieved the body. She was alarmed, but in one piece. The wardrobe however did not escape unscathed. It sustained no damage from the fall, but Father, cursing the bastarding thing to hell, attacked it with an axe, smashed it to pieces and threw it out the bedroom window into the back garden.

'We never had any luck of that wardrobe anyway,' he said later in self-vindication.

The wood from the dismantled wardrobe gave out great heat.

Shortly after that things became unpleasant for Mother and her Catholic co-workers at the Fermanagh Warehouse and Linen Mills, where they sewed business suits and gay tuxedos for American executives and flies-by-night. The Fermanagh was located in the Village, a Protestant stronghold on the other side of bogs and the motorway. There was a precarious arrangement and one often strained by the daily violence. Remarks would be passed by the Protestant majority, allegations would be whispered in lift and the canteen. But work was scarce and, as Mother kept insisting, no one was going to put her out of her job until she was ready to go. She had no sense that there was any real danger. But then, Father said, she had no sense.

He used to collect her every day from work at four-thirty. Often they would give lifts to the girls who lived near us. They were all young women, about eighteen or twenty. But Mother was the sample worker and worked harder and faster than any of them.

'They're only half my age,' she would say, 'but I wouldn't see them in my way.' She thought most of them were rough and ignorant. 'They fairly let the Catholics down,' she complained constantly, 'but God love them, they don't know any better.'

One Friday Mother rang home about four o'clock. I took the call.

'Annie? Oh thank God! I was worried you might be at opera rehearsal.'

'No, where are you?'

'At work. There's a bit of trouble down here. There's a crowd at the gates, waiting for us. I don't know how we're going to get out.' She sounded more excited than afraid.

'You mean Protestant?'

'Yes, they're angry about the bombings this week. They're demanding we get the sack or something. Listen, when your daddy comes home tell him to come and get us immediately. I'll have Angela and Josie and wee Marie with me. We're all going to stick together. Your daddy shouldn't be long, he gets out early on a Friday.'

'Is that m'mammy?' Sinead asked coming to the phone.

'Yes, now be quiet. Mammy? I'll let m'daddy know, but stay where you are, don't be going out to the gates.'

'We won't. Tell your daddy we'll be watching for him, and tell him to sound the horn.'

'Can I speak to her?' asked Sinead. I shook my head threateningly. 'Tell her there was shooting but I'm OK. I hid in the nasturtiums,' said Sinead. I pushed her away from the phone.

'I'll tell him.'

'I'd better go now. See you later, love. Is Sinead all right?'

'Yes, she's here now.'

'Well I have to go.'

'Mammy . . .' but she'd already hung up. I half suspected she was enjoying herself.

'What's up?' Sinead wanted to know.

'Nothing, why?' I said innocently.

'Is m'mammy coming home soon?'

'Aye, but she wants to get some messages first.'

Father arrived home a few minutes late. I met him at the door and gave him the word from the battle front. He was furious.

'What's up?' Sinead asked again.

'Shut up,' I ordered.

'You see, your bloody mother . . .' he said, breaking off in exasperation. Sinead was beginning to look alarmed. 'How many times have I told her to get out of that bloody dive?' He ran through the house and out into the back garden.

'I know,' I agreed soothingly, 'but she likes the work.'
He was opening the shed next to the coal-hole.

'Well she'll not like being battered to death by a mob
from the Village.' He rummaged around inside the shed,
among the garden tools and his picture-framing and the
stacks of wood for kindling. He emerged clutching a
hatchet.

'What's that for?' I asked, stupidly. Sinead began to cry.

'What do you think?' He hurried up the path and got into
the car, me scurrying behind, Sinead wailing behind me.

'What are you going to do?'

'I'm going to get your mother.' He drove off at speed. It
wouldn't matter, there would be no policemen in the area
to stop him. I gave Sinead a good smack across the arse to
make her stop crying and made her go in and do her
spelling.

The car pulled up an hour later. Thomas and Brendan
had come home by that time. We went out to see if the
father had brought back the wee woman. He had. She and
a crowd of young women climbed out of the car, laughing
and giggling.

'Rescued!' they yelled triumphantly. They appeared to
be intact.

'What happened?' Thomas demanded.

'Your father rescued us!' Mother declared delightedly.
'He just drove up to the gates and they let him in. We were
all waiting and we piled into the car and away he went out
the gates again before the Prods knew what was happening.'

The girls roared with laughter again at the thought of it.

'But why did they let you in the gates?' I asked Father.

'Sure they didn't know who the hell I was. I just gave
them a smile and a salute, flashed my Hughes Bakery pass
and they waved me on.'

'You showed them your pass to Hughes! You were lucky
they didn't drag you out of the car,' Thomas said severely.

'Sure they didn't know what I was showing them. They
were too keen to get at your mother and company.'

'But didn't they see you all in the car when you drove out?'

'They did, but your father was hanging out of the window, one hand on the wheel, the other waving the oul' hatchet at the Prods, driving like a lunatic. So they all backed off. We were halfway up Dover Street before they realised.'

The stitchers retrieved their belongings from the chaos at the back of the car, thanked Father again and went off home.

'I needn't tell you, Bernie, that's the end of the Fermanagh. We don't need the money that badly.'

Mother said nothing at first, and then ventured: 'There's never been any trouble before.'

'Well there'll be no more from now on because you're not going back there.'

'We'll see how it goes. Mr McCleod said he would get us police protection in future.'

'Aye. You can imagine the RUC protecting you. You're not going back, Bernie, that's final.'

'We'll see what happens,' she said pleasantly, not meaning to be stubborn.

She took Monday and Tuesday off and she and the others started back stitching the pink tuxedos the following Wednesday. Policemen were in evidence at the Fermanagh gates every evening from then on, but Father was still obliged to go and rescue them several times over the next eighteen months until it became obvious, even to Mother, that it would be bound to end badly. She finally, reluctantly, handed in her resignation.

'It's heartbreaking,' she said at the time, 'that was the loveliest material I ever worked with.'

8

Invasions

I awoke to the insidious sounds of the invasion. Scurryings in the street below, the high-pitched whine of the saracens, the sound of officers calling out commands. Louder by the minute. It was still very early but I could hear my father in the next room tuning his radio to the police messages. Thomas was on the landing, yawning, bleary-eyed.

'The Brits have moved in.'

'Did they wreck the barricades?'

'Must 'av.'

'But where were the boys? There wasn't any shooting.'

'Dunno. They must have been expecting it.'

I'd have to get up then. I'd die a death if they came in and caught me in my nightie. One leg out of the blankets and straight into the jeans that were left, the legs neatly accordioned for easy entry, for just such an emergency. A quick cold wash, a lick and a promise. No time to turn on the immersion.

We slipped down the stairs, furtive in our own home, and watched the proceedings from the front window. The place was alive with soldiers, milling about like a colony of ants. A sense of contained panic. Bunbeg was lined with saracens, jeeps, ferrets, and there were assorted armoured units stretching up Macroom Gardens like a great khaki serpent.

A group of officers stood directing operations from the crossroads opposite our house. We could hear them discussing the geography of the estate with their fruity Sandhurst accents.

'Macwoom Woad is ova tha, sa, and just ova ha we have Macwoom Gadens, sa!'

'Jaysus,' Thomas chortled, 'it's like something out of Biggles.'

'Have they lifted anyone yet?' inquired Father appearing in his wool simit and very little else.

'Don't think so. They haven't started searching the houses yet.'

'Bastards.'

'Aidan, would you for Christ's sake put on your trousers. It'll be great if they come to get you, and you in your bare arse.'

'It's as fine an arse as you'll see this side of Cork.'

But he disappeared upstairs, a man being at his most vulnerable with his trousers off.

The army stomped around for another fifteen minutes, apparently doing very little, then gathered for a brief conference on the green opposite the house. The soldiers then spread out in all directions, some up Carnan Way, some up and down Bunbeg, others up Macroom Gardens. There were hundreds of them. They had the place entirely surrounded.

Father had turned on all his radios. He tuned one to Radio Ulster and the other half-dozen to the police messages. We learned that we were in the middle of Operation Motorman. The breaking down of the barricades, the end of the no-go areas, the flushing out of the IRA. An optimistic view on the part of the security forces. We watched, more with amusement than alarm.

Our neighbours had begun to appear at their doors. Probing heads at first, then whole substantial bodies stood in doorways, arms akimbo, daring the Brits to violate the sanctity of an Irish home. Mr McIlhone could be seen hurrying as usual down the garden path, his lunchbox under his arm. On his way to work. Not quite. He was approached by an officer and two soldiers who evidently ordered him back into the house. Other men emerged to go to work, in dungarees and overalls, well-intentioned respectability. They were all sent back indoors. We were all under house arrest.

'How are we supposed to work?' Mother wondered.

'There'll be no work today, Bernie,' said Father with ill-concealed relish. 'They have the whole area cordoned off. They'll be searching all the houses. There'll be a lot of arrests today.'

'We'll not be able to go to school,' I said, secretly delighted, glad of any excuse.

'No, and we'll not even be able to have fresh bap for breakfast,' Thomas moaned.

We were indeed reduced to tea and toast. We all ate at the window, anxious to bear witness to this historic event. The army seemed to be doing a lot of waiting or planning or maybe thinking. It wasn't until seven that they got started on searching the houses. Half-a-dozen squads of soldiers set out in different directions and commenced house-to-house searches on every row. Methodical, if threatening. At first it seemed routine, but then the first man was escorted from his home, marched down the garden path and forced into the back of a saracen. We didn't quite believe it at first.

'Are they arresting him?' Mother wondered.

'What do you think they're doing with him?'

'But sure, he's a quiet wee man. He wouldn't be in anything.'

'They don't need an excuse, Bernie.'

Within minutes a handful of other men were led, more or less quietly to the waiting saracen. But anger was mounting behind the dozens of picture windows surrounding the green and the intersection. The inhabitants began to emerge at doors and onto porches. From the three-storey maisonettes at the top of Macroom people came out to hang over the ugly cement balconies. At first there was little said, realisation was setting in. But gradually the first indignant whimpers of protest could be heard from the neighbours of the arrested men.

'Where are you taking them?' someone called out to the soldiers.

But the response was undiplomatic: 'None of your bloody business. Now get inside!' The soldier raised a gun and pointed it at the inquirer. Other soldiers stationed near other houses did likewise: containing the local population.

But the order went unheeded. Rather it had the effect of inciting those who were generally unhappy with the morning's proceedings. Like Mrs French. She quickly became quite vocal. She left the warmth of her living-room window, threw open the front door and sashayed down the garden path, her big hips lumbering from left to right. We were all crowded around the front door at this stage and got a terrific view of the entire performance. Two or three soldiers squatting at her low garden wall looked around in alarm at this assault from the rear. They levelled their rifles at the generous target of Mrs French. She spat at one of them with admirable force. A blob of smoker's phlegm lodged on his cheek and he jumped up in horror, wiping off the spit. He was very young, no more than eighteen and obviously no match for Mrs French. She advanced unmolested, bosoms swinging, and stood threateningly at the top of the path surveying operations.

'Do your worst!' she yelled suddenly, addressing those in command. 'Every dog must have its day and this is yours. The British army has always been great at attacking the defenceless and the downtrodden . . .' She paused to draw on the cigarette.

The army looked at her with interest, not quite sure how to manage this intrusion into their tightly scheduled day. They had anticipated concerted armed resistance, spontaneous riots, sniper attacks, but they had not anticipated Mrs French. They were thrown long enough to give her her head.

'Do whatever depredations you will,' she invited reck-

lessly, 'and you will have them visited upon yer own heads
tenfold. We've been fighting yez for eight hundred years
and yez haven't beaten us down. Not through massacre or
the penal laws or the famine – ' Dramatic pause, neighbours and army alike watched in fascination. 'You,' she
bellowed, singling out a soldier who was leaning against a
parked car, 'just take a good look at the faces of every man
yez take away today, for those faces will haunt you for the
rest of yer life. I see you, I know yer regiment and I know
what you look like and if I was you I wouldn't sleep
soundly from this day on.' The soldier began to shuffle
uncomfortably. 'And that goes for the whole lot of yez. Our
sons, they have sons!' she continued unrelenting.

But at least one officer had had enough. He walked
briskly up the street, commandeered two soldiers and
ordered them to get that woman in off the streets. They
managed eventually to do so, but only because Mrs French
offered minimal resistance. She was probably anxious to be
back in front of the fire. We noticed that Bernadette and
Niall were the only other people in the house that day.
Mickey the father, Mickey the son and Danny the holy
terror having conveniently cleared the scene.

The searchings and the arrests continued. As the day
progressed the army's search technique improved. They
could do a three-bedroom house in no time. Except for the
French residence, which was something of a learning
experience. It was about one o'clock when they started
down our side of the street. The first few homes were
uneventful. We watched from the front door as the para-
troopers moved purposefully up and down the garden
paths, or took up defensive and unnecessarily contorted
positions at harmless house corners or behind inoffensive
parked cars. Now and again we heard the sound of rubber
bullets exploding somewhere nearby. Pockets, no doubt, of
isolated resistance.

Oddly, Mrs French had been quiet for the past couple of
hours. 'God knows what she's up to,' said Father.

But she was lying in wait. The morning's verbal skirmish would be only a foretaste of protests to come. The soldiers had just finished at the Gilroys' and now crossed the lawn into the Frenches' garden. The very second they set foot on French territory the front windows of the house were thrown open and the deafening sound of pipes and drums blasted all over the street. An auditory counter attack. The 'Irish Soldier Laddie'. It hit the English soldier laddies like a bucket of cold water. They halted all at once, assaulted by the incredible din that made the house vibrate, and carried over the road, over the green and right up Macroom.

'Christ!' yelled the soldier nearest the front door, 'what the hell is that?'

It was an alternative Irish welcome. But the chorus was even louder than the verses:

Ahhhhh – Will you stand in the van like a true Irish man?
We're going to fight the forces of the crownnnn!
And will you ahhhh-march ah-with O'Neill to an Irish
    battlefield?
For tonight we're going to ahhhh-free old Wexford town!

One of the stirring renditions. Rendition. A rending of the ear-drums. The paras looked rent. They stood dotted among the knee-length weeds of the garden, some covering their ears, awaiting direction. A business-like corporal moved from a nearby jeep, made his way officiously up the path. The officers camped out on the corner watched with glum interest.

'What's this then, lads?' the corporal yelled above the music, 'put off by a bit of a song, are we?'

The paras advanced again, half seriously, half in fun, rifles now levelled at the front window. One banged at the door with the butt of his rifle.

'Open up now, please. Search in progress.'

The door remained closed against them. The soldier

grinned at his companions, banged again. Another tapped
on the window.

'Hello in there. Open up, please. Routine search in
progress.'

'He should say "Open in the name of the Queen",'
Brendan suggested.

At that moment, Mrs French flung open the front door,
looked the soldier up and down and placed her womanly
bulk in the doorway. Manning the barricades. Finding his
way so amply blocked the soldier hesitated. Mrs French
eyed him, drew deeply on a cigarette and pushed back her
newly dyed golden hair.

'Yes? What is it?' she inquired with exaggerated dignity.
This morning's outpourings had been merely spontaneous,
now she was at her best. 'Can I help you?'

The corporal moved up to the porch. 'We're conducting
a house-to-house search, ma'am. We'd like to take a look
inside.'

'Oh would you indeed?' she retorted, giving him the
once-over. 'It seems to be you've been taking a bloody good
look in the windows for the past five minutes.'

'We want to search the premises, ma'am.'

'And who, may I ask, are "we" exactly?'

'The British army, ma'am,' he responded sharply.

'Oh the British army, is it? Her Britannic Majesty's
peeping toms. And may I ask what the hell right yez have
to come searching my house? I would remind you that this
is Ireland. A sovereign nation. This is no bloody British
colony.'

Now the corporal was very sure of his ground here. 'With
respect, ma'am, Ulster is a part of the United Kingdom.'

'Ulster me arse. Sure yez don't even know what Ulster
is.' She leaned towards him and enunciated very carefully,
as if talking to a deaf simpleton. 'I do not recognise British
jurisdiction in Ireland. Now put that up yer arse and
scratch it!'

The corporal paused momentarily: 'Nevertheless we're

coming in and we're going to search the house. We'll do it with or without your cooperation.'

'I'm not stopping yez,' she declared, a sudden shift in tactics. She stood to one side. 'Come on in, lads,' she signalled to the soldiers in the garden, 'I've nothing to hide. Come in and look all yez want. Wreck the place if yez like, tear up the floorboards, terrorise my children. But just remember I'm admitting yez under protest.'

They filed past her, rifles discreetly lowered parallel with legs, anxious not to provoke her.

'Just remember when yer tearing this home apart that every one of ye is infringing my human rights. This will be reported directly to the Commission on Human Rights in Strasbourg. England's name'll be dragged through the mud again. This is a violation of my privacy.'

We could hear the soldiers moving about the house and Mrs French moving after them, filling their ears with threats and curses. A soldier appeared at the door, 'Eh take a look at this, lads.' He spoke in a cheery north-country accent and held up a cardboard placard, 'One Man, One Vote.' He handed it to a soldier on the path who passed it in relay down to the waiting jeep.

'Where the hell's gates are yez going with my placards?' Mrs French shrilled from the hall.

'Confiscating them, missus,' advised the northerner.

We missed the fulsome response as another soldier crowded her out of the hall and handed several more placards out the door. 'Ireland Unfree Shall Never Be At Peace'; 'Up The IRA'; 'Victory To The Provos'; 'Brits Out'. The paras laughed at each new slogan and erupted entirely when the corporal appeared at the door with a basket full of straggly kittens.

'Leave them cats alone,' she yelled; then, turning to her neighbours, 'Do yez see what the great British army has come to? Waging war on helpless animals. I suppose they think the bloody cats is IRA couriers.'

'We aren't arresting the cats, but we will arrest you if
you don't stop disturbing the peace,' said the corporal.

'Peace me arse!' she ejaculated. 'You know what you can
do with your fucking peace!'

But she quietened down after that as the soldiers com-
pleted their search. She stood causing an obstruction in the
doorway, quoting Pearse: 'They think that they have paci-
fied Ireland.' She was addressing the people of Bunbeg and
Andersonstown generally. 'They think that they have purchased the half of us and intimidated the other half.' Two
soldiers squeezed by carrying piles of Republican newspapers. 'They think they have foreseen everything, they
think they have provided against everything; but the fools,
the fools, the fools! They have left us our Fenian dead, and
while Ireland holds these graves, Ireland unfree shall never
be at peace.'

'Holy God!' exclaimed Father with admiration. 'She got
that all right.'

Mother glared up at him. 'I don't care if she did, she's
letting the whole street down in front of them.'

The army did not dawdle chez French. There were a few
minor confiscations, nothing, Mrs French assured Father
later, that would seriously impair the advancement of the
cause.

We were next.

'Search, sir?' asked a soldier hopefully, uncertainly.

Father considered for a second then stood back to let him
enter. The soldier crowded into the little hall with us,
followed by four or five others. One lanky enthusiast set
foot on the first stair.

'Just hold on there,' Father commanded.

The lank stopped where he was, turned to look at Father.

'If you're going to search this house I want to be with
you at all times.'

The lank looked surprised. 'OK then,' he said, and he left
his rifle down in one corner of the hall.

Father passed him on the stair, led the way. The soldiers

followed in a thudding line of khaki, us behind them. We filled the landing and the stairs.

'Right, in here then,' said the lank as Father escorted him into the little bathroom.

The oppressed people confronted the occupying forces across hotpress and toilet bowl.

'Fine, thank you. And are, eh, these the bedrooms?'

Father nodded morosely, pushed open the door of the parental chamber to reveal an unmade bed, sock-strewn floor and a dressing table littered with personal debris. Brendan, dangerously straddling the stairwell with one foot on the banisters and the other halfway up the wall, looked over the soldier's head and tittered. They set about searching. Embarrassingly thorough. They rummaged in drawers, felt in coat and trouser pockets, squatted down to look under the bed and chest of drawers. Mother was mortified, the traditional mortification of the Irish mother. Father was only quietly angry. The soldiers did not find what they were looking for in the master bedroom. They trooped out again and stepped up the landing, over fishing gear and assorted boots to the room I shared with Sinead.

One tightly constructed little para lifted the frill of the bedspread and peered underneath.

'Would you look at the dust under your bed,' hissed Mother, 'you could make a man of it.'

I gave her a discreet, dirty look. The pot calling the kettle black. But I held my tongue, for she would not have forborne to thump me in front of our visitors.

The boys' room was so small as to warrant no more than a quick rotation of the head. No hiding place. But even so it was in a state of chassis. The paras were disinclined to paw around among the piles of clothing, tatty books, comics and tangles of fishing line lethally threaded with vicious hooks. They shuffled past us, then paused at the head of the stairs. The lank looked overhead. 'What's that?' he asked, pointing to the roofspace cover.

'The glory hole,' said Sinead. He looked at her warily. He may have assumed she was a simpleton.

'Can we get up there?'

'If you're game,' said Father without enthusiasm. 'We have no ladder.' A little green lie.

The others gave the lank a leg up. As he swayed six feet above us he pushed at the square plywood cover.

'There's a latch,' Father advised bristling.

The lank managed it, raised the cover in one hand and stuck his long head into the darkness beyond. The head swivelled. 'I tell you what, there's room for a regiment up here.'

He pulled himself up by the elbows, legs flailing, then one last heave and he was sitting on the edge of the square hole. 'I'd better have a look around then.'

'Watch yer foot doesn't go through the ceiling,' warned Father, 'walk on the planks.'

'Right-O.'

We heard him clumping about, checking behind the water tank and hoaking among the thigh-high piles of back-issues of the *Irish News*.

'Anything up there?' called a colleague-in-arms through the black hole.

'Not really,' he called down. A load of old rubbish, is what he meant.

His shorn head appeared again out of the gloom. 'I'm coming down.'

Legs first, swinging wildly about for a foothold, not daring to steady himself by getting a footgrip on the wallpaper, such as it was. One soldier supported him on his shoulders as he fumbled to replace the cover. He descended with a thud, a deep and painful bending of the knees. He was covered in the grey fluff of roof insulation. He picked it out of his hair and off his chest. A hunter-gatherer activity. We clattered downstairs again past the front door where English voices could still be heard calling out orders. They found nothing of interest, no threat to national security in the living room, kitchen or dinette. They omitted to look in the combined coal-bunker/garden shed.

'Like they're very thorough,' whispered Father sardonically as we followed them out. 'We could have had the entire Belfast Brigade out in the shed.'

They left without a word. As they set off down the path I noticed the rifle still propped in the corner of the hall beside the meter box.

'Daddy, they forgot this rifle.' Brendan poked his finger down the barrel, twirled it on its butt. 'Should we keep it? They'll hardly notice one mangy wee rifle.'

Thomas hesitated. A grievous temptation.

'For Christ's sake wise up,' said Father, irritated. 'They'd just love you to keep it.' He was already out on the path.

'Hey you!' he called, 'do you not want this rifle or what?'

The lank blanched.

'Hand me that up, Annie. For God's sake don't be pointing it at your mother!'

I lifted the rifle. It was much heavier than it appeared. I held it for a few seconds by the barrel, and felt sick. Surprisingly, unaccountably sick. I thought fleetingly that it wouldn't be so easy to shoot someone in the head after all. The lank appeared at the door, alarmed. I couldn't shoot him now, I was thinking, he was too stupid. Relieved I handed over the very offensive weapon.

'Thanks,' he said as he turned to go. 'Wouldn't do to leave this behind.' But Father only glared suspiciously.

We thought that was it and moved back onto the porch to witness the rest of the day's proceedings. But not so fast. A second detail of paras now descended on us, crowding the path and the strip of side garden, trampling the deadly nightshade and the sweet-scented stock.

'Which of you is . . . Ay-Dan . . . Mc Feelmc?'

We laughed at his pronunciation, but blood pressures soared.

'That's me,' Father owned up.

'Why? What do you want him for?'

'If we could just have you out here, please.'

Mother opened her mouth to protest but only gulped. The beginnings of panicked tears.

They led Father down the path, told him to stand against the gable wall. I remembered this scene from numerous movies. Helpless Jews lined up against weeping walls by Nazi death squads, Mexican revolutionaries before firing squads, the St Valentine's Day massacre. Father was going to be traditionally riddled against a wall. Against the very wall where for years I played 'A-bouncey Mrs Brown'. I'll tell you a story of Crock McCrory, a hole in the wall, and that's it all. A bullet hole. So that's what happened to Crock? Taken out and riddled by the Brits. And Father was next. They were going to eliminate him, pepper him with bullets, perhaps from the very gun I had so helpfully returned, in front of the Murrays and MacShanes and Frenches and Gilroys. A blatant atrocity. I wondered if it was because of the two guns wrapped in the carpet.

Father's earliest memory of his own father was of Granda on top of an armoured police van, battering all round him with a hurley stick as half-a-dozen RUC men attempted to apprehend him from below. I didn't want my last memory of Father to be of his sinking into a pool of warm blood on the grey Housing Trust concrete of Bunbeg Gardens. Mother would be a widow and then the Brits would be sorry. She would not go gently . . .

'If the army ever killed any of mine,' she used to threaten, 'by Christ I'd go over to London and chain myself to the gates of Buckingham Palace, naked!' – we would be in a kink laughing at this point – 'caesarian scar and all,' – Brendan had been a caesarian – 'and I'd tell the world. I'd soon make them sit up and listen. By God they'd rue the day they touched any of Bernie McPhelimy's family.' The trouble was, she meant it.

And now Father was up against a wall, a soldier on each side and nowhere to run. Mrs French, lured by the promise of an atrocity, sidled across her garden and stood facing Father.

'What are they going to do to you, Aidan?'

'I think they're going to take my photo actually, Patsy.'

He was right. A camera was produced from the back of a jeep. A soldier stood focusing. 'Don't smile, mate,' he warned.

'To hell with that, Aidan,' said Mrs French. 'Smile all you want, you're in your own country.'

He burst out laughing. The soldier looked unhappy but snapped anyway.

'What are you going to do with that?' demanded Mother.

'It's just for our files.'

'You mean he's a suspect?'

'No, it's just routine, for the files.'

'It's routine in a police state, you see, Bernie,' added La French.

'That's true,' said Father. 'We have no civil rights.'

The cameraman moved away, but the other soldiers stayed on the path beside Father. Maybe they were going to arrest him and were just waiting for the order. An authoritative nod. What would we do? I could imagine the goes of Mother. She'd lie down in the middle of the road, naked of course, and block the path of the saracen taking him away. If they beat him . . . His retina might detach itself again. His ulcer might burst under questioning and he'd bleed to death in the Andersonstown barracks . . . But just then the soldiers moved on and we withdrew to make a cup of tea.

Later that afternoon. There were fewer soldiers around now. The army had begun to pull out. But we were still confined to houses. About three o'clock we heard the discharge of a plastic bullet and the shattering of glass very nearby. Then screams; shrill, angry screams. Women's voices.

Mother went out to the door, called to a soldier in the front garden, 'What's going on? What's happened?'

'Get inside,' he answered. He seemed tense, fearful.

Mrs Gilroy was on her doorstep, looking up the street. 'Do you hear that, Bernie?' she shouted. 'That screaming's damnable. Something must be up.'

'Who is it?'

'It seems to be coming from one of the houses just round the bend. But they don't seem to have taken any more men away.'

The screaming continued. People began to leave their gardens, to wander up the pavement, cross the road. The soldiers were too distracted to notice. I followed Mother and Mrs Gilroy a few doors up the bend. The screaming was coming from the Nolans'. The house was surrounded by soldiers and there was shouting too. Someone was abusing the soldiers. 'Vicious evil bastards! Murdering bastards!'

It was Nuala Nolan, a big mild-mannered senior from St Catherine's. It wasn't like her.

'You didn't have to do that. She wasn't doing anything. She was only opening the window in her own house.'

Her younger sister Mairead came out of the house, she too was in a state. 'Come in, Nuala. Mammy wants you.'

She led the distraught sister back inside. An officer appeared at the door.

'Get these people out of here,' he commanded.

'What happened?' someone called to Nolans' next-door neighbour.

'Ellen got shot in the face. With a rubber bullet. All she was doing was opening her window,' the woman wiped her eyes, 'God help her, you should see the state of her. She'll be blinded for life. I saw the one that did it. It was a skittery big get with sandy hair and a wee moustache. Oh he's not here now. The bugger disappeared right after. They got him out for fear the people would lynch him. But I seen who done it. And I'm not afraid to say it.'

At that moment a line of soldiers moved towards us, ordering us back to our homes.

'Inside on the double, please.'

'Why? So you can shoot more of us like you did that poor woman?'

'You get inside or you'll get the same bloody thing.'

I couldn't believe he said that. Really undiplomatic. Two or three of them were aiming rubber bullets at us. Big, black, lethal. We cooperated. We heard later that Ellen Nolan's skull had been smashed by the impact of the bullet, caving in her face. She had lost the sight of both eyes.

The army was gone by teatime. A strange, unsettled feeling hung over the place. The tenuous sense of security provided by the barricades had gone. The British had occupied again. Father was pacing in and out of the house muttering curses under his breath, exchanging a few words with neighbours who stood around on the footpath, waiting for the next instalment.

'Aidan. Come here and see this.' Mother called him in out of the hall. She was standing at the picture window looking down the street.

'What is it?'

'Do you see who's coming up?'

We crowded round, not wanting to miss anything. There was a group of men ambling up Bunbeg, looking relaxed, swaggering even. They greeted a number of the locals, exchanged a few words about the invasion. Laughed easily.

'It's the boys, isn't it?' demanded Mother.

'It is aye,' said Father. 'Christ! The Brits don't seem to have got too many of them.'

'No but they got poor wee Mr Carney and that oul' eejit Waters who isn't right in the head. Just because they were interned years ago.'

'They'll let them out again. Sure Dan Cushnan from Gartree Place is home already,' Mr Gilroy assured Mother.

'But they shouldn't have been taken at all. Where was the IRA when it was happening? Where were they when they should have been protecting the people? What's the point in having them if they don't defend the people. Look at poor Mrs Nolan.'

'Jesus, Bernie, you can't blame the IRA on that.'

'They should have been there. But here they are, big and ugly as you please and not a scratch on them.'

'What did you expect them to do against a whole bloody regiment? Sure there's only a handful of them and damn all weapons. They're fighting a guerrilla war, Bernie. They choose the time and place. That's the only chance they have.'

'Well, they still should have been here.'

Andersonstown was no longer a no-go area, officially that is. It was still not a popular spot for soldiers and police. But the barricades, the physical ones at least, were down: the army established a series of military posts, and token patrols of the area were undertaken more or less regularly. Houses continued to be searched, men to be lifted, night-raids increased in frequency. It would be an exaggeration to say that the people became united, but they found common ground in their opposition to the security forces.

9

The Raven of Battle

There was a great restlessness in the area that night. It is hard to explain the ethereal, collective anxiety, the niggling tension that pervades a street and soaks into the houses until the occupants wander uneasily through the rooms checking the locks on the back door, peeping through the spaces between blind and window frames. There seemed to be little movement in the street below; the odd passer-by, one or two dogs out digging up gardens. But there was a clear expectation of trouble.

It was some time after eleven. I was reading in bed, something by Evelyn Waugh. A novel that smacked of Winchester and men's clubs and cucumber sandwiches. At first I heard the rumble of the saracens up on the Glen Road, the high-pitched whirr of their engines. They came closer. They had turned into Carnan. Out in force. They would be coming for somebody. As they approached I heard for the first time the piercing of whistles in the distance, then closer and closer, then more and more whistles blown powerfully from houses and gardens all over the estate. The dogs joined in, barking, yelping, howling, disturbed by the din, and more so by the panic it induced. In no time women appeared on the street crying that the soldiers were coming. Dozens of men all over Andersonstown slipped out of their houses under cover of the dark and the bloody awful racket set up to warn them.

I had dressed quickly and joined my parents in the street where they stood with a group of neighbours.

'If they're coming for us at least they'll not find us lying

down,' declared Mr Gilroy boldly. But then Mr Gilroy was
a bus driver who had never so much as let his dog foul the
pavement. It was unlikely that he would be a prime target
of the security forces.

'Never you worry yourself, Mr Gilroy,' said Mrs French
reassuringly, 'they'll have to take you over my dead body.'

The army continued its thunderous advance, making
brief stops at street corners. I could chart their path by the
sounds of alarm that preceeded them. But it still wasn't
enough, this noisy cacophony of warning. It lacked the
resonant threat of the Lambeg drum. It had no rhythm.
Then someone somewhere had an inspiration. They banged
a bin-lid on the concrete of a garden path. A full and
satisfying metallic clatter erupted from the clash of concrete and steel. The sound carried, vibrating painfully on
the ear, the rhythm battered out powerfully over the
whistles and cries. A new instrument had been added to
the community repertoire, a struck instrument. Soon bin-
lids appeared on every path, on the road, the pavements,
against gable walls. The chorus of banging bin-lids drowned
even the advance of the saracens. A powerful response to
the threat of re-invasion, a new tribal call that would
rebound for years to come off shops and homes and eating
houses, drinking establishments and other places of worship, betting offices and public amenities, schools and bus
stations and unemployment offices. The great and wholly
original tinny howl of the people.

The army came anyway, swooped into Bunbeg, blocked
the roads and got out of their vehicles. The three officers
commanding the operation were not intimidated by the
noise and hostility of the thickening crowds. But they were
too late. They broke into two houses in Macroom and
found only smouldering hearths and empty beds. The next
day another government instrument, the Northern Ireland
Housing Trust, was obliged to send out teams of carpenters
to repair the damage. The soldiers turned their attention to
a row of flats and maisonettes.

'The bastards are after Desy McIlhone,' Mrs French proclaimed with authority. She was an auxiliary, she knew all the boys. She was standing on the road, bin-lid in one hand, whistle in the other, a cigarette decorating the corner of her mouth.

'I take it he cleared off out in time?' Father speculated, his mouth white with Gelusil tablets, one hand in his shirt nursing his ulcer.

'Oh aye, he's well away by this time. Those bastards won't catch Desy in a hurry.'

We stood watching the soldiers leave the house and return to the ring of army vehicles stretched out blocking the intersection.

'Look,' yelled Mrs French with sudden indignation. She took off like a shot up Macroom towards the maisonettes. 'The gets are raiding Doran's!' she screamed behind her.

She was surprisingly agile for a woman of her weight. She bounded up the street, haunches swaying heavily, and commenced battering her bin-lid on the side of an army jeep, chanting: 'Brits out! Brits out!'

Others joined in, encouraged by her bold disregard of the soldiers who moved forward, their guns pointed at her hostile amplitude. A stocky sergeant intervened. He raised a calming hand in the direction of the soldiers and briskly approached Mrs French. 'That's enough now,' he said in a strong London accent, 'we can't 'ave you bashing 'ere on the side of an army vehicle.'

'Oh can't we indeed?' she demanded with a reasonable imitation of his accent, 'yer buckin' lucky we're not bashin' yiz on the bloody heads.'

He took her firmly by the arm, pulled her away from the jeep and pushed her roughly down the street. She did not go quietly. She rounded on him, arms swinging, bin-lid flying, and clapped the aluminium dome right down on the top of his head.

'See how ye like that, ye bastardin' coward!' she yelled,

incensed. 'That's what ye get for raisin' yer hand to an Irishwoman.'

He reeled, staggered, fell heavily onto the road, not at all sure what had hit him. A roar of approval went up from the bin-lid brigade. Three or four young soldiers ran to the sergeant's aid. They dragged him hurriedly to his feet, helped him over to a saracen. Others produced batons and moved threateningly towards the crowd, which backed off with a great derisive howl of laughter, and stopped no more than fifty yards away, ready for the next skirmish.

Meanwhile the search detail emerged from Doran's dejected, empty-handed. A frail little woman stood on the porch sobbing and visibly trembling, one hand covering her anguished mouth.

'Are ye all right, Minnie?' some of the neighbours called to her.

She nodded tearfully, wiped her hand across her streaming eyes. Her old brown dressing gown flapped about her bird-like legs. She stood watching the soldiers, seemed embarrassed by the attention of the crowd.

'Oh the British army is a noble body of men!' declared Mrs French with heavy irony. 'Look at the way they're able to bash and harass defenceless women!'

She singled out a rotund little captain and addressed further unflattering remarks to him. He looked tired and uncomfortable. Around him his men smirked and one or two laughed outright. The neighbours watched the antics of Mrs French with amusement, disgust or pride. Mrs Gilroy lowered her head, muttering, 'For the love and honour of God you'd think her man would take her in off the street. What must the soldiers think of us?'

'Sure her man's on the run this week back,' advised Mr Curran from lower Bunbeg, 'and anyway, who gives a bollocks what the British think of us?'

Mrs French was beating on the bin-lid again, this time with a portion of paving stone torn up by local youths some days before for use as an anti-army missile. She beat out a rhythmic chant on the tinny instrument and began singing in time:

> Through the little streets of Belfast
> In the dark of early morn
> British soldiers came marauding,
> Wrecking little homes with scorn.
> Heedless of the crying children,
> Dragging fathers from their beds,
> Beating sons while helpless mothers
> Watched the blood flow from their heads.

The women around her took up the next verse while the soldiers left the last of the flats being searched and regrouped at the main vehicles.

> Round the world the truth will echo.
> Cromwell's men are here again;
> England's name again is sullied
> In the eyes of honest men.

Cromwell's men climbed, disgruntled, back into their jeeps and armoured cars and set off in convoy, looking tired and bitter. A bad night's takings, nothing but bloody rain and abuse. A few of them hung out the back of the jeeps as they passed the chanting women, let fly one or two offensive remarks.

'Go on, you stupid ole bats. We're not fru wiv you yet. We'll be back. You'll see. We'll be back.'

They were as good as their word. They came back that Saturday afternoon, for Mickey French. Nobody was ever sure what, if anything, Mr French did to warrant being arrested and interned. I don't think he was in the IRA – not exactly. But he may have been an auxiliary. Father suspected he was a courier. And he sold the *Republican News* in the pubs and drinking clubs. 'They wouldn't let him into the IRA,' Father maintained. 'He's too fond of the drink. They might use him occasionally, but not with anything important.'

Mr French had disappeared about ten days before. His wife gave out that he was on the run, wanted for his involvement in an operation which she wouldn't go into . . . He reappeared every couple of days. On Friday night, for a noisy party hosted by Mrs French, and he collected his boru money in person. We were beginning to think that the security forces couldn't want him too badly. But the army finally came for him anyway. They kept a low profile as they drove into the street and pulled up outside the French house. A mere four vehicles; about twenty soldiers. A string of them filed up the path, knocked at the front door, like the breadman calling to settle the weekly account. For once they caught Mrs French unawares. She was in bed asleep when Mickey himself, who happened to be making a flying visit, opened the door to them, let them in. Well, he wasn't going to make a fuss and maybe get shot in the back trying to escape. That was an old favourite with these boyos. It was clear they had him this time. He'd go quietly. He didn't think it worthwhile disturbing the wife just at that moment. Young Niall was at home, he could tell his ma when she got up.

'She's not very well, the wife,' said Mickey as he put on his overcoat, 'I don't want to get her upset. She's really not strong.'

The sergeant in charge raised his eyebrows incredulously. He had had the opportunity of witnessing Mrs French in action. 'Right. Outside please,' he ordered.

They led Mickey down the path before an audience of gaping neighbours. I think he enjoyed the brief moment of glory. His manful walk into custody was not overshadowed by the usual accompaniment of Mrs French's verbal assault. He was in the armoured car before she even made it down the stairs. Young Niall had wakened her after all. She crashed through the front door as the army vehicles started up.

'Mickey!' she yelled in a voice designed to penetrate the thickest of British armoured steel. 'Mickey, where are you? Come out. Let him out, you bastards.' She ran down the path, her great sagging breasts flopping under her flannelette nightdress, her hair wild about her. We could hear the soldiers burst out laughing in the back of one of the jeeps. She reached the armoured car, began battering on its side, demanding the release of her husband. When the vehicles gathered speed she took off after them down Bunbeg, hair and curses still flying as they gradually left her behind. She stopped just before the shop. It was at that point she turned on the neighbours, delivered to them the fullness of her anger.

'Why the hell did yez let them take him?' she demanded to know. 'Why didn't yez stop them? Ye cowardly bastards. He's out fucking fighting for Ireland, for your freedom, and yez wouldn't even strike a blow just this once. Yez don't deserve men like Mickey French. Ye snivelling dogs, scum, lackeys. Ye deserve to be under the British thumb. Just don't come to me the next time the Brits is after one of your men!' She mustered unaccustomed dignity and flung into the house, banging the door behind her.

'God love oul' Mickey,' said Father, 'but he's better off where he is.'

La French was remarkably popular with journalists. She would give interviews and provide photo opportunities regularly without thought of gain. She made herself conspicuous during riots and other confrontations with the army; she sold the *Republican News* and other publications which the army considered seditious literature, she claimed to know the entire local battalion and their movements and she told great stories. Even on an utterly uneventful day Mrs French could be depended on to produce a story.

A few days after Mickey's arrest Bernadette French came

to our front door. I was sitting with Mother beside the fire, sock-soles in the warm hearth. We were having a pot of tea and Paris buns with butter. Bernadette came straight to the point.

'My mammy sez could you lend her a bottle of milk because this journalist has come to see her and there's no milk for a cup of tea.'

'What's his name, love?' asked Mother with interest.

'Peter Leicester. He's English, but he sez he'll tell the truth anyway.'

Mother got the milk and Bernadette left with her usual insolent toss of the head. I could see that Mother had something on her mind.

'Fancy *that* representing the estate,' she muttered bitterly.

'What?'

'Oul' Ma French. She talks to every TV and newspaper man that comes into Andersonstown. The world must get a lovely picture of us. They'd only have to see the state of that woman's house . . . Talk about the bog Irish . . .'

'I wouldn't worry about it. Any journalist in their right mind would know the kind of her.'

We lapsed into a silence disturbed only by the chewing of the crumbly buns, the slurping of the hot tea. Mother had abandoned her book, she was reading *Rebecca*, and was staring purposefully into the fire. Finally she said, 'Annie, go in next door and tell Mr Leicester that when he's finished with Mrs French I have a story for him, and that I dare him to publish it. That'll get him in.'

I rose reluctantly, straightened my skirt and went over to the French house. As usual the front door was open. Even from there I could smell the stale stink of undisturbed filth.

'Hello?' I called through the small hallway into the living room.

'Come on in, love,' called out Mrs French invitingly, 'we're in here.'

Ireland of the welcomes. *Cead Mille Failte.*

'Oh it's young Annie from next door,' she declared by way of introduction to her visitor. He sat on one side of the fire, a big man with a balding head and black-rimmed spectacles. He had a shrewd, pleasant face, a certain charm. He rose to shake hands with me.

'Sit down there, love,' Mrs French offered, indicating the dingy old settee, 'sit down and give us a bit of your crack.'

'No, you're all right, Mrs French, I can't stay. I've homework to do. I just called in for a minute.'

I had glanced around the room and seen enough to send me flying straight out the door. The fireplace was black and grey with coal dust and cigarette ash. Through the grime a small oasis of cream tile could be seen where puddles of tea had been spilt and left to dry. Strings of dried spittle hung from the fire surround, having missed their mark. The mantelpiece was covered in papers, beer bottles, cracked ornaments, socks, ties, belts and a hundred other items that had no place being there.

The room was largely empty of furniture, but the settee and two easy chairs sagged shapelessly, caked with dirt. The carpet might at one time have been patterned, but the design was now indiscernible under the layer of engrimed clay, ash and spillings. The thin curtains hung like rags at the window. Empty bottles of beer and spirits were piled up in the corners with old newspapers and sticks for lighting the fire. There was no door into the dinette. It had been removed and used as firewood during the winter. The whole house reeked of stale food, cigarettes, alcohol and cats. Mrs French sat with her fat bare legs exposed, her ankles spilled over bottle-green socks. She looked as though she had just risen from bed, although it was four in the afternoon.

'I was just showing Peter the *Republican News* that Mickey was arrested for having in his possession.'

'I know,' I said politely, 'it's terrible. I just came in to say that when you're finished here, Mr Leicester, my mother would like to give you a story and she dares you to publish it.' I winked at the woman of the house.

Leicester was clearly interested and said that he would be over shortly. I made my escape. As I hurried down the path I breathed deeply. I had been holding my breath the whole time I was chez French.

He called in shortly afterwards. It seems he hadn't stayed for tea. I introduced him to Mother, gave him one of the good chairs by the fire. He sat with his hands forming a pyramid under his chin, doubtless waiting for Mother to speak. She was talking about the cold and the price of coal.

'There was something you wanted to tell me, I think?' he ventured at last, his tone mildly encouraging, unmistakably sensitive.

'Em,' said Mother, and she paused, 'well not exactly. I mean I don't have a story for you, that was a bit of a lie.'

'Oh?' he said, more intrigued than disappointed.

'No.' Mother leaned forward in her chair. Leicester obligingly leaned forward in his. 'Actually,' she was speaking confidentially now, 'actually I was wanting to warn you.'

He recoiled a fraction. 'Warn me? Why? Is something the matter?' He had grown suddenly nervous.

'Ah no, no, nothing like that,' she hastened to reassure him, having understood his fears, 'no, it was just about that woman . . .'

'Mrs French?'

'Yes, her. I just wanted to tell you not to believe a word she says. She's not to be trusted.'

'I see.'

'She's an awful liar, she'd say anything to get her name in the paper. Take no notice of her.'

'Right.'

'What did she tell you?'

'Eh . . . nothing much really. She was telling me about her husband's arrest mostly.'

'Aye, poor oul' Mickey, I feel sorry for him, and for the kids.'

I looked at the wee woman sideways. She hated the French kids.

'How will they manage without him?' Leicester inquired with just the right amount of concern.

'It'll hardly make any difference. He never worked. He drinks you see, they both do. Even young Michael drinks. He was vomiting up against the wall there one night, not two weeks since.'

'Really?'

'So you see, you couldn't believe a thing they said. If I can ever be of help you know where I am, but don't be depending on that woman.'

He thanked her warmly and rose to go.

'Are you here for a while?' she inquired as she showed him to the door.

'Yes, for a couple of months at least. I'm staying at the Belfast Europa.'

She laughed. 'You wouldn't get much sleep then.' The Europa was bombed on a regular basis.

'No, but the breakfasts are wonderful.'

They parted amicably. He said he'd be in touch; she said she'd be delighted to see him again. He was not entirely repulsive, for an Englishman.

It had been unusually quiet for two or three nights. There had been no raids, no patrols, no riots. Such unexplained lulls in hostilities occurred from time to time. Maybe a regrouping of forces on both sides. It was a week-night. I was trying to fall asleep when I heard the first tinny bang of bin-lid. I rolled over, listened, waited. It continued. The familiar din, but different. The sound was close, yet lacked body. It lacked accompaniment. There were no whistles, no shouts, no cries of alarm, no Dr Martins thudding up the pavement carrying the word about troop movements.

This was a solo instrument. There were no other bin-lids
banging out of unison, rending the ears of the night.

I got up, went over to the window, carefully padding so
as not to rouse the house, raised the blind an inch. I could
see now why it was so loud. A solitary bin-lid banger
squatted awkwardly at the top of our path, lid in hand,
bashing rhythmically on the pavement. One alone. He
himself alone, his rear end clearly displaying a male mus-
cularity. A man, of all things. That seemed a bit odd. A bin-
lid is essentially a domestic guerrilla appliance, and more
usually wielded by woman or young boy. And he wasn't
dressed for it. He wore a heavy overcoat, tailored, navy
wool. Odder still, he wore a hat. A tweedish, rimmed hat.

As he turned his head the light went on in Murray's
porch, lit up the frame of his spectacles. He turned right
round. Not a young man, but I knew the face. It was Peter
Leicester. Peter Leicester. God knows why. There was no
sign of soldier nor saracen. The pavement was gleaming
from the rain. People would be in their beds, except perhaps
Mr Murray who would be standing dourly in the doorway,
offering moral support. But there he was, the solitary
banger, trying to rouse the district. The populace may have
sensed the beat of a different bin-lid, an alien rhythm. For
they failed to respond. I wondered about the media.

10

The Wail of the Bean Sidhe

There was a big, ignorant knock on the door and Brendan limped out to investigate. He had fallen off the coal-shed roof the week before, playing Davy Crockett in the Rocky Mountains. A voice spoke past him: 'Is your Annie in?' A big, ignorant voice.

I went out to the door, out of interest. Three or four young women crowded into the hall. I recognised two of them. They were Mother's colleagues from the Fermanagh: wee Marie the fancy stitcher and Josephine who never did a hand's turn. There were no preliminaries.

'You speak French, don't you?' Josephine demanded to know.

'Eh . . . yes, sort of,' I was being cautious. I imagined the wee woman would have told them I was fluent. I had spent the summer in Brittany, one of a hundred celtic teenagers succoured temporarily by *L'Organisation de Secours Internationale Coltique*. It was a dull summer. The family who were my saviours worked during the day and played Irish music abominably in the evenings. There had been no one to talk to. My French had not profited noticeably. But the young women were now demanding my services as translator. Before I could protest they had taken me by the elbows and frog-marched me down to Bunbeg Walk.

Something was going on. There were army jeeps and RUC armoured cars blocking the street. A crowd had gathered outside one house, and rows of soldiers flanked the path and doorway.

'You'll have to talk to these French journalists,' one of

my escorts explained. 'The army's raiding the house, and God love wee Mrs Monaghan, her man's in Crumlin jail.'

'What did he do?'

'Nothing.'

'What did they say he did?'

'Ballykinlar.'

That got my blood up. Everybody was in for Ballykinlar.

'OK. I'll talk to them.'

They led me up to the house, past the soldiers. They made no attempt to stop us. Wee Marie went inside, signalled for me to follow. The living room was packed with army personnel, RUC men and the French connection, who were waving lights about above head level. At the centre of it stood a small dark-haired woman, looking unhappy and bewildered, and beside her stood Mrs French, helping to facilitate the international exchange.

'Here's wee Annie now,' she announced effusively. 'Come on in, love, and tell these French fellas the right way of it.'

She hauled me into the centre of the room, introduced me to the woman of the house. 'Now tell them,' she commanded.

I glanced around the room. A dozen dour faces fixed me in their sights. 'What? Tell who what?'

'Them,' she indicated the three slim, sallow foreigners who were watching me eagerly. 'Tell them the truth.'

I wanted to be helpful, to be cooperative, so I cleared my throat and asked the journalists what they wanted. They looked relieved to hear my halting, careful pronunciation. They wanted to know why the man of the house had been arrested and when. I turned to Mrs French. 'They want to know when Mr Monaghan was lifted and why.'

She gave me the details. I conveyed them as best I could to the visitors. The man asking the questions nodded gravely. He understood. Then he turned to an army officer standing directly behind him and asked if he knew anything about the case against Mr Monaghan. The officer, whose face seemed to be entirely devoid of expression, answered in French which would have been perfect, except that his accent did not at all deviate from English received pronunciation. He had nothing to add to what I had said that would be of any assistance. The Frenchman nodded again, turned back to me and asked me if the army usually conducted such orderly searches. I translated the question for Mrs French.

She let out a loud, hollow laugh and slapped me on the back. 'Christ, that's a good one,' she cawed, her breasts heaving in mirth, 'orderly! Did you hear that?' – she was now calling through the hallway, addressing the crowd outside – 'these boyos want to know if the British army always conducts such orderly searches!'

The crowd roared with delight at the idea of it. The Frenchmen probably got the picture, but I struggled to translate faithfully most of the lengthy response supplied by Mrs French. It was necessarily a free translation. I could not put French on 'bastarding cunts'. But the journalists understood entirely, made furious notes. And what, they wanted to know, were the army looking for here today?

'Guns, ammunition, explosives, subversive literature,' Mrs French advised.

I did my best, but I had never learned the French for explosives. I paused mid-sentence, trying to think of an appropriate word. The journalist was bending over me, concentrating intensely on what I was attempting to say. The policemen and soldiers looked bored. My eyes flicked round the walls of the room in a futile search for a Harrap's English-French dictionary. They came to rest on the expressionless officer. The very thing. I would ask him.

'How do you say explosives in French?' I asked him without thinking.

The whole room turned to him to gauge his reaction. Would he collaborate? He looked surprised, an expression at last, and then, without reflecting blurted out, '*Plastiques*, it's *plastiques*.'

I gave him a generous smile and finished my translation. He kept an uncomfortable eye on me for the rest of the interview.

'That was a good one, him tellin' ye the word for explosives,' chuckled Mrs French as the journalists packed up. 'They'll knock his bollocks in when they get him back to the barracks,' she added with satisfaction. I was dismissed.

That evening wee Marie called. She had a present for me. A tube of mascara and a palette of assorted eyeshadows.

'These are for you,' she said, holding them out to me.

'Me? Why?' I was overcome.

'I just thought you'd like them. The young fellas hijacked a van going to the chemist's in Leenadoon, and there was all these cosmetics in it. There's stacks of other stuff too. I'll get you some lipstick if you like.'

'No, you're all right, Marie, this is terrific.' I gratefully accepted the little gold-encased offerings and carried them off to my room to marvel at them.

The wee woman stuck her head in the door some time later. 'Your daddy says wee Marie was up,' she said.

'Yeah, so she was.'

'He said she gave you some make-up out of that hijacked van.'

'Yeah.'

She came over to admire it, studied the eyeshadows under the light. 'Very nice,' was the verdict. 'Now you're not to be wearing it.'

'No.' Pointless arguing. I would wear it in the privacy of my own boudoir.

Mother went towards the door. She paused, turned: 'Was there anything else in that van they hijacked?'

'I don't know. I think she said there was . . .' I knew what she was after.

'I wonder if there was any tablets?' she asked nonchalantly.

'Probably.'

That was all the encouragement she needed. She disappeared mysteriously into the twilight and reappeared at bedtime, her handbag stuffed with little boxes which she hid in her jewellery case. The hijackings became all the rage.

He was bringing up the rear as they passed our house, the last soldier in the foot patrol. The saracen sat in the middle of the road down at the shop, an unhelpful distance. The shots came from behind a house on the corner of Bunbeg Walk. The last soldier dropped his SLR and fell over clutching his left side. The others froze, panicked, scattered. They did not return fire at first, instead they scattered towards the saracen, keeping low, trying to bury their heads between hunched shoulders. One or two recovered once they reached the shelter of armour plating, took up firing positions and searched for a target. We could hear them shouting to each other, shrill, frightened voices.

'Did they get one?' Father inquired as he came down the stairs, carrying a radio tuned to the police messages. He could be callous. Mother was out having her hair done.

'Yeah, there he is, right outside.' The soldier was lying where our car would have been if it wasn't in the garage again for repairs.

Another burst of fire came from the row of houses behind the saracen. They thought themselves surrounded. One yelled out in fear, triggered a second wave of panic among the men crouching behind the lumbering vehicle. As a third burst of fire came from their right they hurriedly backed into the mouth of the saracen, scurried up inside and pulled the door closed. They had abandoned their fallen comrade. It all happened in less than a minute.

'They left the wounded one,' Brendan observed. 'Will the Provos kill him?'

'Not at all,' said Father. 'They'll be away already. The army will be back with reinforcements.' He paused, he was eyeing the khaki figure lying in front of the house. 'I suppose I'd better go out and see how he is.'

We followed him outside and gathered around the wounded soldier. He was lying with his back half on the curb, half in the wet gutter, groaning in pain. He was young, about eighteen. He looked terrified. A dark, wet stain was spreading over his left side, up his shirt, over the top of his trousers. Father knelt down beside him and the soldier cringed away in terror.

'There now, there now,' Father, irritated, tried to soothe him, 'I'm not going to touch you, you'll be all right.'

'Will I call an ambulance?' asked Thomas.

'The soldiers will have done that already, but I suppose you could, just in case.'

Mrs French's door opened at that moment, she came out onto the front step. 'Is he dead, Aidan?' she called pleasantly across the garden.

'No, he's OK, he's been shot in the side.'

She went back inside and came out again carrying a cushion. 'Here,' she offered the cushion, it was strawberry crushed velvet, 'stick that under his head, Aidan.'

Father took the cushion, laid it on the pavement and bent down close to the soldier. 'Now, I'm going to lift you up onto the pavement,' he explained, 'you'll be more comfortable.'

The soldier whimpered, tried to shake his head.

'You'll be all right now,' Father reassured, 'I won't hurt you.'

But the soldier tried to protest. Mrs French leaned down, her face close to his and shouted, 'Why don't you just shut up and do what you're bloody well told. You're bloody lucky the IRA don't come and finish ye off.'

A little cry sounded in the soldier's throat as he twisted away from the hideous face hovering above. As he arched his back Father saw his chance, slipped a big arm under his spine and raised him gently onto the pavement. He settled the fair head onto the cushion. 'There, isn't that better? Are you OK?'

The soldier only groaned in response.

'What's your name, son?' Father asked softly.

'Lionel . . .' the boy whimpered, 'Thurston.'

'I'm going to take a look at the wound now, Lionel, to see if I can stop the blood.' Father carefully removed the belt hung with little pouches and packets of soldierly necessities, opened his jacket and eased his T-shirt gently up to reveal the wound.

'Yuck!' cried Brendan, gagging and covering his mouth.

Father gave him a foul look. 'It's not as bad as it looks,' he pronounced.

The young soldier turned towards him and spoke in a feeble, breathy voice: 'Am I going to die?' He had a cockney accent.

'No of course not,' said Father, 'it's not that bad, and they'll have an ambulance here in no time.'

'Christ I hope they remember,' Mrs French butted in, 'the last I seen of yer mates they didn't seem too worried about ye. They were shittin' themselves to get away out of here.' She drew on her cigarette, flicked the ash over the soldier's legs, and leaned over to inspect the wound. 'Jaysus, Aidan, he's losin' a lot of blood. You might be a gonner yet,' she added, addressing the soldier.

Father couldn't help but smile; Mrs French always entertained him. 'It looks worse than it is,' he repeated. He smiled encouragingly at the soldier. 'Now I'm going to press down here to try to stop the flow of blood, so you just relax.'

Thomas came back and handed Father a clean towel to mop up the blood. 'The ambulance is on its way.'

'There you are,' said Father, 'you'll be safe in hospital in no time.'

'I only arrived last week,' the soldier gasped.

'Did you? Well you've had a warm enough welcome. They'll probably send you home now.'

'I hope so, and I'm not coming back.'

'If you hadn't come in the first place you wouldn't be
lying here now in a pool of your own blood,' Mrs French
pointed out. 'Go back to your own country and leave ours
be. Eight hundred years of occupation is enough.'

A siren sounded in the distance. 'That'll be the ambulance now.'

It was. It came zooming round the corner down Bunbeg
and braked to a halt beside us. It was from the Royal. There
was no army escort, no other vehicle of any description.
Three men jumped out, brought the stretcher immediately.
The driver kept the engine running. They quickly
inspected the damage.

'Right,' said one burly paramedic, 'let's get him in.'

'Aren't you going to put on a bandage or something first?'
Father inquired.

'In this place? Are you mad, mister?' responded the burl.
'We can do that in the ambulance, we want to clear out
while we've got an ambulance to go in.'

They hoisted the soldier onto the stretcher. He cried out
in pain. 'You'll be fine in a minute,' said the burl, 'we'll
just get you out of here.'

They all but threw him into the back of the ambulance
and two of them climbed in with him. The burl swung up
beside the driver, banged the door, and the ambulance shot
off towards the Shaw's Road. We were left standing in a
circle around the strawberry crushed velvet cushion. There
was nothing left of the young soldier but a dark red stain
on the pavement.

11

Valentines

It wasn't all violence. There was sex too. I first heard about sex when I was eleven, from Anna-Maria Donnelly. We were sitting on the ground inside an enormous bush in the Falls Park, sucking ice-lollies. Unintentionally phallic.

'Do you know how you get babies?' asked Anna-Maria out of the blue.

'Of course, my mother told me when I was only three and she was having Brendan. Out of the mother's stomach.'

'Yeah, but do you know how the baby gets in there?'

'My mother said that the couple pray to God for a baby and that if they're lucky he puts one in the woman's stomach.' I smiled tolerantly, God was something of a problem. 'I suppose it's just nature.'

'You know what I heard?'

'What?'

'I heard that the man puts his thing in the woman's thing . . .'

'What thing?'

'You know . . . his thing, down there.'

'You mean his wee man!'

'Yes, and anyway . . .'

'Where does he put it?'

'You know . . . down there, your wee purse, where you go to the toilet . . . and he puts the seed inside her.'

'Ach, rubbish!'

'No, it's true.'

'That's disgusting, Anna-Maria, absolutely disgusting. I never heard the like of it! It's absolute nonsense. Sure it wouldn't fit!' I was horrified. I couldn't imagine a more ludicrous arrangement.

'I asked our Ursula and she said it's true.'

'She's having you on. Anyway what would she know? It's just a rumour. You remember the rumour about the statue of Our Lady that's hands moved? Well it's the same sort of thing, sheer nonsense. I mean . . . it wouldn't even be hygienic.'

I had convinced her, she conceded that maybe she'd heard wrong. 'Well I don't think you should go around telling anybody else. All right?'

'All right.'

We crawled out from under the bush and spent the rest of the afternoon trying to identify the debris in the outdoor swimming pool.

I continued for years in this retarded way. My love life was nothing to speak of. I like to think that came from not being let out of the house. Or perhaps it was just me. Or just men. Many's the man may want a bride, Maloney wants a drink. Drink certainly seemed to be a priority with the grown men of my acquaintance – drunken uncles, alcoholic cousins abounded. But I don't discount the possibility that I may just have been physically repulsive and utterly without charm. Like Hilda.

Hilda was my best friend, very clever, very creative, well-intentioned. Yet she seemed to repel people. They felt uncomfortable with her. I couldn't understand it. I could see that she lacked charm, but she had wit. And she did everything so well. She was the cleverest girl in the school; she wrote beautifully, sang and acted rather well, was gifted in the plastic arts and kept her clothes and belongings in perfect condition for years. When we were all running round with our elbows out of our jumpers and holes in our tights, she was a picture. She did things so flawlessly that I called my most perfect doll after her. But she was without arrogance and was the most tolerant of souls. And yet everyone avoided her.

Her physique was not up to the standard of her other attributes. She was squatly square, somehow seemed shapeless, although only slightly overweight. She had a long, rectangular face with a shadow of the masculine somewhere about it. And perfect white teeth. In all the greasy teenage years of our acquaintance she never had a pimple. And yet she never had a boy either.

If girls found her difficult, boys considered her impossible. I remember one time trying to get her fixed up for a *ceilidh*. I had been invited as a result of parental pressure, by a friend of Thomas's, one of the few young men of my acquaintance. Of course it was not to be a date in the accepted sense. It was more that my mother had arranged with his mother for him to escort me both to and from the *ceilidh* at a woefully early hour. Bill's function was to prevent my being dragged into the back of an army saracen, or shot in crossfire during some insignificant nightly skirmish. He was very decent about it.

Thomas was also to be there, as were a number of his classmates, produce of the Christian Brothers to a man.

'Did oul' Donovan really put his hand on your thigh?'

'He tried, but I put my boot up his arse.'

'He'd have enjoyed that, the same oul' fart.'

Hilda, who had also planned to go to the *ceilidh*, was without an escort. I sought to remedy the omission. It was two nights before the *ceilidh* and Thomas and friends were in the sitting room. I opened the door and waited for the smoke to clear and the stereo to be lowered. A Leonard Cohen lament. Definitely not the way to say goodbye. There were boys sprawled all over the room. A very intimidating sight. They all looked up, awkwardly.

'Hello, Annie,' one or two of them mumbled, feeling they had to. Thomas eyed me sternly. A sister was clearly an embarrassment to him. A matter of principle.

'What is it?' he demanded irritably.

'I was just wondering . . . were any of you going to
Clonard Hall on Saturday night?'

There was a howl of affirmation, some unwarranted
snickering.

'Well, do you all have partners?'

'Na, not yet,' said wee Bobby McCarney, 'but just wait
till the women see us. They'll be round us like flies round
shite.'

More hysterical laughter, a smattering of good-natured
insults.

'I was just wondering,' I persisted, 'because I've got a
friend who's going and she hasn't got a partner . . .'

Thomas groaned, but the others were clearly interested.

'What's she like?' Bobby wanted to know. He was usually
game for anything.

'She's a very nice girl.'

I got no further. Thomas and Bill had cracked up.

'It's bloody Hilda, isn't it?' Thomas said accusingly.

'Yes,' — I had to admit it — 'but she's a really nice person.
She's very interesting to talk to.'

Thomas and Bill were by now falling all over each other,
in fits of laughter.

'She doesn't live very far, it would be no trouble taking
her home.'

'But she's an ugly bitch,' Thomas roared, delighted at the
joke.

'Is she?' asked big Pat Boomer, who had been interested
for a minute.

'Aye, she's a bit of a boot,' said Bill with a laugh. 'No
offence, Annie, but you have to admit like, she's not very
attractive.'

'Not very attractive?' Thomas whooped, 'not very *attractive*? Jaysus, that's a goodun, she's a buckin' ugly bitch.
And she's fat too.'

'She's got great bone structure,' I said in her defence. But
that was the last straw. The whole lot of them collapsed in
a pile on the floor, rolling and laughing and yelling: 'Great

bone structure, Christ that's a goodun, great bone structure!'

Hilda went to the *ceilidh* unescorted. She left the same way.

Still, she took a real interest in men, and was always supportive in the matter of my liaisons, which were almost entirely imaginary. Certainly my relationship with Jimmy Cane never got out of the realm of fantasy. My infatuation for him stretched over four years and came to a bitterly painful and sudden conclusion. I remember the first time I took him under my notice.

I was fourteen, walking down Bunbeg Gardens one Sunday morning, going to get the ice-cream for dessert. We usually had dessert only once a week.

He was coming up the way, towards me. I hardly noticed him at first. It wasn't until I realised that he was staring hard at me that I looked into his face. I had an impression of hair falling over his eyes, and stubble, and a sour look. So I thought. I gave him a dirty look in turn and went off around the corner.

It was about a fortnight later when I saw him again. I was with Hilda that day. We were going down to her house to mind her grossly precocious brother while her mother went to a dance: St Agnes' Confraternity annual dinner dance. Great crack. Hilda's father was spending a few months in a sanatorium as a result of alcohol poisoning and something to do with restless legs.

We were at the bottom of Bunbeg when I saw him coming towards us with a very slow, almost rhythmic walk.

'You see him coming up the street?'

She peered through her spectacles. She must have needed the lenses changed again. 'Yeah, what about him?'

'He gave me a dirty look the other week.'

'What for?'

'Nothing. He was just comin' up the street and he gave me a dirty look. I didn't do anything.'

'Do you know him?'

'I never saw him before. He's a hateful pig.' I had decided to take umbrage against him.

'Well he's staring at you again.'

'Oh is he indeed? Well I'll just stare back. The ignorant pig.'

He was nearing us now and looking right at me. The sort of look that was disconcerting, a lazy look, but piercing with it. I decided it would be better just to ignore him. We walked quickly past him, me staring straight ahead.

'I wouldn't give him the satisfaction of taking him under my notice,' I declared.

'You know, I don't think he was giving you a dirty look,' said Hilda thoughtfully. 'I mean, he didn't seem to be angry or anything.'

'No?'

'No. I thought it was more of . . . a sexy look, actually.'

'A sexy look? What do you mean?'

'You know, a sort of sexy look, like this.'

She narrowed her eyes and pursed her lips. Hilda had very red, well-shaped lips.

'But why?' – this was entirely new to me.

'I don't know, maybe he fancies you.'

'Ach don't be ridiculous.' I'm only a child, I was thinking. He seemed very old to be fancying girls our age.

'What age would you say he was?'

'I don't know. About nineteen maybe?'

'Well, I think he was just giving me a dirty look.'

But the next time I saw him I wasn't so sure. I had been to Leila Barnwell's house. She was an old friend of my mother's and had made me a hotpants suit. She thought it was lovely; airforce blue with patterned collar and cuffs. A suede belt shaped like a chain of butterflies.

'Thanks very much, Leila, it's gorgeous.'

'It's lovely on you, why don't you wear it home? It'll save you changing.'

'Do you think I should?'

It may have been the height of fashion, but I wasn't keen to be seen in it. It was so short: I was so self-conscious.

'Of course you should, you look terrific in it. A real smasher. Now tell your mammy I'll be up on Monday night with the curtains.'

She abandoned me on the doorstep, leaving me to walk all the way up Bunbeg, a good quarter of a mile, with my white thighs bare to the world. Still, it was teatime, maybe nobody would see me. But Jimmy Cane did. He and his friends were sitting on a low brick wall outside Brogan's shop. Real corner boys, all jeans and Dr Martins. They had piles of rocks and broken bricks at their feet, waiting for the soldiers to drive past.

There was no scope for detour. I would have to brazen it out and hope they wouldn't notice me. But already I could feel his eyes on me, doubtless appraising white blubber. I would stay on this side of the street, pretend I hadn't noticed him. This time he was smiling, a very easy, relaxed smile. Very sure of himself. He had stood up and was leaning with his back to some railings, his arms folded, long legs stuck out taking up most of the pavement. He watched me all the way up the street and I felt the chill on my legs. I was wearing high suede boots, which had fallen off the back of a lorry in the direction of my cousin Terry. I felt like an eejit.

He kept staring, mercilessly. I hated him more than ever. I was right opposite him when I heard someone say: 'I like your hotpants.'

I didn't know if it was him or one of his friends, but I wanted to die. I wished a saracen would come round the corner and drive over me, flatten me all over the road. To create a diversion. I passed on. They were still calling after me. I was too agitated to hear properly. All I could think of was my hotpants, providing no cover for my ignominious retreat, and my backside, spreading hugely across the pavement. I would never wear hotpants ever again.

I never entirely recovered from this humiliating experience, which occurred largely in my own head. But having passed through childhood happily unconscious of my looks and the effect image could work on others, I had learned at last the torment of being self-conscious.

I don't know where he disappeared to, but I didn't see him again for almost a year and then he could be seen in Bunbeg regularly three or four times a week. But I made bloody sure that he didn't see me. I would watch him from the upstairs window. It was my first chance to get a good look at him. I don't know what came over me in my fifteenth year, but I had stopped hating him. Worse. Now I thought he was gorgeous.

He was tall, about six feet, with a big chest and shoulders, and long legs. Much like the heroes of my daydreams. He had a broad, strong face, and longish brown hair, and, best of all, stubble. It was through Jimmy Cane that I became fatally attracted to stubble and big thighs. He had big muscular thighs which I could imagine being put to great use. Use of an undefined nature. And he had a slothful, provoking smile. As if he was always laughing at everyone. But I didn't care. I was entirely fascinated by him. Yet I would walk a mile out of my way to avoid him and all the wee hard men who ran around with him.

One summer evening I was invited to Eileen Duffy's sister's engagement party. Eileen was a friend who had been granted the seal of parental approval. Maybe they'd let me go.

'I don't mind,' said Mother. 'But you'd better ask your father, you know what he's like about parties.'

'Daddy, can I go to a party tonight? Marie Duffy's getting engaged.'

'Ask your mother.'

'I did, she said I can go, but I have to ask you.'

'Where is the party?'

'Just round the corner, Carnan Gardens. In Martin's house. He's the fiancé.'

'And are Eileen's parents going to be there?'

'Ach Daddy!'

'Wise up, Da!' Thomas was always scornful of the failure of the parental imagination.

'It's only for young people, Daddy.'

'Will there be drink there?'

'No! Of course not. Martin's very good-living.'

'Well . . . you can go – ' I was ecstatic already – 'provided you're back by nine o'clock.'

'Oh no! It doesn't start until half-nine!'

Negotiations ensued. I was finally allowed to stay until ten o'clock. I was to make Martin and Marie and Eileen walk me back home, I was to behave myself. We were to steer clear of foot patrols. Eileen accepted the terms. My friends all knew that my parents were weird and pitied me accordingly. So I went to the party. He was there. His presence was entirely unexpected. He was a friend of Martin's, who was happy to tell me all about him: his name; that he lived in Creeshlough Drive, just two streets away from me; that his father was dead and that he lived alone with his mother. That he had asthma and was in the IRA. That he was twenty-one and had a job. It was a pity about the asthma, but the rest was fine, and anyway he was very well-built and with care might get over it.

The evening was partly thrilling and partly an ordeal. There were only a few girls present, no more sophisticated, no more pimple-free than Eileen and myself. But there were plenty of shuffling, awkward boys weighing us up and talking disparagingly about us behind each other's backs. There was the pleasant manly smell of fresh sweat. It was disturbing. I was out of my depth. Especially when I saw him, sitting on the other side of the room with a glass of Guinness in his hand, looking moody, a fine growth of stubble on his chin. He had seen and looked away. I wondered if he would talk to me. If he was interested at all this was his chance. I was clearly unescorted. But he was more interested in downing the pints.

Eileen and I entertained each other most of the time.

Martin and Marie were kissing out in the hall. The unattached men kept well clear of us, like at the Thursday novena: incline unto my aid, Oh God, Oh Lord make haste to help me. I was actually bored. There was no room to dance, but even if there had been we couldn't possibly stand up and disgrace ourselves in front of so many boys. We did not move with natural rhythm or even with grace, and we had little practice.

I can't remember how it happened, but somebody introduced me to Joe Smith.

'Is that your real name?' I asked, for something to say.

It was, and it suited him. He was tall, too tall, with a soft, pretty face entirely free of stubble. He had lovely black hair and cornflower-coloured eyes. The kind of fella you'd look twice at in the street. My first impression was that his eyes were slightly bland, even vacant. But at least he was talking to me. He must therefore have some discernment. After a while he got me another lemonade, the glass dripping only a little, and began to tell me about his work. It was not fascinating. He was a carpenter's apprentice and told me all about dovetail joints. There were no sexual overtones in his talk of dowels and couplings. He was a little less boring than the party.

It was ten to ten. I stood up to go home, trying at the same time to pull down my too-short skirt. It was a bad moment. Surely everybody was looking at me, probably scathingly. Martin and Marie were out in the hall again, having another court. Eileen had promised to see me home. She stood up with me now and Joe offered to walk us round to Bunbeg. We left without my even looking at Jimmy Cane. I think he was still drinking steadily.

Eileen was helpfully discreet. She dropped behind as we made our way up Carnan Gardens and appeared to give her attention to the night-dark gardens on either side.

'Where have you been all my life?' he asked mournfully as we walked.

'Round the corner by the looks of things,' I responded.

'It's strange we haven't seen each other before.'

'Yes.'

He was even taller than I thought. I had a slight pain in my neck from looking up at him by the time we reached the corner of Bunbeg. He put his hands on my arms and turned me to face him. Eileen was standing a little way off with her hands in her pockets, examining her shoes.

'Would you mind if I kissed you?' he asked timidly.

I found this polite, if disappointing. I thought for a moment. 'OK then.'

'Right.' He got ready.

He glanced quickly at Eileen then leaned down, his spine painfully curved, and manoeuvred one arm around my shoulder. I wasn't sure what to do with my arms. I think I was waiting to be told. I put one hand on his shoulder, more a gesture of defence than invitation.

'OK,' he said and bent his face over mine.

Our noses collided. They were both reasonably long noses. He drew back awkwardly, surveyed the target area and moved in for a second try. Our lips connected without thrill. His seemed remarkably soft and I wondered if mine were too. Perhaps it was in the nature of lips. His lips opened softly and mine followed suit. There was nothing in the middle. It was rather wet and empty. After about thirty seconds of hollow-mouthing a saracen droned past on patrol and the soldiers cheered out the back. We separated quickly.

'Well?'

'Is that it?' I asked. I think I wiped my mouth with the back of my hand.

'Eh . . . yes. What do you mean?' He looked worried.

'Well there's not much substance to it,' I said, 'I mean, it doesn't seem to have a centre. There's nothing at the heart of it. I sort of thought it would be firmer . . . somehow.'

'Did you?'

'Yeah.'

'No, that's it,' he assured me. I was prepared to give him the benefit of the doubt.

We stood in silence for a moment.

'Well, I better be going,' I declared in a fairly business-like manner, 'I've only two minutes to get in or my father will be out looking for me.'

'OK. Can I see you again?'

'I'm not allowed to go with boys.'

'You don't have to tell your da.'

'I suppose I could say I was going to Eileen's.'

'Yeah. So where should we meet? Is here all right?'

'No, meet me down at the Holy Child.'

'About eight?'

'I usually have to be back by nine.'

'OK then, seven.'

He kissed me again, just briefly, and I walked down Bunbeg.

They didn't tell me for months after, but my parents had watched this first illicit encounter from the bend in the street. Mother had restrained Father, he had wanted to come up and murder Joe.

Now both of them were standing cross-armed and cross-faced on the garden path. They both seemed to be pulsing with anger. Father was dancing up and down on the heels of his carpet slippers, his two hands in fists.

'What's wrong?' I inquired feebly.

'Get in,' Mother spat through her clenched teeth. It was remarkable how she could talk with her teeth sealed together like that.

'Get in, ye filthy bitch,' added Father, who saw visions of my early moral decline.

'Why? What's up?'

He gave me the rounds of the kitchen, he called me a whore. I might as well have been entertaining a regiment. But he never mentioned Joe, so that when I was eventually driven up to bed I was still more puzzled than annoyed. As I lay awake with my heart thumping fearfully in my chest

I thought about that wet, hollow kiss and decided it wasn't worth it.

Somehow I reached an arrangement with my parents the following night and was released to visit Eileen. I met Joe as planned for my first official date. He took me to a civil rights rally on the Andersonstown Road, and then on to a disco. We went together for three weeks and then had an argument about the friend he introduced to Eileen. Now Eileen was a lovely looking girl, and intelligent and refined into the bargain. Joe's mate, I think they called him Bowser, was an overweight, inarticulate skinhead with his jeans halfway up his calves. She didn't like him. Loyalty prevailed over base physical attraction; I went off with Eileen and Joe was left with Bowser.

Joe didn't amount to much, but he took my mind off Jimmy Cane for almost a month. I saw Jimmy a fair bit that summer. Now that we had a mutual acquaintance and had met in respectable circumstances he could no longer make smart remarks from the other side of the street. Now when we passed each other in the street he would nod gravely and I would nod grimly back.

It wasn't long after Operation Motorman. Andersonstown was no longer a no-go area for soldiers and police and so we had riots and shooting almost every night. Of course Jimmy was too old and too tough to be stoning the soldiers, but he was always about whenever there was trouble, manoeuvring in the dark. It was a wonder he wasn't interned with half the other fellas from the area. I decided he was too shrewd, too quick to get caught.

The jangle of bin-lids will carry well on the night air. It will alert volunteers, rouse the locality and unsettle the nerves of foreign troops. But it is not always enough. Sometimes greater extremities are called for. Mrs French was not the woman to shrink from extremities. To provide a more *puissant* system of alarm, to upgrade technological

capacity, Mrs French introduced the siren and experi-
mented to achieve maximum effect. We learned of her
latest acquisition about 2.00 am one Saturday morning.
The house was silent, the street deserted. Sinead may have
been asleep. The siren went off. It felt like an explosion in
my head, but unlike an explosion it failed to come to an
end. It would be one of my bad dreams.

Sinead, more asleep than awake, threw herself on top of
me in dozy panic. I struggled up in fright, we fell heavily
out of bed. We were fully awake now, but the nightmare
continued. I think we screamed, but the sound was lost in
the merciless wail which, like the lament of a thousand
banshees, rose and rose and expanded to fill the night. It
damaged the ear and the nerve endings, it left the hearer
shattered, disoriented. We were still lying in a tangle of
bedclothes on our rose-coloured rug when Father appeared
in his simit, waving a flashlamp.

'What . . .?' we could hear Thomas inquire shakily from
the boxroom. Even Brendan had not slept through it.

'It's OK,' Father yelled above the din, 'it's only a siren,
the army's on the estate. Stay where you are. Go back to
sleep.' He went to investigate.

The French home was set back further from the road
than our house, so that our gable wall and path ran along
the side of their neglected front garden. Having procured a
factory siren from sources unknown, Mrs French had
strategically placed it on our path, facing our gable, to
ensure quality amplification of the sound. It was heard all
over Andersonstown. Hilda's father, returning home from
a local illegal drinking establishment, heard it as he fumbled for the keys to their lovely bungalow in Gransha.
Eileen's sister and her fiancé, courting late in the sitting
room, heard it down in Riverdale. Alex and Kitty had just
got Benedict off to sleep up in Leenadoon when he was
awakened by the noise. And we heard it most clearly of all.
It was our own private Blitz. The house throbbed in agony.
It was to throb for many nights to come. Before long the

whole of West Belfast knew of Bunbeg's early warning system. Mother recognised the voice of the siren. 'It sounded like the siren from Mackie's Foundry,' she commented the next morning as she lay with her aching head on the arm of her chair. She was right. Mackie's Protestant foundry horn had been requisitioned for the national cause. It was never to sound hometime ever again.

Our apparent inability to secure reasonable male companionship was the principal distress of our girlhood. It may have been the result of a population imbalance, or an effect of the revolutionary activities of many young men who expended all their energies on the cause. It was incomprehensible. But for secluded hours on end we would lament and analyse our manless condition.

'I mean, it's not as if we're really ugly or anything,' Eileen would say. 'I mean, we're not gross.'

'I have a horrible smile,' I led off the litany of defects. 'My brothers call me acre-arse.'

'Ach, Annie, you're always saying that.'

'The facts never change.'

'But we have good personalities.' Hilda was sure this should count for something. 'And we're intelligent.'

'Exactly, that's the problem. Boys don't like intelligent girls. I mean look at our Marie. She's always letting on to Martin that she's dimmer than she is. He likes that.'

'I know, you scare them off if you're too clever. The only thing is, we never get to meet any boys in the first place to scare off.'

'I can't understand it,' said Hilda, 'we all have assets.'

This was an interesting notion.

'What, for instance?' I demanded.

'Well, for example, Eileen . . . you have gorgeous big brown eyes, and you're slim.'

'Yeah,' agreed Eileen bitterly, 'I have no bust.'

'And you, Annie, you have fine eyebrows and a lovely speaking voice.'

'Oh Jaysus! Terrific! God help us if that's it. A lovely speaking voice. Fellas don't give a shit about a lovely speaking voice.'

'Right. Fellas like blond hair and big breasts. You're depressing me, Hilda. I didn't think that was all you could say about me . . . frog eyes and no figure.'

'I didn't say that, Eileen, I mean you're so dainty and petite. I wish I was slim. I'd give anything to be slim. Look at Patricia Breen. She's so skinny, and she can get all the men she wants.'

'That's because she's got so many brothers. They keep bringing their friends into the house. I mean Patricia has actual contact with the opposite sex! But you should see her in her nightdress. I saw her when we were on retreat at St Gerard's. God, it was pathetic. Pure Biafra.'

'It doesn't matter,' Hilda insisted, 'I'd give anything to be skinny.'

'Would you drop your IQ by twenty points?'

'Yeah,' she responded gloomily.

'Christ, we must be desperate!'

'We must be . . .'

'Well,' said I, trying to raise Hilda's spirits, 'you really do have the loveliest cheekbones.'

My parents, unlike those of most of my friends, talked to us about boys and sex. Mother was an authority on intimate relations.

'No man would lift you on a shovel. No man wants to marry a woman who's not a virgin.'

'OK.'

'There's nothing like kneeling with your husband at the altar rails and knowing that you've kept yourself only for him.'

'And what about the man?' Thomas wanted to know.

'The man too, of course.'

'So did m'daddy save himself up for you?' Thomas looked up from the fiddle he was mending and winked.

'Of course he did.'

'How do you know?' he demanded brazenly.

'I know. A woman knows,' she replied enigmatically.

'Sure!' he mocked with a great, crude cackling laugh.

'Our Thomas's got awful ignorant since he went to the Christian Brothers'. I thought they would have made a gentleman out of him.' She dismissed him with a dirty look.

'So were you afraid on your honeymoon . . . you know?'

'Oh aye, I was nervous. But your da was a real cod. He made me laugh till I nearly wet myself.'

'What did he do?'

'He marched up and down the bedroom with the po on his head.'

'The po! On his wedding night!' shrieked Thomas from the kitchen where he had begun to heat up a pot of animal glue, 'Christ, Mother, yous must have been mad with passion.'

'I hope you're as good to your wife as your daddy was to me. That's if you can ever get anybody to marry you.'

'No problem, Moar! The women'll be lining up when they hear I'm on the market for a wife.'

'I can imagine. We'll be batin' them away from the door.'

'So you will. But no woman'll trap me for many's the long day. So don't get your hopes up.'

'Get my hopes up? Christ, I can just imagine the sort of hussey you'll bring in. What's that awful smell? Thomas, if you're boiling that oul' glue in my milk pan again as true as God I'll massacre you!'

'This is the very best of animal glue and it's actually good for the pots. It seasons them.'

'I'll season you if you're not careful. And I bet your wife won't let you boil that oul' muck in her pots and pans, and

soak dirty goat skins in the bath.' Thomas was making a
bodhran (the hand-held Irish drum).

'Look, Mother, I'll be the boss in my own house. My
wife'll do what she's told.'

'We'll see about that. Whoever you bring in I'll tell her
about the animal glue. But I dare say you'll have about as
much luck as yer mate William has with the women.'

William was one of Thomas's friends – strange companions. Thomas with his boldness and verve and bright
wit, wielder of the twinkling fiddle, and William. William
of the immense, unwieldy stature, the watery, flat fair hair,
the acne-scarred visage and porridge-coloured complexion.
Behind thick, horn-rimmed spectacles his vague eyes
watched, unblinking. He was very odd, and that interested
Thomas, who possessed a gold-sprayed rubber bullet and
an ostrich's foot. He was William's only friend, for William
was fiercely anti-social. He despised people generally and
was wary of girls in particular. He didn't mind me. He
didn't see me as female, rather as Thomas's sibling.

He once advised me: 'You should stay away from girls,
they're only after your money.'

I looked up at him. He seemed to be perfectly serious. It
was a Saturday morning. We were in the sitting room,
waiting for Thomas to get up. William had arrived early for
their expedition to the central library, and, working on the
premise that a person like William should never be left
alone, Mother had sent me in to entertain him. We spoke
of libraries, the difficulty of finding books and silence.
Then, from nowhere, he made the remark about girls. Odd.
I, of course, nodded in agreement.

William was concerned about money. Thomas said he
was as mean as cat's shite. He invariably worked through
the holidays, although there was no call for it, for his father
was a wealthy bookie with interests in a chain of public
houses. One summer William worked in the morgue of the
Royal Belfast Hospital, washing corpses. He told us how he

could make double time by working through his lunch-break.

'You mean a mortified limb in one hand and a hot sausage roll in the other?' Thomas inquired stingingly.

'Yes,' he replied, 'it saves wasting time.'

He saved up all his time to study. He needed to, he was no better than average intellectually, yet he was determined to become an academic. He wanted to be Dr Deveny. He was working towards this goal by studying for eight hours every day. He had been a swot for fourteen years. Consequently he had no conversation. Our entire family took an interest in him. We wavered between contempt, amusement and incredulity. Mother was sure that he could be redeemed by the love of a good woman. Mrs Deveny quite liked me. But I did not feel drawn to William. He was not only dull and weird, he was unhygienic. He smelled like the corpses he washed.

One February however, I thought I'd try to bring him out of himself. I decided to send him a St Valentine's day card. An anonymous thrill. He would get a kick out of that. It would be good for him to have a normal, adolescent experience, for he had been wearing three-piece suits since primary school. Eileen helped me choose the card. The appropriate blend of provocative romance, harmless humour. We wrote it during maths class, covering it in verses collected from all corners of the school. I wish I was a bar of soap that you held in your hand . . . It would give him a laugh and he might even think some poor girl fancied him. It would be good for his self-confidence.

The night of February 13th was freezing, moonless and threatening snow. But just after nine I muffled up and set off up the street and down the Andersonstown Road to William's. I had left it late enough to ensure that there would be no one about. It was a wild night when I put my face out of the door. There wasn't a soul on the road. I could see the Deveny home, large and imposing on the corner of the Andersonstown Road and Gunn's Crescent.

The house at the crossroads. The intersection of two major thoroughfares. There were no lights at the front of the house. The family would be in the back room, studying. Mother and all, poring over her knitting patterns.

It was a huge, complicated structure of a house with alcoves and recesses and flying buttresses and archways in blank walls. I approached through Mr Deveny's rose garden, bald after the Christmas flowering, the ground cracked and frozen, tinged with frost. There was a gravel path leading to the front porch. I rose on tip-toe for minimal scrunching. I stopped at the porch. No sounds from the house. I slipped the white envelope out of my dexter pocket and laid it noiselessly on the coconut mat outside the front door. I straightened. Still no sign of life. I turned and retreated silently, out the opened gate, and hurried home.

No one could have anticipated the consequences of this inane act of goodwill. I heard it all from Thomas the next day. It seems William came to the front door about ten o'clock to leave out the milk bottles. The hall light illuminated the white patch on the coconut mat. He saw it through the glass and was immediately on his guard. He opened the door with extreme caution and peeped out at the envelope. He knew instantly that it was a letter bomb. He drew back, slammed the door and roused the house. His mother was in fits. His father took charge. He rang the army and the police. The army would come right away. The RUC were reluctant to come at all. Up to Andersonstown at this hour of the night? It could be an ambush. Mr Deveny tried to reassure them, a God-fearing man, his life and the lives of his family in danger.

Within ten minutes the army had surrounded the house and cordoned off the Andersonstown Road and Gunn's Crescent. No one was allowed past. The two main roads into the area were thrown into chaos. The traffic was diverted for miles. Queues of cars formed at all four points of the intersection. The Devenys were evacuated. Their neighbours were evacuated. They spent the next four hours up the road in the White Horse Inn.

The army sent for the bomb disposal squad, but they were occupied elsewhere and didn't arrive for an hour and threequarters. It started to snow. The media arrived. William and his father tried to imagine why they had become a target.

When the bomb squad arrived the regular soldiers were pulled back for their own safety while the RUC tried to reason with the waiting motorists.

'You'll have to turn around, sir, I'm afraid we could be some time yet.'

'Like turn round *where* exactly? There's no other way in.'

'You could go down the Lisburn Road, sir, and through the town and up the Falls Road.'

'Wise up! I haven't got all night. I'm comin' through here. Yez know it's only a bloody hoax anyway. I wouldn't be surprised if it was yous that put it there.'

It was a bad night all round.

The bomb disposal experts pumped an explosion-absorbing foam into the Deveny's hallway. The marble flooring disappeared under the white spume. Then they sent in the robot, an awkward, unstable creature on wheels, like a mobile document holder. It set off a small charge. There was a harmless pouff of smoke and it was all over. My Valentine card was in tatters, the police were in stitches, the soldiers didn't know what to make of it.

Mr Deveny was infuriated but his wife was quite pleased that at last some foolish girl had taken William under her notice. William was delighted with himself, recounting the incident over and over at school. They told him he was a dark horse and a terrible divil. He said it was awful the way girls ran after you. I think it was the only Valentine card he ever got, but he got great mileage out of it all the same.

12

Strength, Purity, Truth

While, like any God-fearing Catholic, Mr Deveny deplored internment in principle, he was frightened and repulsed by the reality of protest. It was by coincidence that Thomas and I happened to be visiting William on the morning of an anti-internment march. It was like any other August day in Belfast – very wet, very tense, very troubled. But in Andersonstown one day was as good as another for public protest, the unemployment rate being so high that a decent crowd could always be guaranteed.

The three of us had somehow managed to be included, as a musical trio, on a concert programme designed to entertain the old people of Divis Flats. At the time Father had commented that the old people would be better off praying for a happy death. But the organisers of the concert had been warned not to expect too much of the Tin Whistlers, for Thomas had told them that I could not sing, and was only being tolerated as a performer while wee Bobby was recovering from tonsillitis.

That morning we had gone to the Devenys' to rehearse. Mrs Deveny had shown us into the room which she called the parlour, but which her husband referred to as the drawing room. The front rooms of the house looked out onto the Andersonstown Road and already local traffic had been brought to a halt by march stewards who signalled their authority by means of green armbands. William's father was clearly agitated. He paced from room to room interrupting the rehearsal when he paused to deplore the antics of the gathering crowds.

'They'll sit on no wall of mine today, by God,' he threatened, his face contorted with as much menace as he could summon.

We politely murmured support. During a march the previous month a group of boys had watched the spectacle from his garden wall and in their excitement had picked the heads off all his roses. The entire road had heard the story. One more grave injustice in the dark night of the Irish soul. But he told us again.

'A line of baldy bushes was all they left. Not a Sam McCready or a Peace rose left. Well, they won't get away with it this time, you mark my words.'

Thomas nodded abstractedly as he adjusted his guitar strings.

'Oh they're all hard men of course, all dark glasses and hurley sticks, but we'll see how hard they are if they come next or near that garden today.'

William looked mildly surprised, but proceeded to rosin his bow while his father made yet another trip up and down the driveway, where he stood at the gate scowling at any young people who happened to pass by.

Before long we heard the aggressive rhythms of martial music approaching. The stamp of multiple Republican feet. The Tom Williams Pipe Band came into sight, leading in advance of the colour party. They were playing 'Roddy McCorley' with more verve than grace. Thomas absent-mindedly picked out the tune on the guitar:

Up the narrow street he steps, smiling proud and young;
About the hemp rope on his neck the golden ringlets clung.
There was never a tear in his blue eye, both glad and bright
were they,
For young Roddy McCorley goes to die on the bridge of
Toome today.

A Druid land, a Druid tune! As the first flag came into sight the crowd joined with the marchers in a chant which could be heard above the band.

'What do we want?' their leader would demand through a megaphone, and they all yelled back with a noble vigour, 'Justice!'

Then, at the top of his magnified vocals he would yell, 'And what do we get?'

And the awful, indignant roar of a wronged people would be hurled back, 'Six months!'

At the first roar Mr Deveny had scurried up the path and slipped in the front door, as though he were somehow responsible for internment. We stood in Mr Deveny's bay window looking down the road to the right. Soon the People's Taxis crawled into view, square and awkward, the black panzers of a civilian struggle. Each of them was impressively surmounted by a four-foot high wire cage, inside which were pasted the poster-sized likenesses of the internees. Canvas banners draped along the windscreen, dangerously interfering with driver visibility, demanded POLITICAL STATUS NOW and, more ambitiously still, FREE THE PRISONERS.

Following the taxis came row upon row of women marching four abreast beneath the tricolour, a present from France, and each carrying a poster inscribed with the name of an internee. Hard-faced women, lacking the soft grace of their Free State sisters. But bitterly determined. Urban amazons. The sight of them more than anything seemed to further agitate Mr Deveny.

'These people don't even think of the disruption they create. I mean . . . what about the shopkeepers, forced to close up for this nonsense, and the suppliers, damned lucky if they don't get hijacked?' His hand went involuntarily to his upset stomach as James Connolly's flag floated by, the starry plough on a midnight-blue backdrop. Banner of the Irish Socialist movement. 'They're killing off what business we have in the area, driving the decent, enterprising men out and they're taking their money with them. Just because this crowd have never worked a day in their lives and they've nothing to lose they're only too ready to sacrifice other people's right to prosperity.'

Thomas and I exchanged glances over his head. No use talking.

'I mean, it's not anti-Irish to want to get on in life. If it wasn't for the Troubles this would be the best place in the world to live. Sure look at the countryside and the beaches. And we're not overcrowded like everywhere else. But . . . Christ . . . the way things are now the government can hardly drag the big international companies here. All the bloody tax concessions and government grants can't help if their factories are blown up and their executives kid-napped. But sure it's pointless talking to these people, they seem to want to glory forever in the misery of their past.'

He moved away from the window and slipped a Gelusil tablet out of his pocket and into his mouth. A flag bearing a yellow sunburst floated into view over the heads of the next division of marchers. It was the Fianna, the young IRA. Inheritors of the lofty, martial tradition of Finn McCool. There were hundreds of them, all of school age, some even wearing their blazers, all with jeans which ended just above the ankle. They were in high spirits, delighted to be on show, happy to be considered a threat to the security forces, although for most of them their appear-ance at marches such as this was their principal contribu-tion to the freedom struggle.

They dandered along, arms swinging freely, nodding proudly to acquaintances who urged them on from the security of the pavement. An army helicopter circled and whirred high above them, intent on drowning out the inspiring thump of the bands. The last of the Fianna filed by; unlikely successors to the noble body of mythical warriors from which they took their name and on whose principles their organisation was founded.

> Strength in our arms
> Purity in our hearts
> Truth on our lips.

And they passed by, cursing the fucking British bastards, the vigilant, hovering enemy.

Next the members of the Miles McGarry Memorial Band filed past, shivering under their thin shirts now penetrated by the light drizzle which had been falling on them for the past half mile. They stepped out regardless, their leader thumping the huge drum slung before him, terrific swing in his saffron pleats.

'That's Donal McGivern,' said William pointing to the drummer.

'Aidan McGivern's son? From Dunmisk Park?' asked his father incredulously.

'Yes, that's him.'

'But I thought he was a decent lad. His father said he got a scholarship to the Belfast Academy of Music.'

'So he did, but he'd sooner have the drums.'

Mr Deveny made some disheartened reply but his words were lost as a great cheer went up from the bystanders. At the heart of the march came the men divided into two sections, some in their uniforms of khaki parkas and black berets, some in civilian dress. There was little to choose between them. Many of them were ex-internees, more of them were unemployed. They marched along like battle-tried soldiers, disillusioned, punished, but determined. They obeyed the smart commands called out in Irish. The only Irish many of them knew. *Right, left, halt, attention.* But they'd fight with the best of them.

The crowd glowed in their presence, the watchers behind curtains and venetian blinds had misgivings. All things to all the people: the boys; soldiers of Eireann; a bunch of thugs; sweet sons of Mother Ireland; sure there's no harm in them; murdering bastards; pack of carried-away ligs; men with a cause; catch yerselves on; fireside Republicans; away and get work; they'd shit if they saw a gun; the boys of the oul' brigade.

The old IRA, men of past campaigns, deplored their lack of security, their big mouths. 'All talk, no discipline. They go up to the drinking clubs and get a feed of drink in them and then they slabber. It's the drink that does the damage. We knew how to keep our mouths shut.'

So they did. A lonely ineffectual campaign betrayed by men like Barry Curran. Yet it had its place. A reminder to the people of St Peter's and Clonard and Beechmount and Ardoyne that a Protestant Ulster for a Protestant people was hardly well disposed to their best interests. So in 1969 when the IRA appeared, disorganised and ill-equipped from quiet corners of the Falls Road, no one was surprised or repulsed. The inevitable return of an old friend. But, as Mr Deveny would point out, men with a poor head for business.

After the march the speeches would be delivered at Casement Park and the riots would follow shortly. Thomas and I decided we had better make our way home. We left William practising his shift to the bridge, while Mr Deveny patrolled his flower beds looking up every other minute to scan the near horizon for approaching rioters.

We walked right into it. The rally had dispersed, the colour party and balaclava'd gunmen had been whisked away in the fastest cars the estate had to offer. The more mature protesters went about their business. Only the youthful element was left with nothing to do. It was likely that they would choose to give voice to the national frustration. If only the Brits would put in a showing. Happily the Brits rarely failed to appear, to overreact, to respond with brutal stupidity. Today was no exception.

As we approached the road junction at the Andersonstown Leisure Centre rain began to fall heavily.

'We'll duck in here for a minute,' said Thomas running under the porch of the leisure centre.

Already the road was littered with broken bottles, smashed paving stones and bricks. A rich collage against a bright mess of paint-bombs which had missed the mark and splattered brilliantly over the pavements, up the walls, across the shop-fronts and the parked cars. A bizarre gaiety in an otherwise desolate scene. The perpetrators could be seen milling on the waste ground behind a row of nearby shops: Hales Fruit and Vegetables, Cosgrove's Pharmaceuticals, etc.

At that moment four mammoth saracens battled heavily down the road and grated to a halt outside the leisure centre. Soldiers in full riot gear issued reluctantly from the vehicles and took up positions clustered behind the armoured doors or squatting beside the wheels. Nothing happened for a few minutes, then suddenly a wild and strangely playful cry went up from behind the shops. The soldiers exchanged glances. The split-second before panic. But professionalism asserts itself: they lowered their face-shields and raised their guns.

Immediately a crowd of about two hundred boys burst from the waste ground armed with rocks, bricks, paint-bombs. They rushed exhilarated to within dangerous proximity of the riot squad and with a climactic choral yell let fly their improvised missiles. The next second, even before the weapons had found or missed their mark, they had turned and retreated as speedily as they attacked. And already the soldiers had released a round of the big, rocket-shaped rubber bullets which went bounding across the road after the disappearing crowd. Few reached the retreating throng. None lethally. The spent bullets were quickly captured by their enterprising targets. Rubber POWs – black gold. Worth a fiver to Yanks and visiting journalists.

We were still sheltering from the rain, unwilling to move on and miss the spectacle. A line of local traffic had begun to pile up not a hundred yards from the riot scene. Suddenly the commanding officer signalled retreat and the soldiers leapt into the saracens, banged the doors shut and took off down the road, almost ramming the queue of cars as they passed. A tactical retreat, more to do with wet thighs than the ferocity of the opposition.

We went on up the road. Outside the Busy Bee a hijacking was in full swing. A burnt-out bus smoked in the mouth of a sidestreet. A group of excited youths were using hurley sticks to remove the last windows from the extinct vehicle. Local cars manoeuvred nervously over the layers of broken glass. A hundred yards further on a huge ice-cream lorry had been parked across the road and was being quickly emptied of its contents by armies of children.

'Is there any Neapolitan?' inquired a passing woman.

I thought briefly of securing dessert, but it would be too cold to carry. I went on home empty-handed.

That night, Radio Ulster.

'There have been reports this evening of an outbreak of food poisoning in the Andersonstown area. Chiefly affected are children and young people, and it is believed that the outbreak could be related to the hijacking of a food transportation van in the area this afternoon. The van was carrying a quantity of ice-cream which had been condemned by a Technical Services health inspector, and was on its way to the city dump to be destroyed.'

13

Holy Week

One night not long before Easter I heard a thump. I sat straight up in bed, immediately awake. No, it wasn't the front door. There was no one charging up the stairs. It was an interior sound. I would not need to dress. I opened my bedroom door, hunched against the cold, and saw the light streaming from the bathroom. The door was half open, my father was lying on the floor.

'Mammy!' A yell that shook the house.

I bent over him, panicked and sick with fear. Christ, was he going to die? He was the colour of old newspapers. His arms were rigid, his mouth hung open. In an instant Mother was behind me, calling to rouse Thomas, a sound sleeper.

'Get up, son. Your father's collapsed.'

He stumbled along the short landing holding up his pyjama bottoms in one hand.

'What the fuck. . .? Jesus!' Thomas bent to feel his pulse.

'He's alive OK. You don't have to do that.'

Mother's head had cleared. She saw that my father was naked and put me out of the bathroom to spare me. I don't remember noticing. I called the ambulance while Thomas helped her lift Father back into bed.

The people of West Belfast are fortunate in living near the Royal Victoria Hospital. The doctors there are remarkably skilled and have made tremendous advances in dealing with trauma victims and half-shot brains. They sorted out the father in no time. His ulcer had burst. He would have to have an operation. He would need time to recover and then he must have peace and quiet, a less stressful lifestyle. That gave him a laugh. Peace and quiet indeed! As it turned out his time in hospital proved to be particularly eventful for the rest of us.

About four o'clock on a grey Holy Thursday afternoon Mary Dillon, wife of Jimmy, mother of twelve, was killed in crossfire by an <u>unidentified bullet</u>. She had just been to the butcher's. A bullet in the chest and two pounds of beef sausages, a quarter of vegetable roll scattered on the damp grass. She should never have got in the line of fire: poor timing on her part.

It began as a routine late-afternoon ambush. Not the best of days for it, too gloomy. The boys, two or three of them, would lie in wait behind the hedgerow at the top of the estate, damp but vigilant. The army would pass down the Glen Road, not in force, a couple of jeeps. Maybe a <u>saracen</u>. The boys would fire a few token shots, nothing serious. If they hit a soldier that would be a bonus. There was a good chance the Brits would not return fire. It would hardly be worth their while. Their assailants would be gone in seconds, behind the white pebbledash garages, through mucky back gardens. They'd be halfway across Andersonstown in minutes.

That afternoon there were two saracens and two jeeps – all the more target. They were passing down the road at a moderate to slow pace when they came under fire, semi-automatic. The first shot, according to eyewitness reports, came from the bushes opposite the Ulster Brewery. It lifted a chink of concrete out of the brewery wall. There were two or three more shots from the hedgerow before the soldiers got organised and returned fire. Neither the IRA nor the army made their target. But one stray bullet from the brief interchange went wide and blasted Mary Dillon in the chest as she turned the corner from Colinview Drive. She wouldn't have known what hit her. An innocu-

ous lead pellet is a remarkable thing. It can tear open a
human being so entirely there's no chance of putting the
pieces back together again.

The shooting stopped when they saw the woman crump-
le. Suddenly people were running towards her from all
directions. Women from the houses fronting the estate,
men from the loading bay of the brewery, dozens of school
kids walking up the road from the bus terminus. The start
of their Easter holidays. They put a coat under her lifeless
head. One elderly man tried to administer first aid. The
soldiers intervened with a medicine chest and tried to clear
the area. Someone called the priest. He arrived from St
Theresa's in a few minutes and administered the last rites.
The Act of Contrition was whispered into deaf ears. Oh
my God, I am very sorry for having sinned against you . . .
and by the help of your Holy Grace I will not sin again. No
danger.

Brendan came home late that day. I was watching for
him at the door. I could smell the brewery. The air was
rich with the warm smell of hops. Finally he ambled round
the corner, dragging his school bag along the ground. He
told us about the shooting. On his way up from school he
had heard the shots, seen the body, the bottle-green coat
dark with blood.

'This man put his jacket over the hole,' he said. He was
white, except for the smears of Easter egg on his mouth
and rosy, wind-raw cheeks. He had broken Lent. He could
not eat his dinner that evening. He was going to take after
Father with his bad stomach. Mother said he was highly
strung.

She was at the hospital visiting Father, so she was not
there to restrain Thomas when he went out to see what
was going on. He wandered back some time later.

'They're rioting up on the road,' he reported, 'hundreds
of them. They've barricaded the top of the estate.'

'Are the soldiers firing rubber bullets?' asked Brendan
hopefully. He was making a collection of rubber bullets.

He sold them to American and German journalists for five pounds apiece, except for the one Mother had sprayed with gold paint and stuck up on the fireboard with the clock and the statuette of Our Lady of Lourdes and the two wooden giraffes she had bought from Colum when he was working on the boats. It looked like a thick golden phallus. She didn't notice.

'It's none of your business,' Thomas snapped, 'and you're not to go up there. Or you might collect a bullet right in the face, like Mrs Nolan.' He reinforced the prohibition with a smack across the head. In Father's absence he had been known to abuse his authority.

'I met Desy McIlhone. He says Liam Corrigan shot Mrs Dillon. He's a stupid bollocks, Corrigan.'

'I thought it was the soldiers?'

'That's what they'll have to say. But the boys know it was that stumer Corrigan.'

'Where is he? I suppose he's over the border by now?'

'No, he's in Desy's brother's house. Now you're not to tell that to anybody.'

'What are they going to do with him?'

'They'll set up an inquiry. He'll have to be disciplined.'

We heard no more about the disciplinary inquiry. For us there were to be other serious consequences of the shooting of Mary Dillon.

Father had been in the Royal for the past fortnight. He had received massive blood transfusions in the first week. The doctors had trouble stopping the internal bleeding. They were keeping him in for at least another ten days. He needed a rest. He needed a break. He probably needed to emigrate. Mother went to see him that Thursday as usual, right after work. There was no crowd outside the factory that day; she reached the Royal unscathed.

*

The sister rang the bell for visiting time and Bernie was first through the heavy, green plastic doors. She could see Aidan at the other end of the ward sagging against the pile of pillows, about the same colour as the sheets. A clear-coloured liquid drip was attached to his left arm. There was a short plastic tube taped into one hairy nostril. Yet he held a small transistor radio close to his left ear, and with his right hand adjusted the tuner on another. The bed was insulated with a covering layer of newpapers: the *Irish News*, the *Belfast Telegraph*, the *Andersonstown News*, *An Phoblact*, *Paris Match*. She leaned over to kiss him, thinking how terrible he looked.

'Did you hear the news?' he asked at once. She had interrupted an on-the-spot report from Ballymurphy where rioting had broken out earlier.

'I heard there was shooting all over Bunbeg.'

'There was a woman killed in the crossfire about four o'clock.'

'Dear God! There was not!'

'Aye, near the Carnan shops.'

'Did it give her name?'

'No details yet. Now listen, Bernie, I want you to go straight home and keep the children in.'

She looked affronted. 'I'm not going home yet, sure I've only arrived. Annie's off school and Thomas'll be home by this time. They'll be all right. Sure they've more sense than to hang around where there's shooting.'

Aidan was waving his transistors around, aerials aloft, hoping to pick up the police messages. 'I wish I had the good radio,' he lamented.

'Sure you'd deafen the other patients. Besides, you're in here to rest and get better, not to be listening to all the bloody troubles. That's what put you here in the first place.'

'It gives me an interest,' he said, a little self-pitying. 'Now do as I say and go home.'

'I'll go in a minute. Do they let you watch the six o'clock news?'

'Aye. They'll be putting it on in a minute.'

A young nurse with a broad bottom and flushed, country cheeks came to switch on the TV. Around the room scrawny heads rose and wavered above their pillows to get a glimpse of the headlines. Mother of twelve shot dead in Andersonstown. Aidan propped himself up on an assemblage of pillows and sent Bernie home.

Mother came in with the wind.

'Did you hear about that woman getting shot up on the road? Your Father was watching it in the ward. He's a good bit better today.' She bustled through the door, shopping bags half the size of herself on each arm.

'That's good. Brendan saw the body,' said Thomas raking up the fire. She was cold-rife and liked to see the flames leaping up the chimney.

'Where is he? Is he all right? He's not out stoning the soldiers is he?'

'No. He's over the road at wee Frankie's. He's OK.'

Relieved, she took off her headscarf and the big sheepskin coat that made her look like a furry mammal.

'Annie, put on the kettle. The road's black with soldiers. Your father's kicking himself that he hasn't got three or four of his good radios in with him. They said he couldn't even sit up to watch the nine o'clock news. He was raging. All the bloody pavements have been dug up. I went over on my ankle at Coolnasilla – look. That'll swell now. Wasn't thon awful about that woman? And her man left with twelve children to rear? I stopped in at Rosaleen's on the way up, for a cup of tea. Paddy Cushnan was there. He lives next door to the Dillons. Apparently the husband's taking it awful bad. God love him. Rosaleen says they know who shot her. Tony had to go out and see about it.'

Rosaleen was yet another of our cousins. Her husband

Tony was one of the boys. Tony had his head well screwed
on. He had managed so far to avoid internment.

'I just said straight out to Tony, this is ridiculous, all this
shooting in broad daylight. He agreed with me, to give him
his due. Especially when the children are coming home
from school and women out doing their shopping. It'll have
to stop. Paddy Cushnan agreed with me. He says there's a
meeting on Monday afternoon down at the Christian
Brothers' school, a meeting of the women of the estate who
want to get the shooting stopped when there's civilians
about. I'm going with Rosaleen and Paddy. He's one of the
organisers. Now don't be telling your father when you see
him,' she said as an afterthought.

We thought no more of it. It never occurred to us to stop
her. It seemed a harmless enough initiative – a group of
local women getting together to improve living conditions.
It would be like bingo, or the Confraternity of the Blessed
Virgin, or like doing the nine Fridays. A little deft negotiation should do it nicely. The adjustment of a few
timetables and everybody would be happy. The IRA could
keep shooting and the women could keep shopping. Father
would be none the wiser.

The meeting was scheduled for 2.00 pm the following
Monday. The Christian Brothers' secondary school was
halfway down the Glen Road, just below the brewery.
Mother set out about half past one, accompanied by a few
neighbours who had heard about the meeting from one
source or other. They collected Rosaleen, and set off for
the school. As the extensive playing fields and the high
steel gates came into view the small party of women were
surprised to see a commotion down at the main entrance.
There were soldiers, a crowd of protesters, a flocking of the
media. The protesters appeared to be preventing cars from
entering the school grounds. The soldiers seemed bent on
ensuring that the cars and their occupants were allowed to

proceed unhindered. Confrontation between soldiers and protesters had inevitably ensued. Nothing to write home about. An exchange of foul language, a few minor scuffles. The media were clearly attempting to record the event. Some said after that they had actually striven to create it.

There was considerable confusion when Mother and her little group reached the gates. No one was quite sure what was going on at the time. No one since has been able to describe accurately what happened next. The crowd of protesters turned out to be local women. Mother greeted a few acquaintances, joined the group in all innocence, assuming that they too had come to negotiate a suitable timetable for armed attack in the area.

'I thought the soldiers were there to arrest any IRA men that might turn up to talk to us,' she later explained.

'Will they not let us in?' she asked at the time.

'No, but they're letting the bloody Women for Peace group in, the bastards,' came the fulsome response.

Just then Mother noticed Mrs Gilroy and her sister pass through the gates under armed escort. At the same time she spotted Mrs French, who stepped boldly from the group of protesters, hurled herself at the gates and yelled: 'Go on, you stinking traitors. Sell us out again! But I seen ye, Maria Gilroy, and I'm telling you now you'll not get away with it, ye filthy traitor.'

Mother was moving from confusion to realisation. The meeting, and the people going to the meeting, were inside the school. Those opposed to such a gathering had collected at the gate. It seemed out of all proportion to what was intended. Why would a few women pose a threat?

'Bernie, I think we're supposed to be in there,' whispered one woman fearfully. 'This crowd's protesting against the meeting.'

'What's the TV here for?' Mother wondered.

'I've no idea, but your Rosaleen's away up home. Her and Mrs McIlhone.'

'Is she? Don't tell me she's afraid of this crowd. Sure

that's only oul' French at the head of them. Come on, stick
by me and we'll beat our way in if we have to.'

They did have to. Half-a-dozen of them fought their way
through the gates under a volley of abuse and stones from
the angry mob. The move may have been unwise, the
gesture uncalled for, even foolish. But Mother is nothing if
not a champion of the right of the individual and no one,
especially not Mrs French, was going to deny her the right
of free assembly. She pushed straight through, past the
crowd now chanting 'Women for Peace Out', past the gates,
past the journalists, past the beleaguered soldiers and into
the school assembly hall cum gymnasium. It was where
we went to mass on Sundays, the congregation of Andersonstown having grown before the chapel could be enlarged
to accommodate it.

Today it presented a very different aspect. In the interior
of the hall the scene was if anything more chaotic than
outside. To begin with there were more reporters than
civilians present, all turmoil and agitation. Six or seven
camera crews battled for the prime vantage points near the
raised dais at the top of the hall. The surrounding space was
a minefield of cameras, spotlights and microphones. An
immense tangle of electrical wires wound in and out
between the chairs on the dais and round the legs of the
speakers' table. Lone photographers hung from the climbing
frames around the walls. One had struggled up onto the
wooden horse. Mother, Mrs Gilroy and her sister, and a few
nodding acquaintances, stood dumbfounded at the bottom
of the hall. Mother noticed Peter Leicester at the other end.

'What's all the fuss about?' Mrs Gilroy wanted to know.
'And who in God's name invited the reporters? It was just
supposed to be a wee local meeting.'

They had no time to reflect, for at that moment the
media descended on them, microphones erect, cameras
aglow with red and yellow and green lights.

'Are you with the Women for Peace group?'

The women looked at each other. Were they? Certainly

they weren't conscious of belonging to any organised group. But yes, they wanted peace. They weren't sure what to say. They said nothing. Disappointed, the reporters abandoned them as suddenly as they had swooped, and made for the side entrance where at that moment a dozen women were being hustled in. But these were women of a different mark. For a start some of them wore hats, and it wasn't even Sunday. They were dressed stylishly, expensively, in tailored suits and coats. Their bags and shoes coordinated, tasteful combinations of navy and white, grey and lemon, brown and beige. They werc all well, if uniformly, coiffed. Wisteria, lilac, silver fox. It must have been they who had arrived in cars.

'They're not off the estate,' pronounced Mrs Gilroy.

'They're not even off the Falls by the look of them. More like the Malone Road.'

'Well they look like they're going to do all the talking.'

'There should be women from around here speaking up.' Mrs Gilroy made a quick survey of her companions.

'You go, Bernie, you're a good speaker. Bernie was President of the Children of Mary,' she said by way of information.

'That was twenty years ago,' Mother protested. 'I wouldn't know what to say.'

'Maybe you won't have to say anything, just go up and let them know where you stand.'

Mother ended up on the platform. A line of women on folding wooden chairs. She failed to recognise any of them. They were marooned on the raised dais, surrounded on all sides by advancing reporters, the focus of a score of cameras. The meeting somehow got started. One suited matron introduced another. She spoke briefly over the din; of the sorry times we live in, of the desirability of peace, of the need for women to band together and show the way. She urged those present to join the Assembly of Women. Audience response appears to have been overshadowed by the fuss and confusion. Mother remembered later that two or three people had said something or other that seemed sensible. It was no more than three minutes into the second speech when the battering began.

The mob at the gate had managed to breach security, break into the school's entrance hall and were now demanding entry to the assembly. They found themselves frustrated. The doors were locked. They naturally began to batter and to give urgent voice to their demands. The floral-draped lady at the microphone stopped speaking and looked around in alarm. Before today she had only ever heard of Andersonstown. She looked around nervously for direction. Mrs Sandra Lockhart, the chairwoman, nodded stern encouragement, motioned her to continue.

She cleared her throat, turned back to the mike and began again: 'It is only by seeking common ground that we can hope to move forward.' She was shouting above the din to make herself heard, she felt her voice was going to break. But Mrs Lockhart was smiling her field-marshal smile. She must carry on. 'Only by reaching a fuller, deeper understanding of each other's needs can we come together peacefully, as one community . . .'

At that point a journalist from a reputable newspaper gave the nod to his photographer and slipped the bolt on the assembly hall doors. The crowd burst in. They were three-hundred strong, mostly good women and true. But a dozen manly specimens urged them on. Together they swept through the hall and made for the stage. They trampled spectators and media representatives alike, indiscriminately. They knocked over chairs in their haste to reach the platform, tripped over the miles of cable and flex and made their stand just below the stage. They were vociferous. Their cries and demands rose to the very roof, resounded around the room. Acoustically pleasing. The rich full voice of an outraged people.

'Traitors!' they yelled. 'Touts. Backfuckingsliders. Out out out!' They made their position quite clear. But lest the meeting's organisers and speakers should be left in any doubt, they reinforced their words with a volley of eggs and tomatoes, the ripest of the ripe, seed-filled and juicy. A hurling of the fat, red tomato bombs splattered on the stage, over the speakers' and chairman's table. An ugly red splurge appeared on Mrs Lockhart's navy jacket. An egg whizzed past the speaker's head and cracked gooey-yellow on the back wall. She thought briefly of hiding herself under the table. But that would be lowering herself to their level, literally. She turned and fled off stage right. She followed other ladies in flight and there were yet others behind her. They took refuge amid the media and covered their faces with the brims of their hats.

Mother and Mrs Gilroy watched in horror from the back of the stage as the visitors retreated in tears, richly decorated with the splatterings of egg and tomato. But just then Mother felt a clutching of manly fingers on her shoulder and Paddy Cushnan bundled both of them down into the green room where they took shelter until the hall had emptied.

In view of the turn taken by the proceedings Mother was not called upon to speak. That is, not until after the deluge, when reporters no longer felt themselves constrained by the earlier tenuous formalities of the meeting. At the time she was not entirely aware that she was speaking on camera.

We sat or sprawled around the principal domestic deities of hearth and television, awaiting the six o'clock news. In an effort to establish a feeling of normality Mother had produced bags of buttered popcorn and chocolate eclairs, and we munched in anticipation. And then, there she was, filling the screen, unlike herself, warily eyeing the microphones thrust up from below. We burst into wild shrieks of laughter and missed her first remarks.

'Shut up!' Thomas hissed, although he too had rolled on the floor in a fit of hilarity.

'I can't hear myself,' protested Mother. 'God, I look a
sight!

'. . . so that at least the children will be able to get home
safely and without any shooting,' my mother's image was
saying as more reporters moved in from behind.

'Oh my God,' said the real thing, 'I sound very Belfast.
That was bloody awful.'

'Is this a move to banish the IRA from Andersonstown,
Mrs McPhelimy?' said one reporter, mispronouncing the
name.

Mother looked blank for a second, assimilating the
question.

'I didn't know he was going to ask me that,' she
explained now.

'No,' responded the image, 'we just want them to stop
shooting when there are civilians about.'

'And how do you feel about what's happened here today?'

'I think it's a disgrace. It's terrible when you can't even
speak out on your own estate.'

At that second Mother's name appeared in white letters
across the bottom of the screem:

Bernie McPhelimy
Assembly of Women

'Christ!' she ejaculated, 'look what they've put. They think
we're with that other crowd.'

But Mother had had her moment in the spotlight; already
the cameras had moved to focus on another woman,
already her name had popped up on the screen:

Deirdre Gorman
Assembly of Women

'Now you see?' squawked Mother in indignation, 'she's not
in the Assembly of Women either. Paddy introduced me to
that woman. Sure, she was asking us if we'd ever heard of

the Assembly of Women. I says no, I've no idea who they are. You see them bloody reporters? They just put whatever the hell they like. They didn't even ask us if we were in it. It was one of them opened the door and let that mob in anyway, the irresponsible gets.'

'It did make great television,' said Thomas.

'Well I'm going to ring Deirdre Gorman, I'm going to get this sorted out or we'll never hear the end of it.'

A feeling of uneasiness had descended. The popcorn lay forgotten, the screen transformed by the inanity of advertisements: Are Your MacLeans Shoween? and Come Home to a Real Fire. We couldn't put reasons on it but we knew that there would be trouble. The reporter's carelessness had changed the nature of the event. The infiltration of Andersonstown by the Assembly of Women – whoever they were – might as well have happened. It had been on the six o'clock news.

Father was not prepared for the interview when he saw it that evening on the six o'clock news, from his hospital bed. He took it badly. The nurse reported later that he was so upset he fought his way out of bed, pulled the drip from his arm and was halfway down the ward, demanding his clothes, before he collapsed and became more amenable to reason. They decided to move his bed as far as possible from the television, and the doctor had insisted on confiscating his radios. The orderlies were warned that he was not to be given the newspapers on any account. Thus, cut off from all electronic and printed communication, Father spent the most miserable few days of his life.

Meanwhile Mother was intent on getting things cleared up. She had phoned Deirdre Gorman and Paddy Cushnan several times. Mr Cushnan seemed uncomfortable. He didn't want to get involved. But Deirdre Gorman had phoned a number of other people, including her councillor, the local branch of Sinn Fein, the president of the Assembly of Women and the Bishop, and the result was that a meeting was held later that night at Deirdre's house up on the Glen Road. It was close to midnight when Mother came back from the meeting.

'What happened?' we asked, nerves rather on edge.

'We formed·a local peace group. Did you ring the Royal? How's your daddy?'

'As well as can be expected.'

'Who formed the peace group?' Thomas wanted to know.

'All of us who were there: Paddy Danagher, Paddy Fehily, Councillor Madden, Mother Brendan from the Holy Cross, the parish priest, Liam Mulvogue, Canon Clancy, Owen Gaffney, ach and a whole lot of others. And we have the full support of the Bishop. He says he's right behind us.' She launched into her nightly ritual. The donning of the head-knickers, the taking of the tablets. 'Liam Mulvogue was great. He gave us a lot of ideas.'

'Who's he?' asked Thomas, not noticeably enthusiastic about this latest development.

'Ach you've heard of him. He's on the Equal Opportunity Commission. He lives in one of those big houses down the road, the one with the wings, does an awful lot of good work. Well he got right onto his contacts at the BBC. Deirdre and I are going to be on the TV again tomorrow, to get this all cleared up. We're going to make it very clear that we've absolutely nothing to do with the Assembly of Women, that we're a local group of concerned residents trying to make the streets safer for our children.'

'What station?'

'BBC, but Liam thinks ITV will be interested too. He's got a few contacts in the media. He's going to talk to some of them tomorrow.'

'What about Daddy? Didn't he say you weren't to be getting up to anything else?'

'We're just trying to undo the damage that's been done. It's too important to let go.'

'What are you going to tell him?'

'I don't think I'll mention about tomorrow, not with him so weak now. I'll tell him later when he's more like himself. Now come on, it's time you were in bed. You're getting away with murder with your father in hospital.'

14

Crosses and Passions

I met Deirdre when she called round the next day to see the wee woman about the broadcast.

'They're sending a taxi for us about eleven o'clock, Bernie,' she said, and Mother went off to respray her hair.

Deirdre was a firm, rounded, rosy woman, about the same age as Mother. She had naturally curly black hair, fine white teeth and an open, handsome face. I liked her immediately. She was very direct.

'Do you support your mother in what she's doing?' she asked me when Mother went out to put on the kettle.

I didn't know what Mother was doing.

'I think she should do what she thinks is right, but I don't know.'

'My eldest daughter is seventeen. She thinks I'm mad getting involved.'

I grunted sympathetically. Deirdre didn't seem like the mother of a seventeen-year-old. She seemed girlish, open-minded, the sort of woman who would let you go to a disco, maybe even out with a boy.

I enjoyed her visit. I was hoping she might prove a good influence on the wee woman. Later we saw her to the door.

'She's not a bit well, God love her,' said Mother as Deirdre disappeared up Bunbeg.

'Is she not? She looked very healthy to me.'

'She keeps having haemorrhages,' Mother whispered confidentially, although we were alone in the house. 'I suppose it's her time of life. I'm glad I had it all taken away. You're far better having it all out at the one time.'

From the following morning's paper, from Peter Leicester in Belfast:

'The Provisional IRA in Belfast has apparently decided to use rather more than mere appeals for solidarity from the movement's leaders to enforce its domination in the Roman Catholic working-class areas of the city.

'A large and well-organised group of supporters succeeded yesterday by plain rudeness, blatant intimidation, and thinly disguised bullying, to break into total disarray a meeting held in Andersonstown by some of the state's more moderate women.

'Thus the first burgeoning of an organised, Catholic-inspired peace campaign would appear to have succumbed to the very intimidation it had hoped to outlaw. It only remains to be seen whether the ugly and disturbing scenes at yesterday's meeting will draw the peaceable together in even greater numbers, or whether the movement will die in its infancy.

'Most of the women who had been bold enough to attend yesterday's meeting, held in a school hall on the estate, were forced to retreat either crying, spattered in broken eggs, or badly shocked and shaken. A mob of 300, mostly young women, but helped by a dozen or so men and youths, took over the school and sang Republican songs to celebrate the rout of the "backsliders" and "traitors".

'Last night the organisers of the moderate protest were licking their wounds and planning their next moves. They were acutely conscious, however, that those of them who still live in Andersonstown would be liable to more unpleasant forms of intimidation if they continue their campaign for peace, and it was not clear what their future moves will be.

'The first stirrings of feminine unease at IRA activity on

the estate began last Thursday night after a woman had
been shot dead during a gun battle between troops and an
IRA active service unit. The IRA claimed that the woman,
Mrs Mary Dillon, had been killed by a British bullet: but the
army and many people on the estate seem convinced that
her death was entirely the fault of the local Provisionals.

'As a result, some of her neighbours got together, bent
on telling the IRA to cool down and "give Mr Brandywell a
chance". During the weekend, the 18-month-old group
known as the Assembly of Women, which has 45 paid-up
members on the estate, heard the murmurings of discon-
tent and decided to organise the protest properly. Mrs
Lockhart, the movement's president, a Protestant from
South Belfast, began to arrange publicity.

'By Sunday evening the sound of protest had become so
deafening that the Provisionals' chief-of-staff apparently
felt it necessary to comment in Londonderry on the need
"to show these good middle-class folk that Andersonstown
is behind the IRA".'

While visiting Father that afternoon Mother left instructions that he was not to be let near a TV that night. We
gathered more fearfully about the set this evening. There
was a good deal less hilarity than on the Monday night. A
sense of bleak expectation. But Thomas and I had some
hope. We had written Mother's text for the interview.

It started off well. Mother and Deirdre sat opposite
Charles Hill on *Ulster Tonight*, behind a quiz-show desk.
Reluctant contestants. They were each labelled on the
bosom with black letters spelling out their names: Bernie
McPhelimy. Housewife. She was beautifully coiffed.

'They did my hair and make-up in the studio,' she
explained, 'they said I'd have disappeared under the lights I
was so pale.'

Deirdre presented very well on camera. She was handsome in the Irish way with her fine complexion and dark,

wavy hair. She spoke up boldly, nostrils flaring, cheeks burning red.

'We just wanted to set the record straight about the meeting in Andersonstown.' She took a deep breath, the interviewer nodded encouragingly. The nostrils dilated again, cheeks flushed right up to the temples.

'That meeting has been wrongly described as a meeting of the Assembly of Women. I would like to state that Bernie and myself are not now, and never have been, members of the Assembly of Women.' Her words fell like blows. 'In fact, we know absolutely nothing about this organisation.'

'And the same goes for you, Mrs McPhelimy?'

'Very definitely. I never heard of these people until after the meeting. I didn't know who they were at the time. I just went down to the school for a meeting of local women, to try to get the shooting stopped in the afternoon.' Mother appeared odd. Her eyelids dipped regularly as she spoke, perhaps because she was reading from the pages Thomas had neatly copied out that morning, my writing being illegible. Her speech slurred noticeably, she seemed unusually relaxed. 'I've been worried about it for some time, but it was the death of Mary Dillon that really made me want to do something.' Her head appeared to be drooping to one side.

'Were you nervous?' asked Thomas.

'Not with five Valium in me,' she replied, still relatively relaxed.

'So it's not your aim to get the IRA out of Andersonstown?' asked Mr Hill.

'No, definitely not,' Mother insisted. 'I believe that I am speaking for a large section of the people of Andersonstown when I say that we want peace and the chance to lead normal lives. However, we are not turning our backs on the IRA, because we do need the IRA for a number of reasons. Firstly we need them to defend us in case of a Protestant backlash – ' Mr Hill's Protestant nostrils flared noticeably,

' – and secondly we need them to maintain law and order within Andersonstown, as we cannot rely on the RUC.

'Some five years ago there was a great deal of house-breaking and gang warfare in the area. However, since the formation of the Provisionals the crime level has dropped greatly. We now want an end to the paint-bombing and bottle throwing that is gradually defacing our estate. The children who are chasing saracens and rioting are only hooligans, and must be stopped before they grow up and turn out like Chicago-type gangsters.

'We appeal to the IRA to stop the rioters from running the streets. There are not, and cannot be any patriotic grounds for destroying our estate by rattling bin-lids and throwing stones. We would like the IRA to use their authority to cut the violence to as low a level as possible, and make Andersonstown a safe place for people to walk the streets without being caught up in a shooting incident or a riot.'

Thomas nodded, relieved, satisfied that the record had been set straight. But the interviewer stretched his eyes involuntarily and straightened his immaculate tie. He shuffled through the papers in front of him.

'And what is your immediate plan of action? What steps do you intend to take to achieve your aims?'

'Well we intend to seek a meeting with the IRA in the Andersonstown area,' said Deirdre, 'to put our point of view and to ask for their cooperation.'

'Do you think you'll succeed?'

'Oh I think so.' She was very definite. 'If they value the support of the people.'

Thomas winced. A bad day at the Christian Brothers'.

'And do you feel that you speak on behalf of the people?'

'I believe we speak on behalf of the majority of people of good sense and goodwill in the area.'

Mr Hill cleared his throat, rounded to face another camera. They had had their innings. 'Ladies, thank you for your time tonight and good luck with your mission.'

Mother started up and nearly knocked her tea all over the hearth.

'Where's the rest?' she demanded, outraged. 'That's not all of it. There was a whole bit in the middle. We talked for a good ten minutes. I said more than that. A lot more.'

I was somewhat thankful that we hadn't heard it. Mother made a beeline for the phone, but Deirdre was already ringing her. There was another meeting at Deirdre's that night. Things happened quickly after that.

Next morning. Letters to the Editor, *Irish News*.

'Facts About Women's Peace Movement.

'Sir – We would like to clear up any misconceptions that may be held by the internees of Cage Six at Long Kesh regarding the peace meeting we attempted to hold in the Glen Road CBS on Easter Monday.

'This meeting was to be an informal gathering of some friends and neighbours of the late Mary Dillon, with a view to discussing ways and means of preventing a recurrence of such a tragic happening.

'Alas it was not to be, and the treatment we received can be likened to that meted out to the Burntollet marchers. We can only assume that the hostility shown to us was organised; or are we to conclude that interested parties usually come to parochial halls with eggs, tomatoes and condemnation posters?

'We would like to make it clear that the Assembly of Women in no way organised this meeting. We take this opportunity to assure the "Men Behind the Wire" that we are acutely aware of the injustices and oppressive laws that have made their struggle and sufferings necessary.

'We hope this letter helps to clear up the Goebbels-type propaganda which has been circulated against our humble efforts towards a peaceful solution of a problem that concerns us all.

'We will continue to work with this aim in view and pray for a just settlement with honour and justice we can all embrace and welcome. – Yours etc. Peace Within the Community Group, Belfast 11.'

I must have been asleep before eleven. I did not know if I was dreaming·at first. I thought that maybe I was almost awake. I could hear thumps or thuds. At the time I did not put a name to the loud, intermittent sounds somewhere nearby. It did not sound like a door or a car door banging. It sounded more like a nun's head bouncing up the stairs. The old ghost story.

'Annie, I'm up one stair. Annie, I'm up two stairs . . .'

I couldn't be awake. It was a nightmare. Thirteen stairs and the landing. Annie, I'm up three stairs. No, I reasoned dopily, I was too big for it to be the nun's head. That was long ago. The head never came.

Then I sensed other voices, and feet on the garden path. The ping of concrete impacting on the night. It was real. Just then I heard Mother call out: 'Thomas, is that you?'

But there were other voices too. More than one, somewhere else, outside. What was Mother doing on the landing, I wondered dreamily, and seemed to lose consciousness again. It was the sound of Thomas and Mother urgently consulting on the landing that brought me back to life.

'Who is it?'

'I don't know, I can't see anything. All the street-lamps are broken.'

'Why? Where are they?'

'They seem to be round the back somewhere.'

They appeared to move through the darkness into the bathroom. I thought I could hear other voices again. A lot of voices, nearby, chanting something. I couldn't make it out. The refrain interspersed with many yells and cat-calls. If I could only make out what it was they were saying . . .

'I'm going out to them.'

I heard *that* clearly enough. This was undeniably Mother. Mother in a rage. Battle-mode. I came to life instantly, reluctantly. It was a nightmare after all. I didn't bother to go through the drill of speed dressing, but hurried out onto the landing to restrain her. Some innate bio-controlled impulse told me it was important to stop her . . . doing anything at all. Thomas shared that impulse. He was standing at the top of the stairs, barring her way.

'No,' he said with a show of reasonableness, 'you're not going out there. There is absolutely nothing you can do. It's only a mob. You can't talk to a mob.'

A mob! Christ! Now I could make out all the chanting and thumping. They were yelling in rhythmic unison.

'Touts out! Touts out!'

Touts! Jaysus Christ and his Holy Mother! It was worse than the nun's head. The worst thing imaginable!

'Where are they? What's all that battering?' It didn't sound as if they were trying to knock in the back door.

'Mammy, would you for Christ's sake wise up!' Thomas struggled manfully with the screaming mother, dragging her back towards her bedroom. I joined forces with him. Tried prying Mother's angry little hands off the banisters.

'Dirty fucking informers.' One martial voice rose above the others.

'That's Niall French,' said Thomas, still keeping a rough hold of Mother, 'I thought I heard the bastard. They're out the back.'

Reinforcements arrived in the shape of Brendan, his red-striped pyjamas at half-mast. He immediately weighed up the situation and grabbed Mother by the feet so that we could lift her bodily and rush her into the bedroom.

'They're on top of the coal-hole,' he yelled as the three of us struggled with the wee woman and the thuds outside the window rose even louder. Sinead appeared at the bedroom door, looking bewildered and frightened. Her hair was wrapped up in rags, for ringlets.

'You'll be all right, love,' said Thomas, who had Mother in an arm-lock, 'come over here and sit with Mammy.' Mammy was abusing him and thumping him in the back.

'Let me go, for God's sake! Let me go!' she demanded, flailing all round her, 'I'll go down and show the bastards who's a tout. They know there's no man here tonight, the stinking cowards. But I'm not afraid to go down to them. I'll kill the bastards.'

But at that second the front window exploded downstairs. The crystalline crashing of glass filled the house. There is something very intimidating about the sound of a breaking window. It seemed to us that our last flimsy defence was down. Even Mother was scared into silence.

'Fuck,' murmured Thomas, '*Kristallnacht*.' But he was now the man of the house, *fearr a ti*, and would do the needful. He armed himself with his hurley stick, a sleek switch of elm, and went downstairs to confront the invader. Brendan was behind him, brandishing two wire coat-hangers. He was going to poke out a few eyes at least. Mother and Sinead and I gathered on the landing, crept down behind them. Everything had gone quiet.

'It's OK,' Thomas assured us coming out into the hall, 'I think they've gone.'

The crowd too had been intimidated by the extremity of shattering glass. They had disappeared into the night. Thomas looked out the front door, but there was no one on the path. Even the French house was dark and quiet.

'It's over for the night,' he pronounced.

We swept up the glass as best we could. Thomas went out and rummaged in the garden shed, coming back with a large rectangle of hardboard.

'This'll keep the draught out for tonight.'

We positioned it in front of the broken picture window, held it in place with the yard brush and went uneasily back to bed.

*

There was a rap at the door early the next morning. Mother went down in her dressing gown to answer it. Whoever it was she kept them at the door and didn't talk for long. I went down for breakfast when I heard the baker call with fresh baps.

'There was a man just here from the BBC,' said Mother pouring out the tea.

'A reporter? What did he want?' I cut into the softness of the bap. It was burnt almost black on the outside. A perfect bap.

'He wanted to interview me about them breaking the window.'

'How did he know so soon?' I plastered on the butter, the traditional half-inch.

'You know this place . . . I said no.'

I was relieved. 'Why?'

'I wouldn't let the Catholics down, Annie, for the sake of a few hoodlums.'

I handed her a slice of bap.

The Housing Trust had the window fixed that very day. Which was much to their credit considering how long we had been on rent and rate strike. The news of the attack on the house was in the evening papers and on the television, yet with the cooperation of the hospital staff we were confident Father wouldn't get to hear of it. We hoped it would blow over. We reckoned without Aunt Kathleen.

The Ford Escort pulled up outside the house and Aunt Kathleen was out before her son-in-law Colum had the engine switched off. Mother was out in a flash to open the door.

'Who broke your windows?' Kathleen demanded at the top of her lungs as she marched up the path.

'Come on in,' said Mother hurriedly. 'Is Colum with you?'

But Kathleen wasn't to be contained by hospitality and

small talk. She had come to voice her outrage at the attack made on her little sister, and voice it she would, all over Bunbeg .

'I know who bloody well broke them, no need to tell me,' she bawled turning, arms akimbo, and facing French's house. 'It was that fucking dirty cowardly bitch that lives next door. Under cover of dark. Some fucking neighbour she is.'

There had been an almost imperceptible twitch of the curtains at Kathleen's first bellow, but now all was still and seemingly lifeless in the French home. But this cowardice only further enraged Aunt Kathleen.

'Patsy French, come out,' she challenged. 'Come on, you dirty stinking coward. I know you're in there. Everybody knows you never shift your fat carcass before the middle of the afternoon, you dirty bitch. Now get the fuck out here, I want to see you about breaking my sister's windows.'

The sight of a stately middle-aged woman in a well-cut suit with matching bag, shoes and gloves, yelling abuse and obscenities was beginning to attract the attention of the street. But Mrs French refused to put in an appearance.

'Come on out, French, you rat,' Kathleen taunted, sauntering onto French's lawn, 'or can you only play your dirty games in the dark, against a helpless woman and her kids, and her man lying bad in the hospital? You're a frigging, cowardly cunt. But let me tell you, I'm not a bit afraid of you. Our Bernie may be too much of a lady to roll in the street with you, but I'm not, and I don't give a shite what anybody says. Now I'm warning you, if you don't come out I'm going up there to break every window in that fucking house, and I won't bloody wait till it gets dark.'

Colum had followed his mother-in-law up the path. She had blocked his way into the house so that he was obliged to stand there, nervously hitching up his trousers while she ranted. He had just recently been released from Long Kesh. He had served two years for membership of the IRA, and had entirely lost his beer-belly in the process, and now none of his trousers fitted properly. He gave another tug at his belt, glanced up and down the street for any sign of the army.

'Come on now, Kathleen, that's enough now,' he said, attempting to be firm. She ignored him.

'Do something, Annie,' Mother hissed, as she tried to hide in the hall, 'for God's sake get her in!'

'What can I do?' I asked helplessly. But I went out and stood uncertainly at Kathleen's elbow. She ignored me too.

Just then French's door opened and Mrs French came out and stood cautiously watching Aunt Kathleen.

'I never broke her window,' she said after a moment, 'I had nothing to do with it.'

'You're a fucking liar, as well as a coward,' was Kathleen's response. 'You were behind it, and I'll bet it was that wee bastard Niall that did it, the obnoxious wee vandal. Not that he licks it off the grass, for you and yours were always scum.' She turned to address the few passers-by who had stopped to watch, and the many neighbours now standing at windows and in doorways. 'I know Patsy White these years back,' she proclaimed, 'long before she was the great Republican. Oh the bold Patsy wasn't always a nationalist. She wasn't during the war anyway. Then she was a soldiers' hoor.' Mrs French gasped, her face contorted with horror. She looked badly shaken. 'Oh, did you not think I remembered that, Patsy? When you were the talk of the Falls? Brits, Americans, RUC men, it didn't matter to Patsy White. She wasn't a bit fussy. She'd lie down with the scum of the earth for a Guinness and a pair of stockings. Sure she used to be at it up Dummy's entry with Sergeant Carew from Hastings Street barracks, and her knickers down around her ankles. Isn't that right now, Patsy?' she goaded, as Mrs French stood trembling, her face by turns white and red.

'You bloody liar,' was all she could manage to hurl back. 'Liar!' But it was lost in the forceful stream of Aunt Kathleen's rhetoric. And the neighbours were laughing, standing wide-eyed and big-eared, taking it all in, making mental notes, looking at Mrs French as if she were a circus exhibit. And Mrs French was blushing, actually burning red.

'That'll do now, Kathleen, that'll do,' coaxed Colum. 'She's not bloody worth it.'

'Colum's right, she's not worth it. Come on in, Kathleen,' Mother urged. But Kathleen wasn't through just yet.

'Listen to me, you dirty bitch, and mark you my words: if you as much as look sideways at my sister again I'll not waste time breaking your windows, I'll have you shot in the fucking head, by both the Provos and the Stickies!' Kathleen generally supported the official IRA, but her sons and sons-in-law were mainly Provisionals. It gave her comprehensive access to the revolutionary forces. 'Now did I make myself quite clear, Patsy?' Kathleen hammered home her point. 'One more peep out of you and you're a gonner. And I don't waste my time making threats.'

It may have been the vicious and libellous nature of the verbal attack, it may have been that it was wholly unexpected, or it may have been the sight of Colum, who was known as a hard man, hovering in the background, but Mrs French said not a word. She went inside, banged her door, and didn't show her face for the rest of the week.

'I hate scum like that,' said Aunt Kathleen as we quietened her down and handed her a cup of tea, 'I can't stand people who use intimidation.'

15

Conclave

The evening after *Kristallnacht* the Provisional IRA approached Mother to arrange a meeting. For some reason never fully explained nor understood, they refused to have Deirdre Gorman present at this first summit. The meeting was organised through our cousin Rosaleen's husband Tony. Tony was a revolutionary in the Che Guevara tradition. A handsome, tanned face – he was a navvy – deep blue eyes, flashing teeth. And all of it in the service of the Republic. Also he had developed muscles, bulges of flesh disconcertingly visible under shirt and T-shirt. He didn't know what to make of Mother involving herself in the security situation. He thought the publicity was a bad idea and he counselled her against it. She became even more determined to have her own way.

'I'll meet them wherever they want,' she insisted when he tried to discourage her, 'over the border, Ballymurphy, anywhere. I just want to talk to them.'

'What'll Aidan say?'

'I'll handle Aidan.' The first note of uncertainty.

Tony managed to set things up fairly quickly. He called later in the week on his way home from work. I answered the door.

'Tell your mother to expect her visitors later.'

It seemed sudden, a bit rude.

'What time?'

He gave me a half-cocked smile. 'Come on, Annie. Do you want them to make a public announcement?'

I remember thinking it would have been a useful way to

combat the rumours, although the clandestine dimension
was not without interest. Mother seemed pleased.

'It's well I left in those few biscuits and the coconut
snowballs. Do you think they'd want their dinner? I mean
if they're on the run . . .'

Thomas advised against it. 'Ma's cooking would hardly
offer aid and comfort,' he commented.

'Will you stay with me, Annie?' she asked. 'I want a
witness, just in case.'

Ready as ever for any diversion, I agreed to be a witness,
although hardly an impartial one. But I had other motives
than that of pure entertainment. I imagined that if a leading
Provisional was dropping in for the evening he would not
come unaccompanied. Indeed he might have an aide-de-
camp, perhaps a second-in-command, and he would certainly require bodyguards. His bodyguards would be young
men, probably tall and well-made. It would be important
that they should know the area well, lest their commander,
in a moment of danger, be forced to flee through the maze
of back gardens, and leap over fences in order to escape a
British raiding party. It would therefore be absolutely
necessary that he be accompanied by volunteers who lived
no further than a couple of streets away. I decided that a
man like Jimmy Cane would be ideal. The Provos would
concur. I had no doubt he would be of the entourage.

I was trembling only slightly when I opened the front door
just after half-seven. Three men stood on the porch. I
immediately ascertained that none of the three was Jimmy
Cane. I gawked. Nothing was said for a second, then Tony
stepped from behind them and pushed open the door.

'Go on in, sir. Annie, these men are here to see your
mother.' He followed them through the little hall.

Jimmy Cane did not amble lazily in behind them. But
that, I decided quickly, was understandable. He would be
more necessary outside the immediate area of the summit

talks, acting as alert sentinel and stalwart buffer in the face of threat. Horatio up on the corner. His relaxed grimness would serve him well. The watcher on the concrete porch. I looked up and down the garden path. There was a long-haired volunteer standing in the passageway between Mrs French's house and our coal-bunker. Nothing to write home about. I scanned the street. There was no man-filled car to be seen, but two or three burly individuals stood conspicuously on the far corner. There was no sign of Cane, neither hide nor straggly hair of him. Only to be expected. The fellas lighting up Woodbines over the road and the stringy adolescent up the path would be decoys. Cane would be part of a strike force, the secret, essential vanguard of military power. A man skilled in the esoterica of revolution. The élite troops would of course be kept in reserve, under cover, but ready to hurl themselves into action at a second's notice, Cane at the head of them, fierce, decisive, gorgeous. He would look magnificent in a saffron cloak and leather leggings. A short tunic in some earthy colour barely covering the big thighs. A disturbing enough image.

Sure that he would be lurking manfully in the vicinity I followed the visitors into the living room. Tony was making the introductions.

'This is Bernie McPhelimy, sir. Bernie, this is the man you wanted to speak to.'

No names mentioned.

'Glad to meet you, Mrs McPhelimy,' said the smallest of the three men as he shook hands with a grave charm. An old-fashioned gentleman. 'Just call me Finbarr,' he added, 'I'll answer to that as well as anything.'

'Will you be all right then?' asked Tony, rubbing his big hands awkwardly.

The little man nodded. 'We'll be fine now, thanks, Tony.'

'I'll be off then. You know where I am if you need me. I'll see you later, Bernie.' He let himself out and Mother

invited the men to sit down. I was wavering uncertainly in
the doorway.

'Come on in,' said Mother, calling me over. 'This is my
daughter Annie,' she explained to the little man who was
prepared to answer to the name of Finbarr. 'Do you mind if
she stays? I'd feel better if she was here.'

'Not at all,' he said easily, smiling warmly up at me.

I sat down beside Mother on the stool to the left of the
hearth.

'I see you're one of the Brown Bombers?' He was referring
to my school and its hideous cocoa-brown uniform. He
was to be sorry he'd opened his mouth. Mother spent the
next few minutes explaining that I was a very brilliant,
talented, responsible, creative and good-living Brown
Bomber. Nor did I drink or smoke. He had the good sense
to agree with her. He seemed a mild-mannered man,
quietly spoken, a soothing, low voice.

As Mother got down to business and told him of the
problems confronting the women of the area he nodded
understandingly, his eyes soft, slightly mournful. Like a
well-intentioned parish priest. I studied him with ill-
concealed curiosity. A low-set man, but sturdy. Grizzled,
grey-black hair and a brown face. He was neatly dressed in
a sports jacket and pressed trousers, a well-knotted tie and
pullover.

Off to one side, in front of the picture window, a satellite
hovered. A discreet, expressionless man of middle age and
middle height. A polite haircut, oil-slicked. The suit-and-
tie brigade. Except when the leader expressly included him
in the conversation he pretended to have no part in the
proceedings. His eyes wandered innocently over the walls.
The Sacred Heart with the pink, shell-shaped votive lamp.
The Mother of Perpetual Succour. Two ceramic plaques, a
gypsy caravan and a fishing village. Wedding presents. He
glanced curiously at the three-tiered Tupperware structure
in the broad windowsill. A nest of bowls in off-white
plastic. Vase, salad bowl and fruit dish combined, sur-

mounted now with a spray of plastic flowers. He eyed it for a moment then turned to study the toes of his shoes. A thorough professional.

The third man was younger. A nimbus of ginger curls ringed his prematurely bald, red head. His jacket too was ginger, and his well-polished loafers. He looked too big for the sofa, his legs spreading all over the carpet. As he sat down his trousers rode up his big red calves, exposing bare ankles. Men on the run maybe don't wear socks, I reflected. Mother had been talking for some minutes now.

'. . . like we realise what you're up against. The only thing is the kids. My heart does be in my mouth every afternoon, in case they'd get hit. Especially our Brendan. He's wild. There's no talking to him. He's at that age you see, just turned thirteen. And all his friends are out stoning the soldiers. I just said to him last week when there was a riot on, you put your foot across that door and I'll break your two legs.'

The leader nodded compassionately, his fine brown hands opening in acceptance of the eternal dilemma of the little Irish mother.

'I don't know what I'd do if one of my children was hurt. I know that a lot of women would be happy to have their sons die for Ireland. But I think they need their heads examined. Like that oul' eejit next door. Oul' Ma French, you must know her?'

'Indeed I've heard of her.' He smiled crookedly.

'Well to hear her you'd think she was second-in-command of the entire Belfast Brigade. She knows everybody. And she knows all that goes on.'

'She thinks she does.'

'Well she makes sure everybody else does too. That woman's dangerous.'

He glanced over at his slick-headed retainer.

'Could we have a word there maybe?' he drawled mildly. It was barely a suggestion, a demure inquiry, but heavy with the thrill of power. The entire interface was beginning to liven up. 'I know what you mean, Mrs McPhelimy, but unfortunately people like Mrs French have their uses.'

'It's the kids I feel sorry for. God love them, they don't know any better. And that woman always quoting Padraig Pearse, "I do not grudge my two strong sons . . .", well I'd bloody begrudge mine. And I won't stand by reciting poetry when their blood's running down the street in the cause of Mother Ireland.'

Unhappily, Thomas came in from the back garden at that moment and caught the end of the monologue. He rolled his eyes in mock alarm and nodded to the visitors with the scant civility he reserved for those who could be of no conceiveable interest or use to him. He passed straight through the room and went on upstairs.

'He has an awful lot of homework,' said Mother by way of expiation. 'Annie, would you make a wee cup of tea?'

I rose gladly. I had been awaiting the opportunity to get into the kitchen and check out the back garden. If I were deploying men to guarantee my safety I would certainly have stationed two or three out the back. One behind the coal-bunker, one by the rockery and one at the back fence, to help me over in an emergency. I sensed that Cane would be out there, deployed behind the lines of washing that constituted the main decoration of the garden. As I arranged the cups and wet the tea I kept one eye on the window. But he was too well concealed. He would not do things in half measures. When I brought in the tea Finbarr was opening a packet of Gelusil.

'Do you have an ulcer?' asked Mother, genuinely concerned, handing him a cup of tea.

'Aye, it's giving me a bit of trouble just now. The Gelusil keep the worst of it at bay.'

'You should be seeing a doctor, though I don't suppose you'd get much chance . . . Here eat something. A dry biscuit might settle it.'

'Ach it's not too bad. The tablets'll see me right.'

'That's what's wrong with my husband you know, an ulcer.'

'So I understand.'

'The doctor says it's all stress. All the shootings and the riots and so on . . .'

'I wouldn't doubt it. That's what it is with me. I'm an oul' worrier. Not for myself. It's these young fellas, on the run for months at a time. I'm responsible for them, and my heart goes out to them sometimes. They've never known a normal life.'

'It's terrible,' Mother nodded sadly.

'And now with all these raids they never get a moment's peace. There's men haven't seen their wives and children since last year. Now if we could get these raids stopped there would be no need for half of the shooting. It's a defensive measure, you see, a deterrent to the army. But of course the British refuse to negotiate with us.'

'Could you not organise a truce of some sort?'

'That should be possible.' He sucked loudly on the tablet. 'But they just refuse to meet with us. We have no way of getting our message across. Now if your group, on the other hand, was to go to Brandywell, and explain our position, the British would listen to you, and we'd certainly be prepared to work something out about the shootings in the area.'

Mother had been listening carefully and now paused to consider. The little man bit into a coconut snowball.

'You mean,' said Mother at last, 'you want us to go to Brandywell and give him a message on your behalf, and if we do you'll stop the violence in Andersonstown?'

He hesitated, found the right words: 'Let me put it this way, Mrs McPhelimy: if the British meet certain of our demands, we would be in a position to . . . change our tactics. I think you would see a real improvement in the situation here.'

'What demands?'

'Well, to begin with, an end to the raids on homes in

West Belfast, no more arrests, the release of the
internees . . .'

'You're asking an awful lot. I mean, we all want to see
an end to the searches, and the men released, but I can't
see them agreeing in a hurry . . .'

'Oh it would have to be negotiated of course, but we
have to start somewhere.'

'Well I'd love to see peace talks myself, but I doubt
they'd listen to us.'

'I think you're wrong there. They'd be more likely to
listen to you than to us. They don't want to be seen talking
to what they call the men of violence.' He took another
Gelusil.

'Do you honestly think so? If I thought I could do
anything to settle all this I'd be only too happy to go to
anybody.'

'I'm delighted to hear you say that, Mrs McPhelimy, it's
the first glimmer of hope I've had since this all started.'

At that moment there was a muffled banging at the front
door. The oilslick went out to investigate. We heard the
door open and a cheerful gruff voice calling out, 'Don't
panic, it's only me. All quiet on the western front!'

He was a big, jittery bear of a man. Fair and pink and
mild-featured. His almost completely bald head shone
above an unlined forehead. He straddled the centre of the
room, boldly displaying a well-developed beer-belly and a
roll of chins. Drinker's chins. A navy padded anorak added
to the bulk of him. Thomas had come downstairs to see
what the commotion was about and now showed the
newcomer into the living room. Mother rose to greet him.

'No, don't get up now, don't get up, Bernie. This is only
a flying visit. I'm a one-man flying column,' he protested
as Mother offered him a seat.

'So do you know each other?' asked the little man with
a happy smile. This might have been a parish social.

'We do surely,' answered Mother brightly. 'I know Cahir
from years back.'

'Sure Bernie's an oul' dancing partner of mine,' Cahir announced, delighted with himself. 'Many's the time we danced the Walls of Limerick together at the Ard Scoil.' Leatherarse.

There was a brief pause. We all looked at each other.

'What was it, Cahir?' inquired his boss in a smooth transition from the social drivel. Down to business.

'We have a man wounded,' announced Cahir heartily, in no way perturbed. 'It's not serious, but we'll have to get it seen to.'

'Is it . . .?' A meaningful shift of the eyebrows.

'Aye, it was bound to happen sooner or later. He's all right.'

'Did you contact a doctor?' asked the little man looking miserable and tossing another Gelusil into his mouth.

'We can't use yer man again, so we're going to try the other fella on the Springfield Road.'

I wondered if they meant Dr Curran. His surgery was on the Springfield. I couldn't imagine him patching up wounded IRA men, with his waistcoats and big stately figure and obvious hairpiece. There was nothing of the rebel about him. I would look at him differently when I had my next bronchial attack.

'Fine. Can you get that organised then, Cahir? I'll not be here much longer. There's just a few things I want to sort out with Mrs McPhelimy.'

'No problem, ample time. I'll pick you up on my way back. I'll go on round then. I'll see you later, Bernie.'

With that he pulled a hanky from his anorak pocket and a heavy wad of ten-pound notes, bound by an elastic band, fell onto the carpet. He may have been the brigade treasurer.

Thomas picked it up, handed it back to him with a sardonic smile. 'Here, it wouldn't do to leave that behind.'

'Jaysus, you're right there, son,' Cahir chuckled, 'I'd be better off leaving my head.' Thomas saw him to the door.

Mother and Finbarr chatted some more over tea. He

asked her about Deirdre, about Canon Clancy and Liam Mulvogue; polite, disinterested inquiries. He asked her what they were planning for the future. She said she honestly didn't know. He said he knew just what she meant, he felt that way himself many's the time.

There was another signal knock at the door. Finbarr's man went into the hall, then came back and gave him the nod.

'I'll have to be going now,' said Finbarr, rising reluctantly, 'I have to see about these boyos. Some of them have hardly slept in a bed these months back. And to tell you the truth, Mrs McPhelimy, since your window was broken a lot of the people on the estate are blaming us and won't take the boys in.'

'Ach, God dekervus. Sure it wasn't the IRA did it! It was bloody oul' French. I know only too well. The boys could stay here if you're ever stuck. I'd hate to think of them doing without their sleep. We'd make beds up for them here, wouldn't we, Annie?' I nodded eagerly. I would offer them the warm welcome of the white Tupperware bowls.

'Not at all, Mrs McPhelimy, sure you have enough to worry you with your man ill and this other business. But the reason we wanted to see you . . . we were wondering if you'd be prepared to attend a meeting this coming Saturday night?'

'Certainly,' Mother agreed eagerly. 'What sort of meeting?'

'Well just with myself and a few of my colleagues, you know, just to sort out a few things. You can bring Mrs Gorman if you like. But we'd be very keen to talk to you again.'

'I'll do anything I can. I think the more we all talk the more chance there is of finding a solution.'

'Hear hear, Mrs McPhelimy, you're absolutely right. If you don't negotiate you get nowhere. I'll be in touch with Tony then. He'll let you know what's happening.' We followed him out to the door. He turned to bid us goodnight and said to me: 'Now study hard and get those exams, we need educated young people.' I nodded cooperatively. Cahir was waiting with the car. Finbarr and his men got in and Mother waved them off. Cahir tooted the horn as they glided down Bunbeg. Still there was no sign of Jimmy Cane. This was taking security too far.

16

Workshopping

It was the first day back after the holidays. The school driveway was speckled with squashed frogs. They came over from the bog for the mating season, and died in their hundreds, under the wheels of teachers' cars. Hilda and I were examining one at the door of our form room when someone came up behind us.

'You never said your mother was in the Assembly of Women.' Patricia Breen looked up at me accusingly, hands on her almost non-existent hips, demanding an explanation.

'She isn't,' I said, surprised, but not yet affronted.

'Well she brought them into Andersonstown.' A smile of entrapment on her skinny mouth.

'No she didn't. She has nothing to do with the Assembly of Women.'

'You'd never guess from the way she gets on.' This from Elizabeth Clarke as she sat on her school bag copying Hilda's physics homework. The entire class seemed suddenly to be standing around waiting to hear my explanation.

'Your mother has no right to bring middle-class Protestants into Andersonstown,' Patricia went on righteously.

'Yeah,' chorused three or four followers.

'She should be more loyal to her own people.'

The voice of the betrayed tribe raised in plaint. I was still hovering between disbelief and annoyance. What the fuck were they talking about? Surely they knew better. They'd been at school with me for years.

'I mean, she's entitled to her own opinion,' said Elizabeth generously, 'but she shouldn't force it on other people.'

I sensed there was nothing I could say to them, but I explained the facts anyway. I wasted my time. They preferred the drama. Only Eileen and Hilda didn't behave differently towards me. A wholly unexpected development. I felt a sudden empathy with flattened frogs and wondered how Thomas and Brendan were managing up at the Christian Brothers'.

Father wasn't doing so well down at the Royal. Aunt Kathleen had tussled with her conscience for a few days and then decided that he'd better know what was going on. She knew Mother would be furious, but she could see that Father was needed at home. She went down to the hospital and told him everything. He discharged himself that afternoon, against doctor's advice and with many severe warnings about his chances of survival. Colum drove him home and helped him into the house.

'Holy God, Aidan! You shouldn't be out of hospital!' Mother declared, horrified at the state of him. He was in no condition to argue.

'And you should have kept your mouth shut and done what I told you,' was all he said. Colum hopped uncomfortably from foot to foot, still hitching up his trousers. He was, Kathleen claimed, a bundle of nerves. Long Kesh had changed him.

'Maybe I'd better get him up to his room, Bernie,' he suggested. Mother stood tight-lipped and nodded. Thomas helped him take Father upstairs.

'You see our Kathleen,' growled Mother as she took her temper out on the fire with the heavy iron poker, 'I'm going to murder her.'

*

We sat in a row on the settee waiting for the Provos to collect Mother. She was standing at the window, watching, her coat already on, holding her big brown handbag under one arm. Our cousin, Tim McGlinchy, had made it in Long Kesh.

'That's lovely workmanship, girl,' she'd said admiringly when Aunt Nora brought the bag round. 'I didn't know Tim was good with his hands.'

'Nor did I,' said Aunt Nora. 'I didn't think he had it in him. But they keep the men busy when they're inside. Sometimes I'm actually glad he's in, Bernie – God forgive me – but I'm not worried about him every minute. It used to be I was driving myself mad all the time wondering where he was sleeping, did he even get a bed for the night? And what he was involved in . . . I was always waiting for them to carry him in dead to me. But thank God, now he's off the drink and he's learning Irish.'

'God, that's great, girl!'

'Aye, well you know our ones, they were never interested in studying like your kids, Bernie.'

'Ah but I beat the studying into them, girl,' Mother declared proudly. She had, too.

Now she was pacing in and out of the hall. 'I wonder if they're coming at all. They said seven o'clock.'

'I hope they don't,' said Father.

'What's that crack supposed to mean?' She was annoyed, defensive.

'You don't know what you're getting yourselves into. They'll give you the runaround,' he warned. He was leaning over the hearth, one hand pressed against his stomach, in pain.

'I don't mind.'

'They'll drive you about all over the place, and in the end you mightn't get to see anybody at all.'

'I don't think so. Anyway, we're willing to take the risk,' she persisted.

'Just be careful what you agree to.'

'We're just going for talks, to find out what they want, what it takes to get peace in this place.'

'Whatever you do, you won't get peace.'

Mother turned on him, angered: 'Why the hell shouldn't we get it? Peace to lead normal bloody lives for once, in this cursed country. That's what's wrong with this place: too many people think like you. You're defeated before you even get started, or you're pro-violence. It's time the rest of us spoke out.'

Father turned to us. 'It's useless talking to your mother.'

Brendan giggled. Father gave him a dirty look. 'Just don't agree to anything,' he went on, 'and don't get any more involved than you are now. Don't be making any promises. These boys are serious.'

'So are we.' She sat down, rummaged in her bag and took out a cracked powder case. She quickly powdered her facial extremities: cheekbones, chin, nose and temples. She sprayed a shower of Blue Grass over her upper body, rearranged her handbag, stood up again. 'And I'll tell you one thing, Aidan: I don't know about the IRA, but Deirdre and I are hellish determined.'

Father shook his head. 'She hasn't a clue.'

The car had arrived. A blue Cortina. It pulled up silently at the front of the house. There were two men in the front, all elbows and shoulders. Father saw her out to the front door.

'Are you sure you'll be all right now?' she asked him.

'Aye, but will you?'

'Don't be silly, Aidan, I'll see you later.' She kissed Sinead goodnight, said a word to the rest of us about homework and left. We watched one of the men get out and open the car door for her. She would like that.

They first went round to pick up Deirdre, then turned down the Glen Road.

'Are you not going to blindfold us?' asked Deirdre good-humouredly.

The driver looked at her in the mirror and smiled easily. 'Ah, I don't think that will be necessary,' he said. He spoke with a Cork accent. Deirdre and Bernie giggled in the back.

'Are you from Cork?' Bernie inquired.

'A policeman wouldn't ask you that, missus, under the circumstances,' said the driver.

'No,' she said, meaning there was nothing behind her question, 'I only asked because I went to Cork for my honeymoon.'

He nodded amiably.

'Not that it was very romantic,' she added, 'all my husband was interested in was visiting the museums, and seeing where the IRA had ambushed the Black and Tans, where this person had been shot, or some bridge blown up, or where Terence McSweeny had lived.

'Who's Terence McSweeny?' asked Deirdre.

'Some oul' Republican,' said Bernie, 'I think he died on hunger strike.'

'He was a great man.' The other man spoke for the first time. The women shut up.

The car was going through the centre of Andersonstown. At one point they passed an army foot patrol. The men appeared unruffled. They drove at last out on to the Andersonstown Road, turned up the Shaw Road and into Stewartstown, a small enclave of private houses. They had taken the circuitous route. They pulled up outside a neat-looking home with well-tended flower beds and lawn.

'Right you are,' said the driver, 'this is it.'

He led them up to the door, handed them over to a tall, thin rake of a man, and left.

'In here then ladies,' said the rake, 'I'll leave you here for a minute. I need to see to a few, eh . . .' He showed them into the sitting room and hastily withdrew.

What next? they wondered. They waited.

'It's a lovely house,' said Bernie after a while.

'Lovely.'

'I like those curtains. I always love anything green.'

They waited for almost half-an-hour.

'What happened to your man? He said he'd only be a minute.'

'I was beginning to think we're the only ones here. The house is so quiet. You don't think we're being set up?'

'Jesus I hope not. Don't be giving me heart failure, Bernie.'

'Well where are they then? They said seven. Look at the time now.'

'It's probably for security reasons . . .'

'Aye, but it's very rude.'

The rake stuck his head in at last.

'Sorry to keep you ladies, but there's been a change of plan. We have another car here to take you to the meeting.'

They rose, tutting in disgust.

'Aidan said this would happen,' Bernie muttered as they got into the brown car. There was only the driver this time. He didn't speak. He took them on a tour of Hannahstown, Leenadoon, Hillhead. They ended up in Riverdale.

'Oh for God's sake,' exclaimed Bernie impatiently when she saw where they were, 'they may as well take me home. Do they think we're stupid, that we don't know where we are? Sure my nephew and his wife have a house down the street and our Annie's friend Eileen lives over the road there.'

'We'll just go along with them anyway. You're better to say nothing.'

Another house, another quiet sitting room, another near-invisible host. And they waited again. There were two further moves, punctuated by periods of waiting, until they found themselves once more in the blue Cortina.

'Now just a wee minute!' Deirdre protested when they saw the familiar driver. 'Are you going to drive us around all bloody night?'

'Sorry ladies, but we're just being extra careful. You never know. We'll be taking you there now.'

It was dark by the time they were led up the final garden path. They were shown into a back room of the house. A ring of men rose to greet them.

'Ah you've got to be joking,' said Bernie as she looked round the room. 'Now we're back where we started!'

The men laughed.

'How did you know?' asked Finbarr, who had come up to greet them.

'Well it's a different room, but the same curtains. I was admiring them earlier.'

'God trust a woman! The curtains! That's a good one.'

Finbarr led them to the discussion table.

'I hope that's not an example of your security measures, for your sakes,' Deirdre said tartly.

His face froze fleetingly, regained the easy grin. He made the anonymous introductions, half-a-dozen grim or stone-faced men. Deirdre and Bernie nodded to each in turn and settled themselves at the table. Negotiations ensued.

'They want us to go to Mr Brandywell,' Mother reported the next day. Mr Brandywell was the British presence incarnate. 'Liam Mulvogue says he'll help us.'

Mr Mulvogue imported delicacies and gourmet fare in a big and lucrative way. But he was also a public figure, entangled from time to time in a range of citizens' action groups and community development committees. He was respected as a man who did much good work, as much for the disaffected as for the downtrodden.

'Liam has plenty of connections with all the work he does. He'll get us to Brandywell. And the Bishop says he's behind us one hundred per cent. He's having all the churches do a special sermon, "Blessed Be the Peacemakers".'

'For they shall inherit the earth – six feet of it,' Father concluded bitterly. There was no use talking to him. And there was no use talking to Mother. She spent the day at Gorman's, making arrangements.

*

'We couldn't go in Aidan's oul' car, we'd only let ourselves down,' said Bernie. She did not mention that Aidan would not be caught dead in that part of Helen's Bay.

'That's where all the top men have houses,' Liam Mulvogue commented, 'the whole Northern Ireland Office. It's easier to protect them down there with only the sea at their back.'

'There are some lovely houses all around there,' said Deirdre, 'you're right, Bernie, we'll have to go in a half-decent car.'

'I'd be glad to take you but I'm flying to Switzerland in the morning.'

'It's well for you. Do you want company?'

He smiled. 'I tell you what. Ambrose Marron would take you. He drives a van for me. I could leave the car for you and ask Ambrose to take you over.'

'Would you? That'd be great. I know Ambrose,' said Deirdre, 'from Cranagh Place.'

'That's him. I'll have a word with him tomorrow.'

So they went in the grey Mercedes, Ambrose providing a guided tour of the road to Helen's Bay. They followed the wooded highway out to the coast and skirted the bay. On both sides of the road mansion-sized houses could be glimpsed through trees and at the ends of long driveways. They passed villas with triple garages and tennis courts, with high stone walls and rampant rhododendrons, with beach access out the back and the masts of yachts bobbing in the bay behind the house.

'Very nice,' mumbled Deirdre.

'Sticking out,' agreed Bernie.

They wondered if they were dressed for the occasion.

The house was at the end of a private lane. They passed under low-arching trees and stopped outside the gate. A man in a dark suit came forward and leaned in to glance around the car.

'These ladies are here to see Mr Irnmonger,' said

Ambrose. Mr Irnmonger was the Executive Liaison Officer
at the Northern Ireland Office.

'You're expected, ladies. Go right on up to the house
please.'

The gates opened somehow and they eased up the driveway. The land fell away to their right, a view over the bay.

'Look out there, Bernie. Thon's magnificent.'

'It is indeed.'

A member of Mr Irnmonger's staff met them at the door.
A young man, already round-shouldered, fair ringlets falling into light blue eyes. He looked worried. He appeared to
be studying his feet. His Winchester accent was particularly pronounced.

'Hello, how are you? I'm Callum Hyde, Mr Irnmonger's
private secretary.' He glanced up anxiously, as though
uncertain how they would take this. 'Mr Irnmonger is just
on the line to London, ladies. He apologises, but it is rather
important,' the young man explained. 'He'll be with you
shortly. Would you like to wait in here?' He showed them
into a room to the left of the entrance hall. It was long and
elegant and looked out over the bay. The decor was entirely
white and gold: the light Persian rugs, the cloud of white
curtains hovering at the open window, the small wood-
inlaid tables scattered around the walls.

'This is glorious,' said Deirdre.

'Perhaps you'd like some tea, ladies, while you're waiting?' He stood some distance from them, just inside the
door. He felt uncomfortable with these sort of people, God
knows their politicians were bad enough. He could think
of nothing to say to them.

'No thanks, we're fine.'

'You've a terrific view here,' Deirdre commented.

'Yes,' he seemed to hesitate, 'yes, it is nice.'

'I suppose you don't get much time to enjoy it.'

'No, not really.'

'I imagine you get homesick?' Bernie suggested.

He didn't know how to respond, only smiled weakly, his

eyes still hovering around his ankles. No doubt they meant well.

'Have you seen much of Ireland?'

'No, not really. Bangor, of course, and Hillsborough. I get so little time . . .

'You should see the west before you go home,' Bernie advised, 'and the Glens of Antrim, and up around the Giant's Causeway.'

'Yes, I really must make the effort. Well, perhaps I'll see if Mr Irnmonger has finished on the phone. Excuse me.' He backed away, withdrew with an ambivalent nod.

'I'd love a cup of tea but I'd be afraid of spilling it,' whispered Bernie.

'You'd swear he was putting that accent on, wouldn't you?'

'I like a nice English accent. Mr Irnmonger has a lovely voice too on the phone.'

They sat down on a scrolled sofa covered in white brocade and studied the ceramics and crystal arranged on tables and shelves around the room. Before long they sensed a low whispering outside the door. It opened, apparently of its own accord and Mr Irnmonger floated into the room. The net curtains billowed out from the windows to greet him. He was a medium sort of man, perhaps in his mid-forties, narrow-shouldered and clean-shaven, well-defined features. His thin, arched eyebrows were darker than his hair, which was almost blond. His eyes were a pale blue. He wore a tie to match them and a silver-grey suit. He clutched a lime-green folder under one arm and extended his hand to Deirdre and Bernie as he advanced.

'Ladies, you're both very welcome, very welcome indeed. It's a pleasure to meet you. I, as you've probably guessed, am Geoffrey Irnmonger.' He smiled brightly at his little joke. 'And I recognise you, Mrs McPhelimy, from your television appearances. You too, Mrs Gorman. I'm very sorry to have kept you waiting, ladies. Couldn't be helped. It's so good to see you at last.' His voice lulled, reassured.

'I do indeed hope that we can achieve something useful together.' He drew up a white matching stool and sat in front of them. 'Now what can we do for you, ladies?'

As he spoke the door opened quietly and a little man entered pushing a small, ironwrought tea-trolley. He wheeled it noiselessly across the carpet, came to a neat halt where the trio sat. Bernie watched him fascinated. He did not ask them if they would like tea, he assumed it. Mr Irnmonger passed them cups, helped them to milk and sugar.

'You shouldn't have gone to so much trouble,' Bernie protested when she saw the plates of tiny cakes and tea-bread.

'Good heavens, Mrs McPhelimy, it's no trouble whatso-ever. It's a pleasure to have company for afternoon tea. Can I offer you one of these?'

Deirdre tried to manage her cup and saucer, but she couldn't eat a bite. She was suddenly very hot. Her face must be glowing. What in God's name would he think of her? A hot flush in the middle of these delicate nego-tiations. She fanned herself with the *Belfast Telegraph* which had been lying on a side table.

'It *is* warm in here,' he responded at once. 'Can I get you a cold drink?'

'Oh not for me, I'm fine,' she lied loudly. She was beginning to feel worse, oddly weak, her heart pumping harder than usual. And it was in her head now too, a rhythmic ache. It grew more painful as she listened to his voice, no longer focusing on the sense. Awful pain now. Bloody awful. It must be like a migraine. What was wrong with her? She wished she could lie down. It wasn't like her . . .

He seemed not to notice. He was talking in his quiet, pained way. 'But of course the media must be held fully responsible for much of the ill will. They exaggerate, they distort, they invent. Some are more responsible than others, of course.'

Bernie nodded. 'I know exactly what you mean, some of them don't give a damn,' she agreed with feeling.

'I have of course spoken to Mr Brandywell regarding your proposal. He would be positively delighted to meet with you. He's always so happy to meet the people, he likes to hear things from the grassroots. He is, you know, very keen to find a solution to the Northern Irish question, and will be most grateful for any assistance.'

Another wave of heat. Heat wave. It swept through Deirdre leaving a kind of nausea. She tried, surreptitiously, to take a deep breath and felt the first cutting cramp in the lower abdomen. She gasped silently, tried to clear her head, breathe in through nose and mouth. A second shot of pain, stronger than before. She leaned forward, curled up for relief, her arm across her middle. Holy Jesus. She sucked air through her teeth, lowered her head and saw the red stain on the sofa beneath her. She studied it for a second, then understood. Shock and shame. She stared as the fresh blood soaked into the sofa, spreading grotesquely over the white brocade. She was bleeding, heavily. A weakness shuddered through her. She let out a small cry.

'Oh Christ!'

'What? What is it?' said Bernie. But then she saw her face, and then the sofa.

'Oh my God! You're haemorrhaging.'

Mr Irmmonger looked at her, mildly surprised, a slight arching of the thin dark eyebrows. Then he noted the blood. His expression did not change.

'Mrs Gorman, are you OK?' A politely pitched tone of urgency.

'I feel awful. I'm really sorry about the sofa . . .'

'Good heavens, don't even think of it!' He laid his hand lightly on her shoulder. She had doubled up in pain.

'I don't know what's come over me . . .'

'I'll send my wife to you immediately.' He slipped silently out of the room. Bernie put her arms around her, pressed her head against her shoulder.

'You'll be all right, love. We'll have to get you to the hospital.'

'No, Bernie, I'll be all right. Just get me home.'

'You'll have to go to the hospital, Deirdre, you're losing a lot of blood.' Bernie felt in her bag for a tissue, tried surreptitiously to mop up the red stain.

'Not the hospital, Bernie, please,' she pleaded. 'This happens to me every now and again, it's not serious. Please let me go home.'

'Are you sure? We'll have to get the doctor up then. You should definitely see a doctor.'

Mrs Irnmonger appeared, big and brocky and complacent. She was quite calm and pleasant, a woman who regularly had visitors haemorrhage on her white brocade sofa.

'Not to worry now,' she soothed, 'we must think of you. Would you like to lie down? Should I call a doctor?'

They finally persuaded her that Deirdre must be sent home at once; she would see her own doctor. They sent a message for Ambrose to bring round the car. Mrs Irnmonger saw them out the door and into the car. She stood in the driveway looking worried and unhappy as they drove away. Her husband, discretion itself, did not reappear.

'Do you think it was very valuable?' asked Deirdre weakly as the car turned into the road.

'What, the sofa? No, not at all. I didn't even like it. I thought it was too gaudy.'

They looked at each other and laughed.

'Never worry yourself, Deirdre.'

'I was worried that it might be an antique.'

'No, I don't think so. That wasn't great material,' said Bernie, based on nothing at all.

'I feel awful . . .'

'I'm not surprised, you've lost a lot of blood.'

'I know, but I feel so ashamed.'

'For God's sake, Deirdre, give yourself peace. You're sick. They understand that.'

'Aye, but it doesn't give a very good impression of the Irish. I'm mortified.'

'Now don't be talking nonsense.'

'Did we decide anything?'

'Eh . . . I don't know, I'm too upset to think, and I'm too worried about you to be bothered.' She was quiet for a minute, then added, 'We're getting to see your man, anyway.'

'That's not so bad then. I hope I don't get it all over Liam's upholstery.'

'I thought Mr Irnmonger was a lovely man,' Bernie volunteered, 'a real gentleman, very charming. He speaks like George Saunders. I wouldn't mind running away with him.'

Deirdre glanced at her sideways: 'I don't think you'd get very far, Bernie, he's a fairy.'

'You're joking! Sure he's married!'

'Well I don't know now, but he struck me as an awful oul' Ginny-Ann. Honestly.'

Bernie thought for a minute, remembered a gesture or two, the way he crossed his legs so daintily, the turn of his foot, 'But what about his wife?'

'I suppose in his job he has to be married. He'd need somebody to act as hostess, and I don't suppose Callum would do.'

They laughcd, then fell silent as the car approached Belfast away from the shelter and privilege of Helen's Bay. They drove past the shipyard. The twin arms of the Harland and Wolf cranes blocked the face of the full moon.

'Just think,' said Bernie, staring out over the black water, 'that's where they built the Titanic.'

'I know, a black hole. I could be doing with a cup of tea, Bernie.'

'Me too, I'm gasping.'

*

They met at the Craigauntlet Hotel, Ulster's finest, tastefully removed from the city centre. It looked like a castle from the outside and overlooked a wide grey-watered lake. Liam Mulvogue accompanied them, as did Canon Clancy. He was a big man, bull-chested, white-headed, a rock of a face, half a ring of carrot-coloured hair just greying in billows above the ears.

'I suppose you eat here all the time, Liam?' the Canon suggested as they got out of the car.

'I do not,' said Liam easily, 'it's too expensive and the food's not that good.'

The manager of the maligned establishment met them at the door and led them into the great foyer. It was glimmering under the light of half-a-dozen chandeliers. The interior was red and black and gold. The gleaming reception desk seemed to stretch into the distance. Waistcoated attendants stood about on corners and in doorways, ready to direct and assist guests. But the manager personally escorted them to the Glenshane Suite where Mr Irnmonger awaited them in an ante-room. He greeted them with his bright, relaxed smile, and spent some time chatting to the women. He didn't mention the haemorrhage incident, merely said: 'You're looking well, Mrs Gorman.' And Deirdre agreed.

A phone rang on a nearby table. Mr Irnmonger excused himself, swept over to pick up the receiver. 'Mr Brandywell is quite ready for you now,' he announced, indicating a door on the left.

'You shut us up if we say the wrong thing, won't you, Liam?' Deirdre whispered as they followed Irnmonger.

'You won't say the wrong thing. Besides the Canon and I are only here as observers, to back you up.'

'I won't open my mouth,' the Canon promised with a chuckle.

Bernie had some lines prepared. She had been saying them over and over again in her mind. But now she hoped that Deirdre would do the talking.

Mr Irnmonger led them to the inner sanctum. It was a disappointing room after the splendours of the façade and lobby, green and gloomy, dominated by a greenish chandelier of cut glass that hung heavily above the table. Mr Brandywell was seated at the top of the table in the centre of the room. He rose as they entered and came to greet them. Mr Irnmonger introduced the deputation. Mr Brandywell bent to shake their hands.

'I've been looking forward to meeting you all very much,' he announced. His great, growling voice seemed to fill the room. He escorted them to their places and saw them comfortably settled, the women at the centre of the table, Mulvogue and the Canon at the far end. Then he returned to his seat at the head of the table. Mr Irnmonger sat on his right and beside him Callum Hyde. Hyde stood up, raised one hand in an awkward salute and dropped back into his seat. On the other side of Brandywell sat a plain little man whom he introduced as George Craven. He nodded, said nothing.

They had noticed at once that Brandywell was so much bigger than he appeared on television: an elephant of a man. He immediately reminded Bernie of Ian Paisley in that way. She had seen Paisley one night at the Lyric Theatre. He was enormous – great hulking shoulders, a chest like an ox and a backside the breadth of Tyrone. And here was this officer of the Crown and him just the same, a big lump of a man. He had a big head too, a thin covering of grey hair plastered down on the right side, a hook nose and an expression like a great, placid bloodhound. It was his eyes. They were long rather than round, responding to gravity with a downward drag. There were bags too, indeed U-valleys sagged mournfully beneath his eyes. His jowls too drooped, and he had a hanging lower lip. Altogether a woeful face. And yet he smiled mildly, continuously. He even appeared shy as he listened to the women telling him about life in Andersonstown. He was a careful listener, he would angle his head attentively, and sponge up the information.

'I do so appreciate you coming and talking to me like this,' he said. 'I have so little knowledge of the real life of the people, the problems they face day to day. And I greatly admire your resilience, your ability to survive in what sounds rather like a war zone.'

'It *is* a war zone, that's why we're so desperate to do something.'

'And how can we help?'

'Well, we're not making any demands, we just want peace in our area,' said Deirdre baldly.

'The IRA are willing to cooperate if you will,' Bernie piped in, 'they've been very good about it.'

Mr Immonger looked at her sideways, his mouth sagged open. 'Have they?'

'They said it has to be a two-sided effort.'

He nodded. He understood.

'Now they have certain demands,' she warned, watching the faces of the men on the other side of the table. 'There are certain conditions.'

'Did they ask you to inform us of these conditions?' interrupted Brandywell, suddenly sharp, severe.

The women exchanged surprised glances.

'Yes, I suppose so,' replied Deirdre.

'Hold on, I've written them down here somewhere. I wrote them down in case I forgot anything.' Bernie rummaged in the Long Kesh bag and held up the folded sheet of an exercise book. 'Here it is, now let me get on my glasses.' She reached into her coat and drew out a pair of spectacles on a gold chain. She put them on, unfolded the paper and read out in a false, faltering voice: 'One, a public declaration that the people of the thirty-two counties of Ireland should decide the future of the country.' She looked up through her spectacles at Mr Brandywell. His eyes appeared to have drooped further. He was looking grave. She cleared her throat, went on: 'Two, the withdrawal of all British troops from Irish soil by New Year's Day, nineteen seventy-five.'

Mr Irnmonger cleared his throat. Hyde was bent double over the table, furiously taking notes. Mr Craven was staring out the window. Bernie, now feeling unhappy but uncertain what else to do, continued: 'Three, pending the full withdrawal, all troops to be withdrawn immediately from sensitive areas, and all house searches to cease forthwith. Four, a general amnesty for all political prisoners, internees and persons on the wanted list.' She paused, looked around the table. 'That's all,' she said simply.

Mr Brandywell leaned back from the table letting out a sigh as he moved. Mr Irnmonger watched him, a frown on his fair forehead.

'They ask for a very great deal, Mrs McPhelimy,' Brandywell announced at last.

She looked at the sheet of paper then back to him. 'It's not us. They just asked us to tell you.'

'All we want is peace,' Deirdre added quickly.

'But not peace at any price?' inquired Brandywell wryly.

The women shifted in their seats. 'What do you mean exactly?'

He rose from his chair, silently, easily for one so bulky, and moved over to the window. He stood for a moment looking out over the greyness of the lake, his hands in his pockets, sucking on his lower lip.

'Those demands go very much further than anything that has been suggested up until now, very much further.'

'Indeed they do,' Mr Irnmonger readily agreed. 'This is asking a great deal.'

'We don't, you see, negotiate with terrorists,' added Brandywell, 'that is Government policy.'

'Oh but I haven't told you, I nearly forgot!' said Bernie.

'Yes?'

'They said they'd be willing to call an immediate cease-fire, didn't they, Deirdre?'

'They did, if you'd be prepared to meet them and discuss their demands.'

Mr Brandywell turned away from the window and stood, the light at his back, considering this latest information. He was looking increasingly grave. He came back to the table but did not sit down. Instead he stood with his hands on the back of his chair staring into the soup-green gloom at the heart of the room. When he spoke his voice was low and strained.

'Ladies, I'm afraid I'm going to have to be very frank with you. It is a difficult and delicate situation you find yourselves in, and I am most concerned that you should come to no harm.'

Deirdre's brown eyes expanded in her head, Bernie felt her throat go dry. Mr Brandywell continued: 'Equally, I am concerned that you should not be used by any group or individual. It is clear to me that you are honest, sincere women without thought of publicity or political ambition, who want only to make a better life for your children and your community.' He spoke nobly, as though addressing a public meeting. 'Now you have come to me, as the representative of Her Majesty's Government, for help, and I feel bound to give you the benefit of my experience and my insight in these matters. Ladies, what I am trying to say, and this is very difficult under the circumstances, is that, in my view – and I do not express that view lightly – the Provisional IRA are not sincere in these demands, and have no intention of calling a ceasefire.'

There was silence in the room. They could hear the honking of water fowl from the lake. Maybe wild geese, Bernie was thinking. She sensed they were losing. She was already wondering what to tell Aidan, she was wondering what to say to Finbarr.

'What makes you say that?' asked Deirdre of Mr Brandywell. 'I mean, that they're not sincere?'

He sat down again, looked over at her kindly, in a fatherly way, his eyes smiling from folds of flesh. 'I can assure you, Mrs Gorman, I do not make the charge lightly. But you see, these demands go so far beyond calls for political status or the end to internment per se – '

'But the IRA has always wanted the British out, it's been their main aim for God knows how long.'

'Yes of course, I do see that, but this is quite different. It's one thing to have long-term aims, but the political reality demands that one works towards those aims by a process of negotiation, compromise, trial and error . . .'

'But you said you wouldn't negotiate with terrorists.'

'No, not as a general rule. You see it would be utter folly to even admit the possibility of holding discussions with the IRA on the basis of these demands.'

'Because of the Protestants? The backlash?'

'Well . . . yes, that too, but for other reasons as well.'

'May I suggest a break for tea?' inquired Mr Irnmonger at that moment.

'Yes of course. Forgive me, ladies. It's a good thing I have Geoffrey to remind me of my duties as host,' and Mr Brandywell slipped smoothly into a more relaxed mode.

The tea was ordered in and served almost at once, as though the hotel staff had been hovering outside the conference room with warming trays and plates of cream biscuits. As the tea-people pattered discreetly about the table the talk turned to the peace movement.

'That is what Mr Brandywell is really interested in, ladies, your brave efforts to bring about peace.'

'Oh yes,' Brandywell declared heartily, 'you find in me your greatest admirer. Now what is your next step, your campaign plan as it were?'

'We don't really know. We have a few ideas. Liam here has been terrific – him and Canon Clancy,' said Bernie, pointing with a Viennese finger. 'We don't know what we'd do without them.'

'Ah, Mrs McPhelimy, I see you have the makings of an astute politician: you already know the value of a good adviser.'

They laughed, sipped tea, admired the view of the lake.

Bernie felt a depression settling in, a sense of hopelessness. They would never be able to explain, to make them understand.

'Actually, Mr Brandywell, I don't see much chance of peace unless you make some move.' She spoke again, a half-nibbled chocolate eclair raised in one hand.

Mr Brandywell coughed lightly to clear his throat. His eyebrows descended. 'Some move? In what sense?'

Bernie felt increasingly uncomfortable, inadequate. She was sorry she'd had that second bun.

'Well I think you should do something first.'

'As an expression of goodwill,' Deirdre interrupted.

'Exactly, and to let the people know you're serious about being prepared to do something about peace.'

'Yes, but what?'

'You could release some of the men, the internees. A lot of them shouldn't be in prison, they're not in anything. Some were lifted just because they were interned during the war. Like the man over the road from me, Seamus Morris. He's never been in the IRA. They wouldn't have him, he's a wee bit simple.'

Mr Brandywell nodded understandingly, he knew the type. He could imagine how selective the IRA could be.

'He's been interned these two months, God knows what for, and his wife's left with five children to rear and no money. And the oldest girl, Brid – plays with our Sinead – is deaf, God help her. The child doesn't know what's going on. Now I don't see any sense in a man like that being interned. It's the family that suffers. And he's not the only one, I could name you a whole lot like that.'

'Indeed? Well, we'll have to think very carefully about what you say.' He was looking graver than ever. 'You see there are so many things to be considered, particularly where security is concerned. But I will think very carefully about it.' He turned to Irnmonger. 'Perhaps we could look into that case; in the meantime, just check the details.'

'Certainly. What was your neighbour's name again, Mrs McPhelimy?'

'Seamus Morris.'

'Morris, right. We'll have that checked out.'

'Thanks very much.'

'But now, ladies, to get back to you. What is your next move?'

Liam Mulvogue spoke for the first time: 'We were thinking of going to the people of the estate.'

'For some expression of the grassroots desire for peace?' suggested Irnmonger. Mulvogue hesitated.

'Well, actually, we were thinking about a petition,' Deirdre explained.

'A petition?'

'Yes.'

'A petition.' He aired the word momentarily, little head cocked up towards the dour, green chandelier, the corners of his neat mouth picked up. 'Yes, that's a good idea. A petition. That might be just the sort of thing one would need. What do you think, sir?'

'I think that would be absolutely splendid, and I'm sure you will have no difficulty getting the necessary support. What do you think, Hyde?'

'There would be useful media coverage in something like that, eh, for the ladies.'

They conferred in low voices at the top of the table.

'Shall we report that you will be organising a petition then? For the newspapers?' asked Irnmonger as the tea things were cleared.

'OK,' said Deirdre, 'but what about the demands? What are we going to tell the IRA?'

17

Chassis

Mother spent hours perched on a stool in the dinette beside the phone, trying to recruit helpers to take up signatures for the petition. Many were called, few were keen. Mrs Gilroy's husband wouldn't let her, Mrs McIlhone didn't have the time, what with looking after wee Siobhan; the girls in work wouldn't have been caught dead doing it and even Eileen's mother was worried because her husband worked with Protestants.

'What's that got to do with it?' demanded Thomas.

'It's just an excuse, that's all. She doesn't want to get involved.'

Still they all offered to sign, provided they could remain anonymous.

'What did you expect?' asked Father, looking up from the *Belfast Telegraph*. 'Did you imagine people were going to stick their necks out?'

'Yes. I did. They all say they want peace, so I expect them to do their bit.'

'Wise up, Bernie,' he muttered in disgust. 'You might be fool enough to put yourself at risk, but most people aren't.'

'That's because they need leadership. That's what's always been wrong with Ireland, no leadership. Or if they do get a leader they shoot him, or turn on him.'

'You're talking nonsense, Bernie.'

'What about Michael Collins? Eh? What about Parnell and his fancy woman?'

'So you're going to be the great leader that Ireland needs?'

'I didn't say that.' She turned to Thomas, Brendan and

me; we were trying to watch a Clint Eastwood movie. 'He always twists everything I say,' she shrieked in anger.

'No I don't! It's your own mind that's twisted. And you're no Michael Collins or – '

'You're bloody right I'm not. They were both failures in the end. Well I'm not going to fail. I'll get peace here if it kills me.'

'There's a good chance that it will.' He went back in behind his paper.

'It'll be worth it, I'll die happy. There's going to be peace here no matter who likes it.'

'You mean you're going to batter the people into a peaceful solution?'

'If need be, yes.'

Father turned to us with mock gravity. 'Your mother,' he pronounced, 'is a militant pacifist.'

In the end the Peace Group abandoned the idea of collecting signatures round the doors of Andersonstown. They decided instead to set up in the foyers and porches of churches and church halls that coming Sunday.

'It was Canon Clancy's idea,' said Mother, 'he says that way we'll reach all the people. And they'll be coming to us, we won't have to go to them.'

'Is the Canon taking up any signatures personally?' Father inquired.

'Well, he's giving a sermon about peace at the eleven o'clock mass and he's going to encourage everybody to sign.' But Father seemed unimpressed. 'And the Bishop's all for it. He's doing a letter to be read out in all the churches, urging the people to call for peace and an end to the violence. He says he's behind us all the way.'

'Aye, well behind you. If he meant the half of it he'd be right out in front of you.'

'He's not a politician, he's doing all he can.'

'Like hell.'

'He is, he's even paying for the printing of these notices.

We're leaving them at all the churches, and having it printed in the papers every day this week.'

The notice read:

A Call For Peace

PEOPLE'S PROTEST

1. We utterly reject and condemn all use of force and violence at the present time.

2. We wish to avail of present opportunities to obtain a just and peaceful settlement of our problems and difficulties.

3. We pledge ourselves to pray and work for these ends, which we believe are shared by the vast majority of the whole people.

Signatures received at:
Foyer of St Theresa's Hall
St Mattias' Oratory
Christian Brothers Secondary School

Sponsored by the Laity and supported by the Bishop and Priests.

'And what do you expect to achieve by all this?'

'If we can get enough signatures somebody will have to listen to us: the army, the IRA, the RUC. If enough people are willing to sign their name we're bound to succeed.'

Father sighed heavily. 'Do you honestly believe that, Bernie?'

She paused, thought for a moment, then said earnestly, 'I do believe it, Aidan, as true as God.'

'Then you're even more stupid than I gave you credit for.'

Bernie failed to recognise Mr Ironmonger's voice when he rang.

'Hello, Mrs McPhelimy? It's Geoffrey . . .'

'I don't know any Geoffrey. Geoffrey who?'

'Actually I'd rather not say.'

The penny dropped. 'Oh! I'm sorry. I didn't recognise your voice at first!' She was careful not to mention his name.

'That's quite all right, Mrs McPhelimy. I do understand. I must apologise for intruding like this.'

'Not a bit of you! It's very nice to hear from you.'

'That's very good of you, Mrs McPhelimy. In fact I did want to have a word.'

'Yes?'

'It was about the matter you raised in relation to your neighbour. I think you know the gentleman I'm referring to?'

'Eh . . . yes, yes.'

'Well, I'm pleased to advise that we may well be able to do something there.'

'Really?'

'Yes, I believe so.'

'That's good news.'

'Yes, I knew you'd be pleased.'

'Thank you.'

'Well, I just thought I'd let you know.'

'I'm delighted, thanks very much.'

'Don't mention it, Mrs McPhelimy.'

'Actually I was wanting to talk to you about that.'

'Yes?'

'Yes. He's not the only one, you see. There's stacks more like him, you know, the same sort of circumstances.'

There was silence at the other end of the phone. But

Bernie persisted. 'I thought, you know, if you could look into one, you could maybe see about the others too.'

'I see,' Mr Irnmonger was sounding a little dry.

'I got that phone number you gave Liam for us. Thanks very much.'

'If you ever need anything I can be contacted at that number.'

'I appreciate that, and, as I say, there are these other cases you might be interested in. I'd only give you a few, of course. I know how busy you are.'

'Let me think about it, Mrs McPhelimy, and I'll be in touch. I probably won't call you directly again. But I'll be in touch through Liam.'

'Fine, that's great. Thanks a lot then.'

'My pleasure. Goodbye, Mrs McPhelimy.'

'Goodbye now, Mr . . .'

For the fortieth time that day army vehicles rumbled past the house causing the nest of Tupperware bowls to shudder one inside the other. It was Saturday and the fine weather brought the young fellas out in force. There had been intermittent riots all morning and still the odd stone or chunk of paving bounced off the armour plating of patrolling saracens. But it was basically the lunch-hour lull. Father had spent the morning in bed and now lay on the settee, a makeshift bed, his face the colour of his old woollen simit, disturbed, brooding. Kitty's Alex sat quietly by the fire, trying to light his pipe. Thomas and Brendan and I were pretending to be studying in the dinette, but we were really watching Alex through the open door, and listening to the parents eating the arses off each other. Their nerves were on edge because the IRA were coming to see the wee woman again. Sinead had been sent round to Kitty's for safekeeping. Mother was washing around the hearth.

'They shouldn't be coming here,' Father pronounced. His voice sounded oddly weak.

'Sure they'll be safe enough here,' said Mother to soothe him.

'There's been too many bloody saracens up and down here all day for my liking.'

'Now don't you be getting upset, Aidan. Sure they'll only be in and out.'

'In and out me arse. The army could have this place surrounded in no time and there would be no chance of them getting away.'

'The army's not thinking of us.'

'You'd no business going to the British anyway.'

'Blame the IRA. It was them that sent us. Besides they'll reach an agreement. They've promised to.'

'Promise be damned! It'll be the old story,' he pulled himself up on one elbow, clutching a handful of blanket, 'there's three things that'll never cease: the wars of the Irish, the pride of the French and the treachery of an Englishman.'

'For Christ's sake don't start, Aidan. They'll be here any minute now.'

Cahir and the man who was prepared to answer to Finbarr arrived about one o'clock. On hearing the rap at the door Mother scurried to pick up the *Irish News* which Father had scattered all over the floor. I opened the door to the visitors and noticed that there was no sign of a car or escort anywhere in the street. After the activity of the morning the place seemed deserted. When Father saw the little Provo a clear flash of recognition crossed his face, but he returned Finbarr's polite greeting with no more than a word and a nod. But Cahir, who had known Father for donkey's years, was all over him, declaring that he looked like a bottle of milk and saying that's what he got for being a teetotaller.

'Take a little wine for yer stomach's sake, Aidan,' Cahir counselled, 'that'll set you up all right.'

'I think it would kill me just at the moment, Cahir,' Father protested smiling. At least he was in a better mood.

Finbarr asked about Father's operation, and Mother was delighted to give him details of stitches and drips and bags of blood. He kept up his face of grave concern, followed her every word.

'That was some operation,' he said when she'd finished. 'You'd better look after him, Mrs McPhelimy.'

'That's right now, Bernie,' Cahir agreed, 'you'll have to feed him up.'

'I'm trying to, but he can't keep a bite down.'

It was Alex who called a halt to the formalities. He leaned forward, tapped out his pipe on the edge of the chimney and said: 'Well, we'd better get this sorted out.'

The three of us, straining to see and hear all, had stopped pretending to be at our books. There was a strategic pause in the living room. Like a chorus the adults looked in to where we sat kneeling on chairs at the big kitchen table. We stared back out at them, expectant. Alex rose and with a wink politely shut the door against us. We couldn't make out the words, but the mumbling went on for almost half-an-hour. It appeared to be amicable. No voice was raised in anger or allegation. We were beginning to get bored.

It was after two. The crowd of boys was gathering again, selecting missiles, making little piles of stones and bricks at the edge of Mrs French's garden wall. Brendan frequently nipped out the back door to glance up the path and check on their progress. Before long the first saracen of the afternoon could be heard rumbling. We could hear the tension of the crowd, preparing to fire and run.

'I'd better tell them,' said Thomas. He boldly opened the door into the living room. Brendan and I saw our opportunity and followed after him: 'Daddy, there's a saracen coming.'

At that minute the saracen thundered into view at the picture window and a hail of rocks immediately descended on its armour-plated sides. The boys yeowed triumphantly and ran in all directions, but the huge vehicle didn't stop, only one or two rubber bullets were emitted from side-slits, and it passed on.

'It looks like it's starting up again,' said Alex to the visitors, 'you might be taking a bit of a risk ... hanging around.'

'Alex is right,' added Father, getting up and going to the window, as if to block the view inside, 'you should get out while you can.'

'We'll be let know if there's any need to make a move,' Finbarr reassured him. They were let know almost immediately. There was an urgent knocking on the door. Thomas went out to answer it. I saw the shapes of two men in the little hall. The smaller of the two was Tony, but the other stepped forward and I felt my heart, blood and pulses pumping fiercely.

He appeared like a vision in the doorway. He was tall and young and powerful and handsome. He looked the part. His hair was something between red and gold, his eyes unsettlingly bright, a strong green colour. His expression bold and intelligent. His sure movements expressed an awareness of his own powers. His eyes skimmed over me, not entirely dismissive. I do not think my mouth fell open.

'It's only Hugh,' said Cahir, visibly relaxing.

Only Hugh indeed! His name was Hugh. Resonance of resonances. Such a well-formed and comely name. A noble nomenclature. I would like to have called him by his name. A vision of bold manfulness.

He took command. 'You have to go, sir, now,' he stressed, standing over Finbarr, 'the army's all over the place. We'll be lucky to get out of here at all.'

No sooner had he spoken than a huge khaki beast of an armoured car flashed past the door, dead-braked just up the street and spewed soldiers from its rear end. It was at that moment that Father's ulcer burst for the second time. He turned in a panic from where he stood at the window, staggered momentarily and collapsed on the carpet with a familiar thud, blood streaming from his purplish lips. He had gone corpse-grey.

'Oh Holy God, Aidan! What is it?' Mother threw herself down on top of him, attempted to administer first aid.

'Christ, he's had it!' exclaimed Cahir in horror as he bent over him.

'No he hasn't,' Alex declared, calm but alert as he checked Father's pulse, 'it's his ulcer, it's gone again. Thomas, phone for an ambulance.'

I was standing stunned and helpless as they leaned over Father, debating whether they should raise his head, trying to give him the kiss of life. I was aware of the vision at the side of the window eyeing the freshly alighted soldiers from the gap between wall and curtain. The crowd had melted inexplicably away. The soldiers ringed the two armoured vehicles, fierce in full riot gear, the big plastic shields, visored helmets, rubber-bullet guns, SLRs in the background.

'Maybe if we sat him up?'

'OK. Here, you take his other arm.'

They hauled Father up and a stream of blood gushed from his throat; he dropped back choking.

'Oh for God's sake somebody help him!' Mother pleaded. 'Do something!'

I was considering having hysterics. But it would attract the soldiers, then we'd all be in shit street.

'Here,' said the vision, handling me out of the way, 'just put this cushion under his head. Keep his airways clear. Make sure he can breathe at all times.' He was completely calm. He moved back to the edge of the curtain, clearly trying to decide whether there was any particular significance in the army being there at that moment, or whether it was just a routine pause for confrontation.

'They always stop there,' Tony reassured him from the hall where he had stationed himself.

At that moment Father came to, struggled up on one

white arm and rasped: 'I told you, you shouldn't be here. The bastards are after you. For Christ's sake get away, get away while you still can.'

'Now you lie back there, Aidan, and don't be upsetting yourself for God's sake. We'll be all right. I'm not going till we get you into the ambulance and if the fucking ambulance doesn't get through I'll take you to the bloody hospital myself,' Cahir declared manfully while Alex and Finbarr tried to hold Father down.

Suddenly an unholy howl went up outside. The local lads had re-emerged from back gardens and behind cars in riotous formation to launch another assault on the latest batch of Brits. Even with the blood still wet on his lips Father struggled to see what was going on.

'Lie down now, Da,' Thomas demanded, 'you'll kill yourself. The ambulance is on its way.'

'It'll never get through,' moaned Mother, 'the roads is all blocked. There's two burnt-out buses down at the Christian Brothers'. Oh Christ, what'll we do?'

Finbarr bent to calm her, one arm around her shoulders, his other hand clasping Father's. 'We'll get him to the hospital, Mrs McPhelimy, if the ambulance isn't here in a few minutes.'

But Father, who had sunk back to the floor, shook his head as furiously as his condition would allow, and gasped out, 'No Kieran, get out now, right away. Hey you,' he feebly called to the vision who was in the kitchen checking the back exit, 'get him out of here right away . . . over the back fence. You'll be in Desy Martin's back garden. Go through the house, Desy'll help you. But for the love and honour of God go now!'

'Aidan, lie back, please,' demanded Mother as she moved to take his head in her lap and began stroking his cheeks.

'Mr McPhelimy's right,' said the vision. 'It's time you were gone.' Marvellously single-minded.

'No,' said the man Father had called Kieran. He was

looking up at the vision without any sign of alarm. No arguments.

'Should we get him onto the sofa?' asked Cahir.

Alex paused thoughtfully, considered the ramifications, the pros and cons, weighed all possible outcomes.

'I think we'd better leave him where he is, Cahir, just to be sure. We wouldn't know what damage we might be doing by lifting him.'

'Will I make a cup of tea?' asked Brendan from the dinette, where he'd been sent and told to stay when Father fell. His normally merry face was white with fear.

'I'm OK, son,' said Father to reassure him.

And then there was a great banging on the door. A banging of biblical proportions, a knocking akin to the McPhelimy death knock. It shuddered through the house causing a draught to fan up the fire, making the Tupperware bowls bounce on the cardinal-red tiles, making all our insides turn instantly to mush.

'Oh fuck!' said Thomas, 'is it the army?' He had expressed the collective thought.

The men all froze, all except the leader who stood up, keeping away from the window, looked towards the back garden, then back to Father who lay face twisted with pain and horror. For the first time I saw him less than confident. Tony was standing in the doorway to the hall, awaiting instructions. But just then the back door banged and Brendan came charging in.

'It's OK,' he said, 'I looked up the path. It's only the ambulance men.'

'Oh thank God!' A heartfelt ejaculation. 'Thomas you go to the door.'

Alex turned to the leader: 'It might be better if you go now.'

'I think you're right. We'll nip out the back. Right, lads, let's be off. Thanks a million, Mrs McPhelimy. And, Aidan, I'll be praying for you. Look after yourself.'

Father nodded, too weak to say anything more. The

vision led them out the back, Tony bringing up the rear. Brendan went out after them to lock the gate that led from the path to the back garden. As they went out the back door the ambulance men came in the front carrying a stretcher, and behind them came two soldiers. Fortunately Father had already passed out again. Brendan immediately came up behind me and quietly closed the door into the dinette, blocking off the view of the long, exposed back garden.

'I think you'd better work as quickly as you can,' prompted Alex.

The ambulance men wasted no time. Ably assisted by the volunteer soldiers they whipped Father onto the stretcher and carted him out the door. As I followed I could see the ambulance parked up the street beyond the army vehicles, its red light smashed, its sides splattered with yellow paint. The army acted as escort as the stretcher was carried to the ambulance, Mother scurrying behind and assisted by Alex as she tried to put on watch and hat and scarf, all at the same time. Thomas was holding Father's hand, reassuring him as he faded in and out of consciousness. Brendan and I followed, in funeral formation.

'I'll go with your mother to the hospital,' said Alex quietly as they put Father into the back of the ambulance. 'I'll ring from the hospital to let you know how he is. I think it might be best if Sinead stayed with Kitty and me tonight.' He paused, struck by a thought. 'In fact it might be best if you all came round to our house later. Just until your father gets out of the hospital.'

'No,' said Thomas immediately. 'We can't leave the house.'

Alex nodded, Thomas was known to be wilful. Mother climbed in beside Father, calling to us to be good and not to be going out and to make our tea.

'We'll be all right,' Thomas told her, a little disgusted. 'Let us know what's happening.'

They closed the ambulance doors. The three of us stood

watching behind the ambulance as the driver negotiated with the soldiers as to the safest way off the estate. The soldiers finally waved them up the street. We went back to the house.

'M'daddy knew that man's name,' said Brendan. 'Did you hear him call him Kieran?'

'Aye,' said Thomas, 'but don't say anything to anybody.'

'Do you think he knows him?'

'He must. Or maybe he just found out who he was.'

'Cahir's funny.'

'Aye, he's an oul' eejit.'

We hurried back inside, looked out the dinette window, but there wasn't so much as the rustle of a leaf in the back garden.

18

Utter Chassis

Eileen and Hilda were beginning to enjoy the saga of the Peace Movement. News of the latest happenings from Bunbeg would brighten their day, dilute the tedium of the academic slog. They welcomed the appearance of the bold Hugh. My dream Hugh made flesh. He was the very image of the Hugh of my fantasies. And he would be high-minded and worthy.

'Did he have hair like a raven?' Hilda inquired, as the three of us walked home up the Falls Road. There had been no buses on the road that week because of the rioting.

'No. I told you, it was coppery gold.'

'Did he have skin like snow?'

'Snowy enough. And not a pimple on him.'

'Did he have cheeks like blood?'

'Christ, I hardly noticed his cheeks.'

'Then he can't have been the man of your desires,' Hilda concluded.

'He is.'

'And what about Jimmy Cane?' Eileen was indignant, she, after all, had wheedled information about Jimmy out of her future brother-in-law. She had a stake in Jimmy.

'Him too. I'm not fussy. Either one would do.'

'But your mother would sooner have Hugh if he's a medical student.' Tony had been good enough to provide some background information.

'But he's on the run now,' Eileen reminded her.

'On the run.' Hilda savoured the phrase. 'A man on his keeping.'

'Sure nobody be's on their keeping these days. Where did you hear that?'

'In Liam O'Flaherty's *Famine*. It was brilliant. I cried my eyes out.'

We stopped at a newsagent's to buy crisps and toffee.

'We're not supposed to be eating in uniform,' Hilda reminded us.

'We'll go through the park then. Nobody will see us,' I proposed, and we crossed the road into the Falls Park, our cheeks and teeth tortured by the effort of mangling hard toffee.

We passed by the beds of small orange and yellow flowers. We didn't know their names. In the distance I saw the great growth of rhododendron; in its dark centre Anna-Maria Donnelly had told me about getting babies, and I hadn't believed her. I thought of Jimmy and Hugh now, and the basic mechanism didn't seem so repellent.

'Will he be coming back?' Eileen interrupted the agreeableness of the reverie.

'Who?'

'Who do you think? *Hugh.*'

'I hope so.'

'Do you think he fancies you?'

I paused to consider this for the fortieth time in twenty-four hours. It seemed unlikely.

'I doubt it. He's too gorgeous. He probably thinks I'm a boot.'

They exuded a sympathetic silence. They were realists. But then he wasn't the only man in my life.

After many weeks deprived of the sight of him I discovered that Jimmy Cane was a friend of Brigid Quinn. Brigid was the brilliant, buxom and improbable President of the Children of Mary at St Catherine's. She was two years older than I was and rich in earthy experiences of men. Real men had passed their naked hands up the back of her jumper, maybe her school jumper, and fumbled with the hooks of her bra. Although she was a big, hefty girl, shapeless even, Brigid had wit and a womanliness that was very appealing to the opposite sex.

Her father had been killed when Protestant paramilitaries threw a grenade into a bus carrying Catholic workmen to a building site in East Belfast. Mr Quinn had deliberately hurled himself on top of the grenade and taken the full blast of the explosion. Yet surprisingly he looked fairly intact lying in the coffin on a bed of brown satin. Only he had a white cap covering the back of his head. I had said to Brigid, 'I'm sorry for your trouble,' and then felt stupid. She seemed very cheerful at the wake. Mr Quinn was given a hero's funeral.

Brigid was very informative. She told me something about Jimmy and kept me up to date over the next year or so. And then he seemed to disappear for a long time. Maybe he was in training over the border, or on the run, or even interned. It was Brigid who finally told me the truth. We were walking home from an opera rehearsal one evening. *The Mikado*. I was Pooh-bah and she was the Daughter-in-law-Elect.

'I haven't seen anything of Jimmy Cane these months,' I mentioned casually as we shared a quarter of chocolate chewing nuts.

'You mean you haven't heard?' she screeched, incredulous.

'No. Heard what?' I was thinking that maybe he'd got married. He was old enough anyway.

'You're kidding! I don't believe you. It was all over the place about him. Do you never go out?'

'No. I'm more or less house-bound. What, anyway?'

'He was an informer! A bloody informer.'

I stopped dead in the middle of the street. Order had dissolved into chaos. A terrible state of chassis.

'What? Who?'

'Jimmy Cane. It turns out he was an informer.'

'An informer? I don't believe it!' I was shaking my head, an involuntary thing.

'It's true. He was responsible for a lot of fellas ending up in Long Kesh.'

'No! I don't believe it!'

'Yes. I couldn't get over it either. I thought you knew.'

'Nobody tells me anything.' I was beginning to sound like Aunt Minnie. I tried to place him as an informer. I could see he was reckless, shiftless, irresponsible, but it never occurred to me that he could be dishonourable. I was devastated.

'How? What happened, for God's sake?'

'I'm not sure if this is the right way of it, but I heard the soldiers dragged him into the back of a saracen and beat the shite out of him until he had an asthma attack.' A standard enough army procedure for the gathering of information.

Even now my heart went out to him.

'So?'

'So he told them all they wanted to know, and they let him go. But they kept coming back for more information, until the boys caught on.'

I tried to take it in. I got a picture of Victor McLaglen hulking across Hollywood-Dublin, winded and panicked, the spare, ruthless men in the trench coats and Sam Browne belts after him, dogging his every frantic step, hounding him relentlessly up entries and over walls. I just couldn't see Jimmy Cane at that sort of thing. So relaxed, so sure of himself, so gorgeous. Now no Irishwoman would lift him on a shovel, whatever the glories of full thighs and darkening chin.

'It's a shame,' said Brigid, 'and him such a stud.'

'Oh did you think so?' I inquired indifferently. The last thing on my mind.

'I always thought he looked like Orson Welles when he was young.'

'Did he? I never noticed.' Jimmy was already in the past tense.

Brigid shared out the last of the chocolate chewing nuts. We chewed in silence as we made our way up Shaw's Road past the burnt-out cars and brick-littered streets.

'Did he get paid for it?' I asked later.

'I dunno. He might have.'

Utter chassis.

'And where is he now?'

'He got away just in time. I hear he's been in England these few months back, living in an army barracks for protection. But the IRA are after him. They'll get him . . . should it take years.'

They always got their man. Victor McLaglen, Barry Curran, Jimmy Cane. Very thorough. From that day I wouldn't let myself think of Jimmy Cane. He was already dead. An informer. Worse than being a married man. Fortunately there was Hugh still left to me. Sadly he too was in no position to take me under his notice.

19

Stormont

The car eased through the gates of black and gold, up the long stretch of avenue as it dipped in the middle, rose and broadly advanced to the radiant stone structure. They had seen it in the distance, high and remote, the summer palace of a Roman emperor. Before them the seat of government sat, brightly reflecting the white of the cloud-spread sky. It grew as they approached. An effulgent looming beyond a neat arrangement of lawn and tarmac.

Liam Mulvogue was himself at the wheel. 'Would you look at that!' He drew their attention to what lay ahead. 'You'd never guess you were in Belfast.'

'It's magnificent,' Bernie agreed. She was sick with nerves. The pressmen would be out in droves today, cameramen and reporters and TV men, and they'd all get it wrong again, the way they distorted things and took it all out of context. They never told the whole story. And they never thought of the consequences. She smoothed the wrinkles out of her dusky pink coat and matching dress. She felt wretched.

'Apparently they built it on a bed of granite, from the Mourne Mountains.'

'Get away!' exclaimed Deirdre.

'Aye, I suppose they wanted it to have some relevance to the country.' Liam laughed.

'It's lovely all the same.'

'They said to go round the back to avoid the press on the way in. There's a road off to the left up here somewhere.'

They forked off the main drive, skirted the administration complex and drew up at the rear of the Parliament buildings. A uniformed RUC man came forward to open the car door. Callum Hyde was waiting on the steps to greet them.

'Thank you so much for coming, ladies, Mr Mulvogue, I'll take you right through. Mr Brandywell and Mr Ironmonger are ready for you. If you'll just follow me. It's a bit of a distance actually.'

'It's a terrific building,' said Deirdre, 'you know, I've lived in Belfast all my life and I've never seen Stormont.'

'Really? What a shame. I do wish we had time for a bit of a tour. It *is* rather special. It was designed by Sir Arnold Thornley you know, in the Greek classical style.' Hyde seemed suddenly different, animated.

'Was it?'

'Yes, the entire exterior is faced in Portland stone, and it's three hundred and sixty-five feet in length.'

'Three hundred and sixty-five? A foot for every day of the year.'

'I suppose so. I hadn't thought of it like that. Some of the plasterwork is remarkable, in the style of the Irish school of the mid-eighteenth century. Still, you're here for something much more important.'

They followed him along a stone corridor and up a wide wooden staircase. He paused at the double doors of the room at the head of the stairs, threw open the door and stood back to let them enter. Mr Brandywell came forward at once and led them into the room. A dozen men rose to greet them and he introduced them to each in turn; his Press Secretary and other members of his staff; Lord somebody or other who had something to do with Development and Community Relations; members of the Advisory Committee on Northern Ireland; men from the Northern Ireland Office.

Flustered, Bernie heard none of their names. She was relieved when Mr Ironmonger seated them in armchairs upholstered in powder-pink damask. They match my

outfit, she noticed as she sat down on the edge of her chair.
She looked around her. The room was sumptuous, but too
big and draughty. She hated the ceiling too, all plaster
vines and bits of fruit and flowers looking as though they
were about to drop. And wee bare-arsed cherubs hanging in
all the corners. She found it ugly and depressing. She tried
to pay attention.

'I understand the petition went extremely well,' Mr
Irnmonger was saying.

'Better than we expected,' Liam answered holding up the
petition. 'Sixty-three thousand signatures.'

'Sixty-three thousand! As many as that?' Mr Brandywell
seemed thrilled, his jowls quivered with pleasure. 'Well
you are all to be congratulated, ladies, this is far, far more
than we could have hoped for.'

There was much talk of numbers and population size
and boundaries in West Belfast. There were warm and
sincere congratulations, they were all delighted with the
Peace Women. And then it was time for the main business
of the day, the official handing over of the petition by the
Peace Group to Mr Brandywell, in front of the media.

'We felt that the steps of the main entrance would be the
spot,' Mr Irnmonger explained. 'I believe the press are ready
for us. Now which of you will be handing over the
petition?'

'Me,' said Deirdre.

'Fine. Callum will be out there in front. He'll give you
your cue. Just watch him, and when he gives the signal
you may formally hand over the signature. Ready, Callum?'

'Ready.'

'Good. The whole thing should take no time at all. The
press have been advised that there will be no questions, no
interviews. This is purely a photo-opportunity as they call
it.' He laughed at the silliness of it. 'So American, isn't it?
But the ordeal will be over before you realise it.'

'I hope so.'

'Shall we proceed then?'

Callum Hyde led the way, followed by Mr Irnmonger,
Mr Brandywell, the Peace Women and the Press Secretaries. Liam Mulvogue was not to take part in the handing
over of the petition. He stayed to chat with the luminaries
in the great, draughty room. Bernie felt her legs trembling
as they went down the stairs and turned off to the right.
Deirdre clutched her elbow as they passed two rows of
portraits of former members of the Northern Ireland Parliament. They had the look of Ballymena men, staunch,
Presbyterian, Orangemen. The women saw the light from
the doorway ahead and found themselves at the top of the
Portland-stone steps. The media advanced.

Mother seemed white and dopey, Deirdre looked flushed, a
bit alarmed. This was live, something terrible could
happen. Ridiculous things happened on the steps of the
Parliament buildings. Belligerent members had once been
carried bodily from Stormont's innards by burly RUC men
who struggled to keep their faces straight in front of the
cameras. The Reverend Doctor Ian Paisley had followed at
speed behind them, demanding: 'Unhand that man, sir!'
He had later deplored the manhandling of Ulster's elected
representatives.

And now here were Mother and friend treading the same
dangerous ground, with the TV in tow. The announcer was
giving out their names as they began to descend the long
flight of steps, Mother and Deirdre with Charles Brandywell between them. Deirdre held up the petition and waved
it triumphantly as she came down towards the press. A
few of them advanced to the bottom of the steps, getting in
front of the TV cameras. The cameraman worked his way
to a better vantage point just in time to catch Deirdre
stumble and slip down onto the next step. Mr Brandywell
put out a hand to help her, but already a thin young man
had nipped in and caught her under the elbow, setting her
on her feet again. Mother was standing on the one spot

smiling a benign Valium smile at the crowd below her. Her
pink coat reflected brightly the early afternoon sun. Her
hair looked stiff, like a Dutch bonnet. She looked a bit out
of it. She hadn't noticed the kerfuffle with Deirdre. They
came down another step or two and stopped. Mr Brandywell turned ceremoniously to Deirdre; she drew herself up
with conscious formality. The pressmen stopped pushing
momentarily. This was it. The camera zoomed in on
Deirdre and Mr Brandywell. A big black mike was thrust
up between them, another in charcoal grey appeared at
Deirdre's left shoulder. And still we missed her first few
words.

'. . . the people of Andersonstown. And so we wish to
thank every one of them for having the courage to sign the
petition and stand up and be counted. And now I'm
delighted to be able to hand this over to Mr Brandywell as
an expression of the desire of the Catholic people of Belfast
for peace.'

Mr Brandywell beamed. They crossed hands as he took
the petition and held it up between them for the
photographers.

'Thank you, thank you,' he said, when the first noise of
scuffling photographers and the buzz of automatic winders
had died down. The cameras moved in for a close-up of Mr
Brandywell saying, 'You've done very well, both of you.'

He turned to Mother on his right, the cameras backed
away to include her as they shook hands.

'. . . very well indeed.' He was really hammering it home.
'Well done. And how many signatures are on the petition,
Mrs McPhelimy?' he inquired. It sounded a bit rehearsed.

'Just over sixty-three thousand, sir,' said Mother with
satisfaction.

'All from Andersonstown?' called out one reporter.

'Definitely,' said Mother.

The camera had moved out again to include all three as
the photographers continued to flash and snap. Deirdre
laughed down at them as they jostled one another out

of the way. She turned again to the beaming politician.

'Are you pleased with us, Mr Brandywell?' she was heard to say over the hum.

'Very pleased,' Mr Brandywell pronounced, a contented growl, 'you've done very well indeed.'

Bernie heard it. The journalists heard it, the TV cameras picked it up, beamed it all over Andersonstown, bounced it off Divis and Collin Mountains until it came back to rest like a damp mist over Bunbeg Gardens. 'You've done very well indeed.' Mr Brandywell's nicely modulated English voice sounded in every ear and heart. The Peace Women had done very well for Mr Brandywell, for the British Government, very well indeed. The image of the smiling politician, looking very, very pleased filled half the screen, and beside him Deirdre smiled up the smile of a winsome colleen; rosy cheeks, bright teeth, black, curling hair. 'Are you pleased with us, Mr Brandywell?' It would echo forever: *Very, very pleased. You've done very well indeed.* Bernie's heart stopped with a thump, her legs weakened, bowels churned. She suddenly understood what they had done, how it would be seen, how useless it all was. At that second her intuition told her that this would be the end, not the start of it. There would be no peace. There could be none.

She felt someone taking her by the elbow, leading her back up the steps away from the microphones and cameras, up the fine Portland-stone steps, back into the seat of Government. She felt relief and fear at the same time; she was beginning to sense a turmoil inside her. She looked up. It was Mr Irnmonger laughing brightly beside her, walking her up the corridor as he joked with Hyde and the Press Secretaries. She glanced over at Deirdre. Deirdre looked back. She looked ashen, her eyes seemed ringed in black.

She knew too, she understood now. They had done very well indeed.

'I hope you ladies will join us for tea before you go?'

Bernie shook her head. 'No, we'd better be going, we'd better get back.'

Deirdre nodded in agreement.

Mr Brandywell came up to shake their hands again. He was very gracious. 'I've had Mr Morris' case looked into,' he said confidentially as he bent over Bernie. 'I don't see a problem there. I expect he'll be released very soon now.'

'Oh, thanks very much.'

'I know from Mr Irnmonger that you've given him some other names since our last meeting. They are being looked into at present. If there are other cases which you feel merit further investigation do please let Mr Irnmonger know. I believe he's given you a telephone number? I want you to know that I'll do everything possible. You've both been very brave. If I can ever help you in any way please do not hesitate to contact me. Goodbye ladies.'

Mr Irnmonger accompanied them to their car. 'Well I must say, it's been a remarkable success. Sixty-three thousand signatures, and from West Belfast alone! It gives a very good indication of what can be achieved with courage and persistence. Congratulations, ladies, you've shown us all how it's done.'

They didn't speak on the drive back to Andersonstown.

That night, after seeing the six o'clock news, Father discharged himself from the hospital for the second time.

Bernie was relieved there was no one in the house when she got home. It was early afternoon. They had been on the lunch-hour news, and would be on again at six. She would go straight over and see Mrs Morris, let her know about Seamus. Eilish Morris was sewing curtains in the dinette.

She took in sewing now that Seamus was interned. It kept them barely solvent, that and the envelope every week from the Prisoners' Dependants Fund. She missed her husband, but mostly she worried about him, worried that the other men would give him a bad time because he was a wee bit slow. That was probably how he'd been caught; he had no sense.

Bernie heard the sewing machine, saw the frail little woman get up to answer the door.

'It's only me, Eilish,' she said, 'I wanted to have a wee word.'

Mrs Morris looked at her, she seemed cold, not as friendly as usual, but nobody was these days.

'Come on in, Bernie, I was just doing a bit of sewing. Here, sit down there.'

For a minute Bernie was conscious of having arrived empty-handed. Since Seamus was lifted she had been bringing small offerings of food and clothes, for the four wee girls, or to take up to Long Kesh with the weekly food parcel. But today she brought good news.

'How are you managing, Eilish?' she asked politely.

'Ach, you know. I'm doing my best. It's the children I get annoyed about. It breaks my heart to see our Angela missing her daddy. She doesn't understand.' Angela, her eldest daughter, was deaf and dumb. 'Some days I just feel like giving up.'

'Don't say that, Eilish. Things'll be better soon.'

'By the help of God they will.' They were silent for a minute.

'Eilish, what I'm going to tell you isn't to go any further,' Bernie began mysteriously, 'now, do I have your word on that?'

Mrs Morris looked affronted. 'If you don't want me to say anything I won't. What is it?'

'It's hard to know where to start really. As part of this Peace Movement thing I've been doing some work behind the scenes to get the men released . . .'

Mrs Morris sat up, her mouth dropped open. 'From Long Kesh, you mean?'

'From anywhere they're being held. Not all the men of course, but certain ones.'

Mrs Morris' heart was racing. 'And?' she croaked.

'And I thought your Seamus was a special case, so I put his name forward too. Now I'm not saying who else is involved, so don't ask me.' She paused. 'But I've just heard today that Seamus is going to be released, very soon.'

The other woman sat silent, stunned.

'You're joking me,' she accused at last.

'Would I joke about a thing like that, Eilish? Of course I don't know when it'll be exactly, but I was told soon.'

'Are you sure, Bernie? Honestly?'

'As true as God.'

'I can't believe it. I can't imagine him home again.'

'Well it shouldn't be long now.'

'Oh thank God.' She was on the verge of tears.

'Well I'd better get over home and see what's in for the dinner. Sinead'll be home soon. I'll see you later. Let me know the minute you hear anything.'

'I will surely.'

Not a word of thanks, Bernie was thinking as she walked home. Still, there was no point annoying herself. She began to peel the potatoes for chips.

Sinead came home about an hour later. She came in the back door, raced through the house and hurled her school bag on the settee. Her face was flushed and she was panting to catch her breath.

'For God's sake what is it?' Bernie demanded. 'Take those wet boots off, Sinead, you'll have muck all over the house.'

'Mr Morris is out!' Sinead gasped at last.

'What?'

'He's out.'

'Are you sure?'

'I saw him getting out of a taxi just a minute ago. He's

away into the house. Bridie was so excited she almost said
something. She squealed, anyway.'

Bernie waited all afternoon for a word from Mrs Morris.
It never came.

20

Siege

School was unbearable after the scene at Stormont. Some girls ignored me, others would stop talking when I came into the room. The teachers were unnaturally good to me, which made things worse. It was bad enough having a mother in the Peace Group, without being the teacher's pet. I tried to concentrate on my O-levels. The examinations were coming up in June. Thomas and Brendan were having a bad time at St Mary's. Thomas never mentioned it, but he became more grumpy and aggressive. Brendan came home one day with his face all cut and bruised.

'What happened?' Thomas demanded as Brendan tried to slip upstairs.

'I fell over my school bag,' he said, looking more afraid of Thomas than anything.

'Sure!' Thomas said scornfully, 'and you fell against the toe of somebody's boot. Come here.' He unceremoniously marched Brendan up the stairs. I followed behind, but they went into their room and Thomas closed the door in my face. I never found out what arrangements they made for handling the matter externally, but Thomas backed up Brendan's story in front of the parents.

At nights we could hear the parents arguing in their bedroom. Every night. It would go on for hours. Sometimes Mother could be heard crying through the walls; other nights we would hear her rising at three or four or some other ungodly hour, to pad shivering downstairs to make herself a cup of tea and take more Doriden. I followed her down one night. She was trying to rekindle the fire.

'What are you doing out of bed?' she demanded, her eyes red and face puffy.

'I couldn't sleep. What's up?'

She opened her mouth to speak and burst into tears. I awkwardly patted her shoulder. 'There, there,' I soothed, 'try to get some sleep.'

'I can't sleep,' she shouted. 'Let me alone. Go back to bed, you have school in the morning.'

'Do you not want to talk?'

'What is there to say? I've made a mess of everything. I think your daddy's started to hate me, and even Thomas is ashamed of me. I thought I was doing the right thing.'

'Everybody has to do what they think is right,' I said, paraphrasing John Wayne; I couldn't think of anything else to say.

'Aidan's whole family will be against me. Not that they ever liked me. I wasn't enough of a Republican for them.'

'Sure who gives a shit what they think?'

'He does, Annie. It's only natural. They're his flesh and blood. He got a letter from Roisin today, and he didn't show it to me. He always shows them to me. I can imagine what she said, her and Una, sitting over there in Australia, well out of it. Oh it's fine for those two big shites, living in peace and all their orders. They give a few dollars to the IRA and say keep up the fight, bomb and shoot rings round you, let the blood flow down the streets, it's all for the cause; but I'm all right sitting here in bloody Melbourne, trying to beat the flies off me. I'm all right Jack. And then they've the cheek to criticise me.'

'You don't know that they did.'

'I know, all right. They're probably feeling sorry for your daddy that he ever married me. They'll be saying I brought shame on the good Republican name of McPhelimy. Well I don't care, I don't regret it.'

'OK, well go to bed then.'

'No, you go, you're only annoying me sitting there. You need your sleep at your age.'

'You need your sleep at any age.'

'I'm not doing exams. I never got the chance. But I saw to it that you did. Now get up to bed. I'll be up shortly.' As I left the room she was reaching down for her handbag, and another couple of Doriden.

On the night before my first O-level exam - I think it was English Literature – we suffered the second attack. I had taken two Valium. To get some sleep. I was in bed by half-ten. I was taking Valium regularly at the time, prescribed and dispensed by Mother in an effort to cure a lifetime of wakefulness. The tablets certainly had an effect. Firstly my mouth and throat would go dry, my speech would slur and my head begin to revolve. Within twenty-five minutes it would be spinning. I would totter upstairs, flop my way through the nightly ablutions and fall onto the mattress, the world still turning around me. Oddly the drug failed to stop me waking as usual several times during the night; but the next day I would come to life with what I supposed was a hangover, and spend the first part of the day in a brightening haze which would lift almost entirely by noon, enabling me to function normally.

That night, with the prospect of the examination, I took an extra tablet. This was a mistake. I was getting ready to go to bed, learning quotes from Thomas Hardy's *Woodlanders*. He smelled like autumn's very brother. I liked that; short, fruity, pithy. Then the protest dirge began. I had been hearing voices for a few minutes. Not celestial voices. I had tried to ignore them. Autumn's very brother. But there was definitely a crowd gathering outside.

'What's going on?' Father demanded. He had been sleeping in front of the fire. He had come home the day before after another brief stay in the hospital, looking frail and sickly. We do not know what passed between him and

Mother before she brought him home, but there was a sourness, a grim accusation in his attitude to her all that day. She had gone about her peacemaking activities without consulting him, and he could not forgive her.

The crowd was growing vocal. We all came to attention. Someone was heard to say loudly something about breaking windows.

'Our windows?' asked Sinead, alarmed.

'I'm going out to them,' Father announced heaving himself up out of the chair and shuffling towards the hall door.

'No you're not, Aidan!' Mother was up and after him. 'You'll end up in hospital again. And you might never come out of it this time.'

'Leave me be, Bernie,' he ordered.

'Stop him, son,' she appealed to Thomas. But it was too late.

Father had made his way into the hall, located the Toledo sword beside the meter box and flung open the front door. Some of the assailants, the French boys among them, had come down the path as far as the porch. Father now raised the sword over their heads. It glinted grey in the light of a street-lamp. They drew back hastily at the sight of it.

'Peace with justice,' they yelled. 'Sell out!'

'Take yourselves off!' Father bawled back at them, more angry than intimidated. I wondered where the breath came from, considering his condition. Thomas appeared beside him, clutching the blond shaft of his hurley stick, the head-cracker. Mrs French was standing, arms akimbo, on her porch, enjoying developments but saying nothing.

'Touts out, touts out, touts out!' The accusation went up on the fringe of the mob. We turned to face them. They were standing on Murray's path, chanting and clapping in time, 'Touts out, touts out, touts out now!' Something familiar about them, the shape of their figures, lumpy thighs and round shoulders. As they grew bolder they moved forward into the light; it was the Murrays, the two generations, our friends and neighbours, hurling abuse,

egging on the crowd. I felt Mother nipping my arm, a signal
that discretion was of the essence.

'The minute you get a chance run round and get Tony.
Tell him what's happening,' she whispered like James
Cagney out of the side of her mouth. I nodded to show that
I understood and would obey. My throat was dry and
seemed to tremble.

'You forged all those signatures,' a young man stepped
angrily over the low privet hedge, shaking his fist.

'That's nonsense and you know it,' Mother shouted at
him.

'Oh yeah? Well I don't know nobody who signed. Do
yous?' he turned to canvass opinions.

'I know one woman signed,' somebody called out, 'but
God love her, she's not all there.' This caused laughter,
more smart remarks, a temporary diffusion of anger. They
had lapsed into debate. It was safe for the moment at least.
I saw my chance, remembered the Alamo, and slipped off
over French's garden in the general direction of help. I
glanced back for a second, no one had noticed me. I
concentrated on producing speed.

I brought one foot down to touch the pavement, became
aware of the spring going through my calf, the ball of the
leg, knee and thigh, on up my body, and I felt myself
momentarily soaring through the air in the dark, weight-
less above the pavement. Then the heel levered, lifted off
the ground again and the other foot touched down. The
wind was invigorating, like autumn's very brother. I could
run for ever rather than arrive. The corner now, just past
Mrs Nolan's house. Poor faceless Mrs Nolan, a rubber
bullet hole where her features should be. She hasn't an eye
in her head, no longer sees around corners. I veer out to the
edge of the pavement like a motorbike on a bend, responding to centrifugal force. I'm round the bend, I certainly am,
up to the top of Bunbeg, a sharp left turn up Carnan. Tony
and Rosaleen lived in the last house in the row. I reached
it finally, panting, wheezing, my breath like a thin whistle

in my chest. I banged on the door, sounded the bell, clattered the letter-box, just in case. I managed to rouse the house, and several others as well. I could hear Rosaleen at the top of the stairs.

'Christ, it's the soldiers!' she cried in panic.

'No it's only me,' I yelled through the letter-box, 'Annie. The house is being attacked. Can Tony come round?'

I heard him thundering down in his sock-soles, he fell near the bottom, cursed and got up to open the door.

'Who is it?' he asked me as he pulled on a shirt. Rosaleen stood holding his parka.

'I don't know – everybody. The Frenches, the Murrays, young fellas, strangers, everybody.'

'All right. Now listen, I'm going to go and get some help. It'll take me a few minutes. Do you think they'll be all right until then?'

'I don't know. Look I have to go back now.'

'No, don't be going back,' said Rosaleen, 'I'll ring Alex and Kitty. You stay here with me. Let Tony and the men handle it. Your mammy wouldn't want you to go back.'

But I was already halfway down Carnan again. I could hear Tony and Rosaleen calling me. They sounded miles away. The journey back was quicker; all down hill. I leaped through someone's garden, cutting the corner into Bunbeg, half-aware that my foot had sunk into a wet, boggy hole. I ran down the centre of the road regardless; I'd see round the bend more quickly that way. I reached the bend, inhaled, dared to look. The house was still there, but so then was the crowd. They'd advanced again. They were all over the front garden, French's garden too. I couldn't see the family. Were the bastards on top of them? I put on a rush of speed. The air was noisy through my nose and I leaped higher than ever from the ground. Big epic leaps, heroic risings from the earth. Going too high, not making enough horizontal progress. Our Lady of Lourdes pray for them. Other ejaculations, unheroic in nature. Still no sign of blood relatives. The crowd was maybe battering them into the ground, standing on their faces, crushing Mother's beautiful little hands, dancing on Father's ulcer spot which was tender just then from the stitches. No they were not! The decent people. I saw Mother in the doorway and the hall light behind her. And that must be Father on the porch. I couldn't see him clearly, tall as he was, through the bodies of protesters who had invaded French's garden raised a little above our path. But they were OK. I paused internally, thinking how to approach, getting out being easier than getting back unharmed. I could sidle up through them, like one of themselves, edge my way up to the door, hope they didn't recognise me. But I decided to just make a run for it, to fight my way through. Sir Knight I fear me a wee bit of alarm, one or two of these sons of Erin might just possibly offer me harm. I attained the outer ranks of the holders-back. Some of them were looking on in bewilderment, others were smiling, enjoying the crack.

There was one young woman up at the front yelling and cursing, the dirt of her words distorting her pretty freckled face. Her long sandy hair was neatly tied back with a black velvet band. I knew the face. She lived, I thought, up the street, round the corner, went to the Cross and Passion. She saw me first.

'There's the daughter,' she screeched, 'get her!'

I wondered if she meant me. But nobody moved as I shoved through them. Someone said: 'She's a girl, leave her alone.' I prayed they would see the wisdom of this little straw of chivalry. The girl ranted on. They stared at her in her bitterness and anger, as she bawled into the night.

'There'll be no fucking peace in this country till Ireland's free. Peace with fucking justice is what we want!' Again that nice distinction. She powered on. She had so transfixed us we hardly noticed the youth edging his way through the crowd right up to the path. He reached just in front of me. He seemed calm, purposeful. I wondered if he'd been sent by Tony to help.

Then I saw Thomas; he had just turned his back on the

crowd to say something to Father. And I saw the youth raise his arms above his head. He had something in his hands. It looked like ... Christ Jesus! It was a hatchet! Father saw at the same second, dashed out yelling, 'Thomas! Behind you!'

Thomas turned to see. The hatchet fell. A scream croaked in my throat as the weapon made contact with head, off centre. Thomas had dodged it well. But the blood poured out down the left side of his head onto the neck of the Levi shirt he was so fond of – the blue one with the metal buttons – down onto his shoulders and back. He stumbled, momentarily weakened; Father grabbed him, put him on the porch out of harm's way.

Thomas stood there dazed, inspecting one bloody hand that had just touched the wound. Mother was merely hysterical. With the first blow well struck Father was now happy to resort to violence. He charged forward, lashed out wildly with the broad edge of the sword, punishing backs and legs and arses. The hatchet man fled and the mob backed off rather than retaliated: the sight of blood had diffused their enthusiasm. The Murrays withdrew behind their canary-yellow front door. Mrs French and her sons, Michael and Niall disappeared. Just then a car zoomed to a halt in the middle of the road. Tony leaped out followed by men in green and brown anoraks – I noted briefly that Hugh was not among them. The Seventh Cavalry turned to face the mob.

'Get the hell out of here,' Tony commanded. 'Get back to your own homes and don't let us catch you at this again. Christ, Thomas!' he cried, noticing the blood. 'Are you hurt bad?'

'I'm all right,' Thomas retorted ungraciously. Mother, who was no longer hysterical but merely sobbing wildly, bundled him into the house with the help of Rosaleen who had appeared, her camelhair coat on over her nightdress.

Once inside I saw the wound for the first time under the light. It was wide and deep and gory; the red of flesh, the white of bone. Flesh of my flesh. Thomas was very pale; I imagined the blood draining from his head, pouring out of the wound, running down over his sky-blue shirt and metal buttons. I snapped. I screamed and screamed and screamed. It rose and filled the house. It reached outside and filled the street. Like Mrs French's siren I could be heard all over Andersonstown, down the Falls, across the bogs, over Belfast Lough. One of the primal screams. But it wasn't enough. I broke away from Rosaleen who was trying to calm me; I rushed into the hall, threw open the door again and screamed in the face of the crowd. They stared, transfixed; Tony's men turned, bewildered; French's door opened a crack. And then I was no longer screaming; I was cursing every one of them, vomiting foul-mouthed abuse at them, one by one. I put the freckled harpy to shame.

'You bastarding cunts!' I heard myself yell. 'You fucking bastarding morons, I damn every one of you to hell. I swear to God you'll rue the night you opened my brother's head. Every single one of you will live to regret it.' I saw their faces white and uncertain under the street-lights, all hostility gone, and I felt the hate pour from me like lava. I turned to the chink of light on the Frenches' porch: 'And you, you evil oul' whore, I curse you and your whole fucking family to the devil. May you never know another day's peace, you oul' – '

I felt the cold hand on the back of my neck, felt myself dragged inside, slapped about the face, told to calm down. It was Tony, shaking me by the shoulders. Mother, sobered by my outburst, hurried upstairs for the bottles of Doriden and Valium. Father had quickly bandaged Thomas' head. The door knocked. It was Alex and Kitty. Kitty cried when she saw Thomas. He was her godson. Mother handed round the tablets; some for me, some for Kitty, some for Rosaleen, some for herself. Thomas absolutely refused to take one.

'We'll have to get him to the hospital,' said Father, 'the cut's bad.'

Alex, calm as ever, considered what arrangements had

best be made for bodies still potentially under threat. 'It
might be better if nobody stayed in the house just at the
moment. If you take Thomas down to the Royal, Aidan,
Kitty and I will follow in my car with Sinead.'

We abandoned the house. Tony's men had managed to
disperse the crowd by this time and the street was decep-
tively still. Father piled us into the car and set off for the
Royal. As the car tore out of the estate Mother switched
on the interior light and leaned over the seat to inspect
Thomas' bandage. It was seeping with blood, Thomas was
whiter than ever, and seemed weak. Mother dissolved into
sobs.

'Stop crying for God's sake, Ma,' Thomas ordered. 'I'm
not dead. It's only my shirt I'm annoyed about,' he added;
'the bastards have ruined my good shirt.'

'At least he hasn't got brain damage,' quipped Father
half-heartedly.

'No more than before,' said Brendan with a grin.

Thomas gave him a companionable thump.

The car streaked down the Glen Road. The barracks, the
bus depot, Milltown, the Falls Park, St Catherine's, passed
in a flash, then St John's, the Canon's parish church,
Whiterock, St James', the Donegal Road, the Beehive Bar,
built by Great-grandfather Mohan, and St Paul's zipped by
in a jumble of graffiti and paint-patched walls. Father
swung into the Royal, ignoring the security post, and
speeded right up to the emergency entrance. The elderly
security guard followed behind, roaring in protest as Father
pulled up in the ambulance bay and helped Thomas out of
the car.

'I'm all right,' Thomas insisted.

'Hey! You can't park here!' bawled the security guard, as
he limped breathless down the entrance road. 'This is for
ambulances only.'

'My son's hurt,' Father called back, flinging the car keys
into the road. 'Here, you move it.'

'I can walk, for Christ's sake,' said Thomas in protest as

Father attempted to lift him. But Mother could not. She hung tearfully on his right arm as Brendan and I tried to advance the party into the emergency room. Once inside the nurses took over. They made a quick inspection of Thomas' head.

'He'll live,' said one. 'He'd better have an X-ray, just in case, and then we'll get it stitched up. But it'll be a while before we're ready for him.'

We were to go to the waiting area, Thomas included. There was no doctor available at the moment. They were all treating victims of an explosion that had gone off earlier in a pub in Ardoyne. Thomas' head would have to wait.

Brendan quickly commandeered two orange, plastic couches, standing back to back in the centre of the waiting area, and we settled down to wait. Alex and Kitty had arrived by then and the men went off to get essential supplies of hot tea. Mother doled out a second round of tablets.

'That's a lot of Valium, Bernie,' Kitty cautioned. 'Never mind those other ones.'

'Sure they have no effect on me,' mumbled Mother through dozy, red eyes. 'It's like throwing buns to a bear.'

'But you should be careful how many you take, Annie love; aren't you starting your O-levels tomorrow?'

'She has her first exam, English Literature isn't it?'

'Yes, but I'm not doing it now. There's no point.' I knew I was chancing my arm, but the wee woman was in no mood to object.

The men came back with trays of tea.

'Any orange juice?' Brendan inquired. Father cut him with a look.

'I phoned Deirdre's to see if they were OK,' he said. 'She's on her way down. She said she'd phone Liam Mulvogue and Canon Clancy.' Then he noticed Thomas wandering along the corridor. 'Christ! Have they not even taken you in yet?'

'Na,' Thomas shrugged, 'there's a whole lot of people up

there covered in blood with bits of them lying all over the floor. I'm all right.'

'Well sit down then, you shouldn't be roaming around with your head like that, it could get infected.'

'Your daddy's right now, Thomas, come and sit down,' Kitty urged in her gentle way.

'It's all my fault,' Mother lamented. Father said nothing to disabuse her of the notion. 'But I thought I was doing the right thing.'

'Look, don't be worrying about that just at the moment, Bernie,' said Alex in his philosophical voice. 'When you think about it, things could be much worse. Basically you're all fine, with the exception of poor Thomas here, and that doesn't appear to be serious. I think you have to count your blessings at this point.'

'That's right,' Kitty agreed, 'just thank God you're all right, Bernie. Look at those people killed in the explosion tonight, five dead so far . . . Here, I brought you this, I thought you might want to wear it until this is all over.' She produced a small relic of St Benedict; a scrap of lint on a red background encased in a bubble of plastic. It was the object she valued most. 'It's very powerful,' she said. 'It was blessed by the Pope.'

Mother grabbed at it, pulled it over her head.

Thomas had been leaning back on the orange plastic couch, his eyes closed. He now turned and considered me with his deep blue, froggy eyes. 'You made an awful eejit of yourself with all that screaming,' he commented.

'I know.' For a flicker I could see the funny side of it.

'I hope to God the wee woman isn't thinking of chaining herself naked to railings in some prominent spot,' he whispered.

'I don't think she would,' I said without conviction.

'I think she might.'

'What do you think will happen now?'

He shrugged.

'Do you think they'll attack us again?'

'Na,' he said confidently, 'that'll do them for a while anyway. The thing about people like that, people who do things in mobs, is that they're basically cowards. If you tackled one of them they'd run a mile.' He was always so level-headed, even with his skull split open.

'But what are we going to do now?'

Before he could answer, Mr Mulvogue hurried into the waiting area, his son following behind. He spotted us and came straight over. 'Are you all right, Bernie? And is this Thomas? How are you, son? Is it bad?'

'No. I'm fine, thanks. It looks worse than it is.'

'Thank God for that at least.' He turned to Mother. 'I'm awful sorry about this, Bernie, I feel responsible . . .'

'Ach Liam . . .' she protested.

'I encouraged you. You mightn't have gone this far if I hadn't . . .' He trailed off helplessly. Father was standing tight-lipped and Mother had begun to sob again.

'No. It's my fault,' she hiccoughed, 'I should have kept my mouth shut.'

'Are you all right, Mrs McPhelimy?' A young nurse approached, took her by the shoulders. 'Can I get you something to calm you down? Will I get the doctor to give you a wee tablet? Would you like me to do that?' Mother nodded meekly.

Kitty opened her mouth to object, to warn against the possible consequences of mixing barbiturates, Valium and God-knows-what else, but Alex frowned at her behind Mother's back and she said nothing. I, too, briefly considered discreetly informing the nurse that the wee woman had been swallowing tablets by the handful, but I thought better of it. Oblivion would be better for her than reality for the next few hours. The nurse returned with two elephant-sized tranquillisers, and Mother gulped them down. She was tottering by the time they took Thomas off to stitch up his head. When Deirdre arrived with Canon Clancy she was incoherent. Father had gone off again in the direction of the phones.

'You'd all better spend the night with us,' Deirdre decided.

'No, Eithne's expecting them,' Mr Mulvogue protested. 'Sure, we have more room.'

'You could come down to my house and welcome,' added the Canon, 'I've five empty bedrooms there.'

'That's very good of you,' said Kitty, 'but they'll be staying with us.'

Mother settled the dispute. 'No. We're going back to our own house,' she said, as firmly as possible under the circumstances.

They argued with her: it would be foolhardy and unpleasant to return to the scene ... She didn't care. Nobody was going to put her out of her own home. Father came back just then. He looked a bit calmer now.

'Bernie says she won't come to our house,' Deirdre complained. 'She's talking about going back to Bunbeg.' She was clearly expecting Father to back her up.

'I think she's right,' he said. 'It'll be all right now. They'll not be trying anything like that again.' Brendan and I exchanged looks. We knew he'd been up to something.

'I think you've both gone mad, Aidan,' Deirdre began.

But Father was not inclined to workshop the options. We lapsed into a dreary silence, well-suited to the wee small hours of the night. Thomas reappeared eventually, smiling, his head bandaged.

'Twelve stitches,' he announced cheerfully. 'The doctor says I've got to come back in a week.'

'Did he give you anything?' asked Mother.

'He gave me a few tablets to take in case I get a headache.'

'Here,' said Mother, holding out her hand, 'I'll mind them for you.'

It was almost 6.00 am when we left the hospital under a hail of abuse from the security guard. Father insisted on going straight to work and Mother agreed to go to Kitty's for breakfast at least. Kitty would keep Brendan and Sinead

for the day. No one would be going to school. My exam
was forgotten for the moment. As we drove back up to
Andersonstown Thomas was asking Kitty if she thought
she'd have anything in the house to take the blood off his
good shirt.

Miss Savage came to get me. We had spent the morning at
Deirdre's house. The phone never stopped. We heard from
Paddy Danagher that reporters and the army and the police
had all been round at our house, looking for us. We were
incommunicado. But of course St Catherine's tracked us
down. Miss Savage was admitted to the sanctuary. By now
the Valium and the lack of sleep were taking effect; my
head felt light and heavy at the same time and my words
wouldn't knit together properly. My tongue was fat and
unmanageable in my mouth, my eyelids felt thick and
clammy, my limbs were weak and limp. Miss Savage
looked at me aghast.

'My God!' she muttered. Then, turning to Mother, 'Is
she all right, Mrs McPhelimy?'

But Mother only shook her head bitterly.

'We heard what happened, it was terrible. I've come to
take Annie to do her exam,' she explained. 'We thought
you wouldn't want her to miss it.'

Sister Bonaventure had sent her. That was just like
Bonaventure – sending someone from Lisburn into Andersonstown. She would have seen it as a learning experience
for Miss Savage. Sister Bonaventure was the head nun at St
Catherine's; stern, courageous, intelligent; and, for a nun,
unconventional, an odd-bod. She was also the only nun
with sex appeal I'd ever met. She was tall and well-made,
with a handsome face, high cheekbones and a fine mouth.
But she was hard as yesterday's baps. Even the masters
were afraid of her.

I knew she held me in high regard. But I wished she
didn't. She had me terrified. I was accused of being her pet,

but I dreaded her more than most of my classmates. My nerve-endings would contract at the sound of her resonant, Free State voice in the corridors. I would try to make myself scarce. Mother thought she was wonderful, but by now the wee woman was too far gone to grasp what was happening. I knew I was too groggy to acquit myself even passably at a three-hour exam.

'I'm not, miss . . . I'm not going, miss,' I mumbled, afraid that even as spaced out as she was, Mother would come down on the side of education and progress.

She started to work on me. She began by being stern and sensible, then reasonable and persuasive. Then she put her arm round me and I began to cry. It was the novelty of physical contact, such a strange thing to be sitting there with Miss Savage's big arm around me. 'But, Annie, you *have* to go. This is one of the most important things in your life.' She was horrified, she could understand none of it.

'No it's not, miss. I thought it was, but it's not. It's just an exam.' I was thinking of the red lip of blood on Thomas' head, the pinkness of the gashed skin. I could not bring myself to think about *The Woodlanders*, but the quote ran through my head, 'He smelled like autumn's very brother.'

'Don't be silly, you've worked too hard for this exam to throw it all away. Hasn't she, Mrs McPhelimy?'

That struck me as odd. I wasn't conscious of having worked hard. But then maybe I had.

Mother was trying to focus. 'She hasn't got any sleep. She's in no fit state to do an exam. Can she not do it another time?'

'They'll probably make her wait till next year.'

'Maybe you should go then, Annie.' Deirdre sided with Miss Savage. 'It may be the best thing for her, Bernie, to take her mind off all this . . .'

Mother nodded: her head must have been clearing. She suddenly rallied, 'Deirdre's right, Annie, you should do your exam. Don't let them spoil everything for you.'

I finally caved in under the threat of Sister Bonaventure. 'If you don't come for me, Annie, you know that Sister Bonaventure will come up herself. She's determined you're not going to miss out on your O-levels.'

I hesitated. I had always been terrified of Bonaventure. They saw my weakness and took advantage of it. Within minutes I was in the car heading for St Catherine's. Miss Savage checked her watch.

'The exam started twenty minutes ago, but they may give you extra time.'

I think I slept briefly in the car. Sister Bonaventure met me at the door of the assembly hall. She squeezed my shoulder meaningfully with her big countrywoman's hand. 'Get on into your exam now. You'd better try to concentrate. They won't be able to give you more time,' she said. 'But you'll manage well enough. I'll see you afterwards.' A terrible prospect.

When Miss Savage led me into the hall a hundred heads lifted off the page. I was conscious of not being in uniform. Everything around me seemed cocoa-brown. I saw Hilda. She was looking at me with alarm. Eileen was waving encouragement from the other side of the hall. Even Patricia Breen was smiling sympathetically. I hated her at that moment; the fucking hypocrite. Her and others like her. I was led to a desk, pens and paper were found for me. They handed me the examination paper. My head felt massively heavy, and was inclined to fall forward. I thumbed through the pages, trying to assimilate the paragraph-long questions.

Question 1
Walter Allen wrote: 'Thomas Hardy turned for his standard of reference to the primitive oral tradition. "We story-tellers," he said, "are all Ancient Mariners," and just as so much of his lyric poetry, based on the rhythms of country dances, country airs, and folk songs, is an expression of an ancient music, so behind his novels we

feel the shaping presence of the ballads of love, passion, and betrayal he knew as a boy when he was a notable fiddler at dances.' Comment on Hardy's use of the oral tradition in *The Woodlanders*.

I could think of nothing to write. Except that somebody smelled like autumn's very brother.

I contemplated murder. Seriously. Patricia Breen maybe, or the entire French family, or that oul' bitch Murray, who should have known better. She would be easily done. I spent time planning it, enjoying the details. The timing would be crucial. It would have to be between four and five, before her husband and daughters came home from work and school.

I could choose a day when I would be alone in the house; Friday. The parents would be shopping, the boys doing sports, and Sinead over playing with wee deaf Bridie. I would slip out the back door, climb over the fence and peep in Murray's kitchen window. The place would be dim and empty. She spends most of her time sitting fat and mournful in front of the fire. I would open the door, slowly, noiselessly, and slip into the kitchen, through the dinette. The living-room door would be open as usual. I would get down on all fours – with the stealth of a great, hunting cat – and crawl behind her foul, beige velvet armchair. I would wait for the right moment. I could wait for an hour if I wanted to. My every movement would be graceful and soundless. My very breathing would be restrained.

The weapon would be the tent mallet. It was heavy, stable, iron-capped. I thought of using the turkey knife. A foot long it was. But Father insisted it wouldn't cut butter, and I was afraid that I might not locate the heart from behind with the first lightning thrust. Bone might intervene, or a leathery belt of intercostal muscle, or the solidity of entrenched fat. It would be the mallet. I would raise it over the chair back while she sat there puffing and wheezing with her asthma. I would rise from the knees, taut as elastic, breathe deeply for fullness of force, and strike, bringing the flat of the mallet crashing down on her dyed head. But always fire twice. My arm would rebound down again. To be sure.

I would immediately, yet with presence of mind and no sense of panic, flee the scene. There would be blood, but I would be wearing my white, see-through plastic mac. I would remove it in the back garden, wrap it up blood and all, and make my way up to the bathroom. There I would rinse the blood off in the bath, dry the mac in the hotpress. Detectives would find no clues. They might suspect Mr Murray, but wouldn't mind if it was only Catholics murdering each other. I planned it in fine detail. I practised throwing my leg over the fence. I hoaked in the coal-hole for the mallet. Lucky for oul' Murray I couldn't find it.

21

Champ

We were making champ, one of the traditional dishes. It was to cheer up the parents; they were both fond of it. A cooperative effort.

'Have you the spuds near mashed yet?' asked Thomas. He was losing interest. 'It says here "cream the potatoes": they don't look creamed to me.' He was leaning on the kitchen counter, one finger on the champ page of *Irish Farmhouse Cooking*. 'Mash harder,' he instructed, adjusting the dressing on his head-wound.

'I'm mashing as hard as I can,' Brendan retorted, his big face red with effort. There was potato on his shirt-cuffs and his school jumper.

'Take your dirty oul' bandage out of that!' Thomas growled. The day before, Brendan had caught his left thumb in the bedroom door, almost severing it; and now the grimy bandage was unravelling into the champ. Sinead was watching me cut up the scallions.

'"Chop scallions finely and set to one side. Meanwhile bring milk to the boil in a saucepan."'

'What's a saucepan?' Sinead wanted to know.

'A pot, just get out a pot.'

'This pot?'

'Any oul' pot. What does it matter? Now, "bring the milk to the boil . . ."'

We heard Mother let herself in at the front door. There were none of her usual demands for help with the shopping, or to empty the car. We kept to our posts in the kitchen, stirring milk and scallions, mashing spuds. Father came in behind her. They didn't speak. The four of us exchanged worried glances. They must have had another fight. There had been nothing but fighting all week; fighting and silence, and Mother crying downstairs in the middle of the night. And no more Peace Group. We didn't know what arrangement they had come to, but Mother had resigned from the Peace Group the day before. She had continued to ring Mr Irnmonger, and other men had been let out of Long Kesh; but it wasn't enough for Father, and he went around with a permanent crease on his forehead. We had hoped the champ would help.

Mother came into the dinette. She took no notice of what we were doing, she just announced: 'We have to leave. We're giving up the house.'

We all suddenly stood still. The look on her face warned us to say nothing. We went on making the champ. She began to cry and went upstairs. A great misery had fallen on us.

'Where are we going?' asked Thomas of Father, who had come in to stand staring out into the back garden.

'I don't know, Thomas,' he answered angrily, 'we'll just have to wait and see.'

'Dinner's ready,' said Thomas. 'Do you want some champ?'

'Na,' said Father, 'I couldn't eat anything. My stomach's giving me terrible jip.'

Mother didn't come down that evening so we had to eat dinner by ourselves. My tears salted the champ. I didn't want to leave Bunbeg. I loved Bunbeg. And now it was all ballsed up. I knew for definite now that life wasn't fucking worth living. Nothing would ever be normal again. It emerged later that the parents had been down to see the Housing Executive, who would attempt to find us somewhere suitable as quickly as possible. For the moment we would have to stay where we were. But we could rest assured, we were on top of the Emergency Housing Intimidation list.

*

We left Bunbeg on a weekday morning. A handful of Provos spent the last night in the house with us. For protection. I opened the bedroom door about six o'clock. Now that the time had come I wanted it to be over quickly. Father was already disappearing down the stairs looking thin and grey-faced. I followed. He eased open the living-room door. Not a stir. Only the heavy smell of sleep-breath and comfortable bodies. He smiled wryly over his shoulder and stepped into the room, over one prone body after another. There were five of them lying in heaps on the floor. The settee was unmolested. One snored intermittently. We picked our way through to the kitchen.

'They could all have been raped in the night and they'd have been none the wiser,' he commented with a nod at the dormant.

He made tea, his own blend, and toast. He stared continually out the window into the back garden.

'Do you mind the time that garden was full of vegetables?'

I nodded. 'Before the Troubles.'

'There was potatoes and beans and peas and lettuce and onions. And you remember the blackcurrants along the fence?'

'Aye, I used to make jam.'

'Aye, but nobody used to eat it.'

We smiled. It was true enough. I used to make it too runny, though not for the want of fruit. It sat in a covered jug on the shelves above the toy cupboard until it went bluemould.

'That was the only instance I ever heard of preserves going bluemould,' he said, 'but then you take after your mother for the cooking.'

'I take after you too – the toast's burning.'

'Ah but nobody can burn toast like me.'

Always the last word.

He brought breakfast in to the night watch, shook them awake. 'Here's a drop of tea.'

'Is it morning?' inquired a fat fella with an Armagh accent who was lying mostly under the coffee table, as if he'd been cheated out of the night.

'It is, aye.'

They came to slowly, from the brink of oblivion, pulled themselves up still dazed and slow from sleep.

'Lazarus come forth,' muttered Father as he handed out the tea.

They had slept fully dressed, jackets and all, and arose now, masses of wrinkles. They were young and passable, apart from the fat gulpin, yet I hadn't the heart to notice. Life being contrary. They chewed in silence. Only the odd agreeable remark, and Father telling them about the old IRA flying columns.

The van was loaded and the oul' car piled to the roof-rack with cardboard boxes and dressing-table drawers. The boot gaped open, tied down with a piece of hairy cord and bulging with suitcases, the small wheelbarrow and the cement garden roller. Despite the spectacle the street was strangely empty – no sign of the crowds that gaze habitually on wedding, ambulance and funeral scenes. Mother was already in the car, with Sinead and Brendan in the back on top of the drawers. Like the wagon-train game. Thomas would ride in the van with Colum and Alex.

'Where's your father?' Mother, tear-stained, called irritably from the car.

'He's gone in to check that we didn't forget anything.'

'Well, tell him to hurry up.'

I went up the path for the last time and into the house. There was an echo already. I found Father on the upstairs landing; he was kneeling down, pulling up the oilcloth and feeling underneath it. He drew out a flattened pile of yellowed papers. Old newspaper clippings: the *Telegraph* and the *Irish News*. He looked through them, oddly absorbed.

'What's up?' I asked. 'What are they?'

He handed them to me without speaking. They were dated 1947. *Michael Matthews Hangs. Death of a Rebel. The Falls*

Road Mourns. There was a photograph of his family at the funeral, among them a younger, slimmer Mrs Murray.

'I was going to slip them under her door,' he said with a half smile.

'What for?'

He looked at me as if I was stupid. 'For revenge. But I suppose there's no point. It would achieve nothing. She's only an oul' fool anyway.' He crumpled the papers into a ball, took aim and fired it through the bathroom door and right into the toilet bowl. 'I was always a terrific shot,' he boasted. 'Come on, we'd better get going.'

We did not look back.

Craigavad Road was a small street on the edge of Andersonstown. It was quiet and green, with a view of the mountains, and it ran down to the M1 motorway. From the front door of our new home we could look out over the bogs, and even see as far as Milltown Cemetery. We moved the day after school broke up for summer holidays. We had only told a few people where we were going. We would lie low all summer.

I could count on the fingers of one hand the number of dances and discos I attended in my youth. The Troubles were a terrific excuse for imposing the convent-like regulations. I was kept house-bound. There appeared to be ample justification for my virtual incarceration: there was usually no transport, no street lighting and almost nowhere to go. And it rained. Every day for fifteen years.

'You'll get your death of cold if you go out in that weather,' Mother would threaten.

'Sure, I'm well hopped up,' I'd say, wrapping a scarf like a winding sheet round my neck and head, 'and I've got my umbrella.'

'If you get a cold on your chest you'll be laid up for a fortnight.'

'Don't worry, I won't get wet.'

Like hell I wouldn't. By the time I reached the top of the street it was all sopping socks and wet thighs. Trickles down the back of the neck, the wind whipping rain and wet hair across the face, on the horizontal plane.

There was almost nowhere to go but to the Blackthorn, a species of cabaret situated on an exposed perch on the lower slopes of the Black Mountain. A perilous out-of-the-way place, inaccessible by public transport. But Hilda and I were desperate for diversion. We would endure reasonable expense and unreasonable discomfort for the prospect of sitting for just a few hours in the shadow of male company.

A typical night out on Titanic Town. There were the parents to be persuaded. We would not be late, we would not drink, smoke or indulge in impure acts. We would not be set upon by gangs of rapists, bag-snatchers or drug-pushers. Nor would we get arrested, or involved in a riot or related incident. We would not travel on a bus which would be hijacked. We would not place ourselves in the path of any bomb, bullet or simple incendiary device. We would not be induced to get into cars full of paramilitaries, especially not if they clapped hands over our mouths and placed black bags over our heads. We would not, in short, be assassinated. We would not be persuaded to give up our studies and run away to join the IRA. My parents between them thought of everything. Hilda's mother was merely anxious that we should remember to take an umbrella.

Fortified with threats and warnings we set out up the Andersonstown Road, to get a taxi. One of the people's taxis, an enterprise of the Free People's Republic of West Belfast. Black awkward things, equipped with flip-up seats and no door handles. But the rides were cheap, if crowded, and the drivers ridiculously obliging. They would take us to the foot of the mountain loney that led to the Blackthorn.

'I'd take yiz up to the door, love, but there's nowhere to turn these yokes, and I'd probably get bogged in the ruts.'

'You're all right, mister, this is great.'

We would get bogged in the ruts ourselves. High heels would sink into muck mixed with gravel, feet would disappear into surprisingly deep potholes as, bent half double, we would toil freezing up the hill. Just when it seemed we would never reach summit camp, just when frostbite seemed imminent, the squat, featureless outline of the Blackthorn would become visible through the fog. The doormen – bouncers really – blocked the entrance; big men with bigger beer-bellies and long drooping moustaches. They would eye us with suspicion, grudgingly let us through the door. It was, after all, their job to maintain standards.

The dance or disco would begin nominally at eight; and certainly the girls would begin to congregate on time, fresh, well-groomed and hopeful. While the boys would devote the early hours to drink, we would dance among ourselves, self-consciously, without abandon. A uniformity of bop. We would have the men under close scrutiny as they besieged the two long bars. Then, with drinks secured – a Guinness and a chaser – they would crowd together in packs to discuss us, the talent. Perhaps they planned strategies for the end of the night. But mostly, we suspected, they would speak of manly, forbidden things. There was small chance that we could ever be of significance to these aloof and fascinating beings. Boys. The ultimate mystery. A no-go area.

Still, some girls got lucky, usually not Hilda or me, and got a dance out of the fellas early in the evening. Usually meaningful eye contact was made during the band's drink break when hearing was more feasible. Discos were passable, but on bad nights we got a live act. Many of the performers were dislocated leftovers from the late fifties. Tony Romano and his Band. They liked to sing 'My, My, My, Delilah', 'Feelings', 'My Way', 'Simple Simon Says' and other assorted cabaret standards. Sadly the older audiences for which their act was tailored had more sense than to come out to hear them. They wore pink cummerbunds and matching dicky-bows, the little knot of satin quivering in time with Tony's opulent vibrato, frilled shirts, long side-burns and short legs.

For some reason the traditional IRA appeal for funds would come after the rendition of 'Bridge Over Troubled Waters'. It seemed to soften up the crowd. There would be a stirring at the back of the main lounge area, crowds of drinkers would part and a hush of respectful approval ripple across the dance floor. Two or three young men in black jumpers and cocky berets would march the length of the room and up to the stage. The band would break into something stirring, like 'The Foggy Dew' or 'The Rifles of the IRA' to underscore the bold rhythm of their passage.

From the stage they would turn smartly and salute. Then their spokesman would step forward and give the address for funds. There was the cause to be fought for. We could not very well depend entirely on subscriptions from Australia and America. There were arms to be purchased, men on the run to be fed and accommodated, Republican publications to be supported, overseas fundraising trips, administration costs . . . Indeed the wonder was that the Provisionals could afford to engage in armed struggle at all. It was not surprising that the Official IRA had been driven to stoop to political persuasion. The support of the local community was the life-blood of any revolution. Please give generously. Up the IRA and Venceremos! Howls of approval would go up from the crowd and pockets would be opened. The collection would take place in a spirit of friendly cooperation, with the assistance of in-house waiters. The colour party would then retire via the back of the stage to tunes of glory, better-heeled than when they arrived.

Later in the evening we would have the equally traditional entrance of an army foot patrol. They however were more inclined to slink into the hall, to disperse and permeate the area one by one, walking backwards, rifles at the ready. They were there to prove a point, to make their presence felt. They were consequently ignored. They usually failed to impact on the evening, and would leave by the front door.

Then the MC would announce the final set. The last chance to touch that evening. This would coincide with the advice that the bar would be closing in fifteen minutes. There would be a dive for liquid supplies. Then, as we jerked dejectedly through the final songs the boys would consider us seriously from behind the froth of the final Guinness of the night. Were we worth dancing with, worth the bother of escorting home? Hilda and I almost never were. We would leave with the rush, unfettered by male admirers, and begin the battle to get home.

One night it was Hilda's turn to see me home. She walked me to the bottom of Corlough Gardens and we turned into Craigavad Road. We were approached by a couple of soldiers. There were others standing behind hedges, kneeling round the corner and behind cars. We jumped with fright as they stepped out to block our way, their faces blackened with boot polish, Kiwi black, their radio antennae waving about behind their heads.

'Where are you going then?' said one in a Yorkshire burr. He looked very young.

'Home,' said we in unison.

'So where's home?' He was a cheeky bugger.

I pointed two doors away. 'Just there, with the white door.'

'I live in Gransha,' Hilda added

'Oh yeah? So what you doing down here then?'

'Em . . . I was just seeing her home.'

'Oh yes? You her escort then?' He smiled, exposing discoloured teeth.

'Can't be too careful, can you, luv?' suggested his mate.

We said nothing.

'What's your name, luv?'

I told him. His companion walked a little way off, said something into a walkie-talkie. 'Just a minute, girls,' he called over. I supposed they were checking us on the computer.

We settled back against the hedge. It would be considerably longer than a minute.

'I'm going to be really late,' Hilda whispered, 'my ma will murder me.'

'So will mine. She'll never let me out again.' I knew that before very long Father would be out at the door watching for me. By ten to eleven he would be strolling up to the garden gate, scanning the street. By eleven he would be walking halfway up Craigavad, getting worried. Five minutes after that he'd have the radio tuned to the police messages to hear if a young woman had been shot in crossfire. At eleven-fifteen he'd be getting the car out to come after me. Then I'd be in for it.

Some time later the soldier's radio crackled, emitted static, and a not noticeably human voice said something indiscernible. The soldier came over to us. 'What's your father's name then?' he asked, looking less friendly. Oddly, I thought of the painting, 'When Did You Last See Your Father?'

'Aidan McPhelimy,' I said, slowly, clearly. I noticed the black leather trim on his khaki beret.

'Very funny,' he retorted. 'Now what's his real name?'

I sighed obviously. 'That is his real name.'

He eyed me suspiciously, deciding whether I was trying to mess him around.

'What was it again?'

'Aidan McPhelimy.'

'Aid An Mac Feel Me? Spell that please.'

We giggled, I spelt it. He jotted it down in a little notebook.

The other soldier suddenly asked: 'Right, who lives at number 14 Carnan Gardens then?'

I shifted from foot to foot, looked at him with calculated disgust. 'My cousin.' That was Rosaleen's address. I glanced down and saw the brass eyelets twinkling on his black boots.

'And her husband,' he prompted. I said nothing. 'So where's the husband right now then?' he asked with a smile. I shrugged. Hilda was looking worried. 'He's in prison isn't he?' the soldier asked.

I wanted to say no. I considered saying he was in a prisoner-of-war camp. But the wee woman would have murdered me, even if the soldiers let me go. I therefore maintained a discreet silence and tried to look bewildered.

And then that voice came out of the dark: 'Annie!' It was Father, sounding thunderous. He was at the garden-gate stage. He had spotted us. I must have jumped, for the soldiers jumped too and started waving their SLRs around, looking for a target. They settled on Father.

'Is that you, Annie?' Father demanded, his voice severe with authority.

'It's my father,' I said hurriedly to the soldiers, 'I have to go now,' as if we were having a pleasant chat in the freshness of the evening. Hilda and I made as if to go. The soldiers did not object. Perhaps they were young enough to recognise the weight of disgruntled parental authority emanating from the garden gate. As we walked towards our house they began to move nervously up the street, walking backwards. Father threw open the gate, took possession of the two of us, ordered us into the house.

'You see what you get yourselves into, gallivanting about at this hour of the night?' he admonished. I opened my mouth to say we weren't gallivanting, then thought better of it. I would hold my wisht.

'Goodnight, luv,' said an English voice from out of the night. Hilda and I walked meekly into the house, and didn't look back.

22

Chez Mulvogue

Through Mother's spurious activities of a public or even political nature we saw a great deal of the Mulvogues. They were almost millionaires, or as near as you'd get on the Falls Road: the Rothschilds of West Belfast. The wee woman spoke very well of the son of the house, young Brian, particularly in my hearing. I consequently walked streets out of my way to avoid him, and pretended not to see him when we were in the same room, even though he was polite and intelligent and good to his mother. The wee woman held it against me, and secretly feared that I preferred wee hard men.

Mr Mulvogue was a highly respected public figure. He was a well-set-up man, tall, silken haired with an unBelfastly tan: a John De Lorean with integrity. He was gentle and gentlemanly, if a bit obtuse, because, Mother explained, he had a lot on his mind. I could well imagine: transport costs, insurance, the rot-rate of port-bound vegetables, the boom in Ferrero Rochers, Strasbourg, international money markets, the planned release of internees, bruised fruit. So he could be a little removed in his treatment of people. He worked endlessly, all hours, commuting about the world, striking, I supposed, a deal for candied jellies here, securing some macaroons there, organising a dozen gross of Chinese gooseberries or monstera deliciosa.

His activities were supported in a passive, almost undetectable way by his wife Eithne. Mrs Mulvogue was a woman predisposed to inertia, anxious not to become upset. She had been ill-placed by the hand of fate, right in the middle of the Falls Road, where trauma was the shared reality. She was small and square with the sort of generous figure that is solid rather than flabby. She had a handsome, blooming face with well-contoured lips, hair making a dignified transition from red to grey, and a wardrobe of striking spectacles.

Although very clever and able, she was averse to activity and spent much of her day in bed. My father insisted that she hibernated from October to May. In her girlhood she had worked as a teacher of speech and drama. But her pupils having failed, for sectarian reasons, it was said at the time, to win one cup at the Belfast Festival, and having lost a kidney at twenty-three, she retired to be pampered by her indulgent father. He sent her to Paris to buy underwear and hats, bought her a grand piano, and even a horse despite the lack of the kidney. Mr Mulvogue came and took her away from all that.

She was in bed the first time I ever met her. I was with Mother that day and we had called about half-past eleven in the morning. A fine-looking girl, one of the seven gorgeous but lethargic Mulvogue daughters, showed us in.

The house was enormous and strange, like a butterfly of glass and wood. A light timber structure set well back to command the road. The entrance hall, lined with acid-etched aluminium, the size of our living room.

'M'mammy's in bed,' said Christine sluggishly, 'go on up, Mrs McPhelimy.' Mother was already an intimate friend.

'Is she not well? I wouldn't like to disturb her.'

'She's just tired,' said Christine, 'but then she's always tired. I have to go out now, so she'll be glad of the company.'

We passed through the hall and made our way up the wide staircase. Mrs Mulvogue was sitting up in bed, a box of Lindt chocolates on her knees and a Harrods catalogue in one hand.

'Ah come in, Bernie, come in do. Excuse the state of me, but I haven't been a bit well.'

'What is it ails you, Eithne?'

'Ach, just that old weakness that comes over me now and then. We were up all night with the rioting. Things are a lot worse with the warm weather and the clear nights coming in. It was wild. But I'm feeling better this morning.' She had the loveliest speaking voice. 'And is this Annie?'

I was duly introduced, behaved well and had good things said about me by Mother and hostess alike. Having done my bit I was free to quietly survey the bedroom.

It should have been a beautiful room, but it lacked order. One length of the glorious blue and white silk curtains had been unceremoniously flung over the back of a wicker chair, another had been squashed in behind the dressing-table mirror. The matching bedspread lay on the floor at the foot of the bed. The wardrobe doors yawned open to reveal an untidy if rich abundance. The floor was strewn with shoes, handbags and books, while a pure white Afghan hound lay stretched unobtrusively on a flokati rug. At its head another half-empty box of chocolates, Mrs Mulvogue not being partial to soft centres.

'And is Liam working today?' Mother inquired.

'He is, God love him,' replied Mrs Mulvogue feelingly, 'sure he hardly gets a minute what with the business and the election coming up. He was off to Singapore on the eight o'clock plane this morning. He's so good, Bernie; he insisted on bringing me up my breakfast, because I haven't had much of an appetite these last few days. But, thanks be to God, I was able to struggle down some bacon, egg and sausage with a wee bit of soda and potato bread. Just to please Liam really. But it's done me some good. It gave me the strength to go through this catalogue to pick out a new dinner service. I was even thinking I might get up for a wee while.'

'That'd be great if you think you're up to it. Would you like me to make you a cup of tea while you're getting dressed?'

'Not at all, Bernie, sure I couldn't impose on you.'

'It'll be no trouble at all. Come on, Annie, I'll show you the kitchen.'

It was an enormous room; quarry tiled, lined with oakwood cupboards, cluttered with every available electrical appliance. And all of them half-cocked. The jafflemaker that lay dismantled on the bench, the juicer filled with old yoghurt and greenmould, the electric knife and can-opener in need of new batteries, the microwave with its interior coated in melted plastic bag.

'This place is a mess.'

'Well, Eithne doesn't be very well a lot of the time.'

'What about the girls?'

'Sure they're lazy big shites. There's a woman comes in to do the cleaning from down the road, but she's not very reliable. Look at thon roast . . .' said Mother, shaking her head over an untouched sirloin that sat exposed on the kitchen table, its nether quarters secure in congealed fat. It had dried out entirely. 'It must have been here from Sunday. I think we'd better throw it out. It's gone off. So much waste . . . Just look at the stuff in the sun room.'

The sun room opened off the kitchen, a large glassed annex furnished with bamboo and glass-topped tables. It looked abandoned. The corners were piled up with boxes of pineapples, oranges, paw-paws and peaches, many of them wilting, shrivelled or rotten. Clouds of small, black midges hovered above the fruity stink. Boxes of Lindt chocolates were melting one into the other on the Papa-San chairs.

'Doesn't anybody ever come in here?'

'Well . . . it's such a big house.'

As Mother wet the tea we heard the heavy clatter of Mrs Mulvogue's wooden loafers on the staircase, souvenir of Mallorca. She swept into the kitchen with surprising grace wearing cream silk and tweed pleats. She looked wonderful; pink, glowing, incandescent with affluence.

'Would you credit that? Liam just left those breakfast

dishes! I suppose he expects me to do them and me not well. He knows Mrs Maguire isn't coming in today, her veins are at her again. Ach, God love you, you've made the tea,' she said with satisfaction. 'We'll bring it into the morning room. There's a chocolate cake up there in the cupboard, I might be able to struggle a bit of that. Would you take a bit, Annie?'

Too straight I would. The tea procession proceeded to the morning room. Off-white and egg-shell blue with great bay windows and a copper-lined hearth. Mrs Mulvogue descended delicately on a green scrolled couch and waited for Mother to serve her tea and a slab of cake. We talked of the election. Liam was to stand as an independent candidate of Nationalist persuasion. My parents had volunteered to lobby throughout Andersonstown and to act as scrutineers on poll day. It sounded promising so I decided to join them. If I couldn't go to discos, politics might take my mind off my dull and nun-ridden scholastic existence. I didn't want to be Pooh-bah again this year. I was anxious to meet men rather than to impersonate them.

'We'll be having a meeting of all the helpers when we get back from North Africa,' said Mrs Mulvogue.

'Are you going with Liam then?'

'Well, he's insisting. He thinks I don't get enough sun, and I need to get some shopping done before Christmas. I can't stand the Christmas rush.' It was mid-May. 'You can get some lovely wee things in Morocco and Tunisia. I just shop all day while Liam's at meetings. It's actually very exhausting.'

'Must be terrible,' agreed Mother without conviction.

I was sitting in the bay window. The house overlooked a luxuriant, shapeless garden bounded by a high stone wall. Beyond it the road. The surface of the road was splashed with the brilliant outburstings of a score of paint-bombs, aimed last night at the odd passing saracen. A gable wall a little up the road had been freshly sprayed in cobalt blue graffiti with white highlights. It read, 'Brits o, IRA 6';

results of the latest close encounter between rocket
launcher and troop-carrier. It was a terrific window from
which to survey a riot or demonstration, a box of Swiss
soft-centres for reassurance. There was something just
about to begin, a certain something in the air – intimations
of hostility. Groups of boys and young men were forming
around the shops on both sides of the road. I thought
maybe there was an army patrol due. Parked near the top
of Divis Road was a car full of older men. They seemed to
be issuing orders, acting in a coordinating role; the lads
awaiting their signal.

Mrs Mulvogue absently offered me a cream puff. 'Sometimes I think Liam isn't with the rest of us, Bernie. He
seems to be in a dream world half the time. Take that car
for instance . . .' She signalled vaguely out the side window.
There was an almost new Audi sitting on the lawn close to
the garages, up to its bumpers in couch grass. It had the air
of a thing abandoned.

'That's a lovely car, Eithne,' commented Mother, 'I was
just noticing it on my way in.'

'Oh it's a nice enough looking car,' she agreed, 'but it's
just not practical. Now you know that I just hate to drive
on this road, what with the army patrols and the riots and
the hijackings. My nerves just won't stand it. So I said to
Liam, I need a small reliable car now, something I can run
into town with and park without any bother. Well, Eileen
Brosnan has a Saab automatic and she said she wouldn't go
past it. Apparently it's a very nippy wee car. I just didn't
like the look of that particular car. I felt the roof was
coming in on me when I sat in the back seat. Not that I
would ever have any cause to sit in the back seat . . .
Anyway, Bernie, I said to Liam, go ahead and get me an
automatic. I left it up to him. So he got this Audi and I
thought, terrific, for it's a nice wee car to drive. Anyway,
to cut a long story short, I went into town one day, the
week after I got the car, and then I took a run up to Clonard
Monastery. It was a Thursday and there's nowhere like

Clonard for the novena. I was doing the nine Fridays for
Liam's shingles at the time.'

'How are his shingles, by the way, Eithne?'

'Great, thanks Bernie. An awful lot better since he's
finished at Strasbourg. Anyway, I was on my way home
and I get as far as Beechmount and here, doesn't the car
stop dead. Well I'm telling you I was furious, Bernie. I
thought to myself, they've landed us with a dud. So I had a
terrible time getting home. It was raining and damned if I
could get a taxi for as long a time. Anyway, I got home and
I'm telling you, I fairly gave Liam a piece of my mind. So
he had it picked up the next day by one of the men from
work and he came home that night with a grin from
shoulder to shoulder. "You know all was wrong with the
car?" he said to me. "Sure you hadn't put petrol in it since
you got it." Well I'm telling you, Bernie, that was the limit.
I really lost my head. "Petrol?" sez I. "You have to put
petrol in it and it supposed to be an automatic! Some
automatic that was you got me!" I just told him straight
out, Bernie. I mean what was the point in getting an
automatic if you have to put petrol in it all the time just
like any other car. Well now, he and young Brian thought
this was a great joke, my imagining you didn't have to put
petrol in the car. But wouldn't you think with all the
advances they've made these days that they could at least
develop a car that ran on self-charging batteries or . . .
mechanically or something?'

'You would.'

'So I just said to Liam, "Well I'm glad you and Brian
think it's such a great joke, but the joke's on you, for I have
no intention of driving that car now. It's not at all what I
had in mind, and I'm not going to set foot in it." And do
you know, Bernie, that car has sat there from that day to
this and I haven't so much as turned the key in the lock.
And it can sit there until it rots for all I care.'

Directly over the garden wall a double decker bus had
been brought to a halt by a cordon of male humanity which

stretched, hostile, purposeful, across the main road. The driver and bus conductor were negotiating uncertainly through the side window. A young man below the window grew tired of reasoning. He walloped the side of the bus with a crowbar whch seemed to appear from nowhere. The busmen drew back and made an attempt to start the engine, which roared momentarily to life then juddered to a halt. The keepers of the bus looked around in desperation. The young man motioned towards the car parked at the top of Divis Road – the gun appeared briefly, just a subtle glimpse. But entirely adequate. The busmen climbed down in something of a hurry. They watched from the shelter of the post office as their bus was quickly set alight. It blazed up with a great whoosh. Even Mrs Mulvogue noticed.

'What in God's name is going on out there, Annie?'

'They're burning a bus. I think they're going to barricade the road.'

'Oh my God! Not again. And Liam not even in the country.'

'I think we might be in for a day of it, Eithne.'

'Is it any wonder I'm not well!' lamented Mrs Mulvogue. 'Come away from the window, Annie, I don't want to draw attention to the house.'

'That's right now, Eithne, the worse thing you can do is make yourself obvious.'

'The trouble with young men like that is they have no interests, nothing to keep them occupied. What they need is a hobby. Sure, Brian was always moaning he had nothing to do until he took up sailing. That's been the making of him. It was the best thing we ever did giving him that boat. Now why can't more of these young thugs take up a sport like that? If they kept themselves occupied there would be less of this rioting.'

'You're right there, Eithne.' Even the wee woman knew it would be useless to point out that the young thugs in question could hardly afford the price of a lifebelt, never mind a sailing boat. But Mrs Mulvogue had paused to draw breath and Mother saw her chance. 'But listen, Eithne, I was forgetting . . . I didn't tell you what happened to Kitty, did I?'

'What was that?'

'Her house was hijacked! The IRA came in and took over, last Saturday, about twelve. Annie was round there when it happened. Weren't you, love?' I confirmed her story. 'They just walked in and ordered Kitty and Alex and Annie into the kitchen.'

'Holy be to God!'

'You see, the back of Kitty's house looks out onto the Shaw's Road and apparently they were waiting to take a shot at the army patrols that come down there regularly.'

'God bless us and save us! And what happened?'

'Well the lads didn't say much of course. They wanted to know if there was anybody else in the house. So Kitty said there was only Benedict, and he was still asleep.'

'And this was twelve o'clock?' asked Mrs Mulvogue, seemingly shocked. Benedict had grown into an awful slug of a boy.

'Aye, Kitty has terrible trouble getting him up in the mornings. He's terrible lazy, and he eats a shocking lot.'

Benedict did like his food. He would eat an entire loaf, a pound of sausages and a half-pound of bacon for breakfast. Kitty didn't like to see him go hungry. And she certainly wasn't keen to waken him before two on a Saturday. However, as the three of us sat under guard in the living room, the five young men with guns and determined expressions were quite adamant that Benedict would have to get up.

'You come up with us, missus, or we'll get him up ourselves,' threatened a youth with the beginnings of a ginger beard and straggling red hair.

'I'll go with her,' said Alex to me as two of the volunteers followed Kitty. We went up the stairs in single file: Kitty, me, the redhead and another of the men who wore a khaki jacket and trousers. Kitty tiptoed into the darkened room. There was a stale smell of breath and fart in the air.

'Benedict,' Kitty whispered, 'it's time to get up, son.' But Benedict was dead to the world. 'Benedict, it's getting late. It's after two.' But Benedict held his ground. Kitty turned nervously to the men in the doorway. 'It's awful hard to get him up in the mornings,' she apologised.

'Come on, missus,' urged the redhead.

Kitty tried again. She gently shook the body under the blankets, 'Come on, son, up you get.'

Benedict growled in response. He had at least come over from the other side.

'Benedict, love, you have to get up right now.'

'Fuck away off,' he snapped.

'Benedict, come on now. The IRA's taken over the house. There's a couple of men here with guns. They want you to get up.'

'Very fucking funny.' He was returning to full consciousness now.

'I'm not joking, son. Now get up, for heaven's sake.'

'Wise up, Ma.'

I took up the cudgels. 'Benedict, your mother's not joking. The house has been hijacked,' I said, attempting to convey a sense of urgency. But Benedict never moved.

The redhead had had enough. He slipped silently into the room, pushed Kitty aside and stood over the hump of bedclothes that was Benedict. In an instant he had placed the barrel of the gun against the back of Benedict's head, and roared: 'Get the fuck up or I'll blow your fucking head off.'

Benedict jerked up in pure terror and ran off the bed into the corner of the room between the wall and the wardrobe, yelling 'Ahhhhhhh' as he fled. He turned to face his assailant, his gross white belly trembling over the top of his dangling pyjama bottoms. 'Holy Jesus fuck!' he cried when he saw the two guns.

'Benedict!' Kitty exclaimed, horrified at the coupling of the expletive and the holy name.

'Downstairs,' the redhead commanded. We obeyed, Benedict going before us, tripping over the bottoms of his pyjama legs. We gathered again in the living room with two guards to watch over us. We sat for over an hour, saying nothing, and nothing happened. Alex, who had spent much of the time studying Esperanto and calmly attempting to light his pipe, turned to the redhead at last and suggested making a cup of tea.

'No. Just sit there.'

Alex considered this for a few minutes and decided to try again. 'I feel that I should point out that we've had no lunch, we were just about to make it when you, eh, arrived. And Benedict there hasn't broken his fast since supper last night.'

The redhead surveyed the mountainous figure of young Benedict, who, with his rolls of fat and oily dark hair, looked remarkably like Oliver Hardy. 'I think he'll survive anyway,' the gunman said with just a shadow of humour.

'I can assure you,' Alex began again, 'you need have no fear that any one of us would in any way jeopardise your operation, whatever you may have in mind. Now you're obviously inconveniencing us to a fair degree, but I do feel it would be compounding the injury if you were to deprive us of our basic human rights. And we do have the right to eat in our own home.' Alex was clearly enjoying himself. Our guards didn't know what to make of him. 'After all, even in Long Kesh prisoners are entitled to eat.'

The redhead thought for a moment, saw that Alex had a point. 'OK. The women can make something, but you two stay here.'

Kitty and I headed thankfully for the kitchen, the khaki guard in tow. 'I think we'll do scrambled eggs,' said Kitty. 'We can put scallions in them to give them a wee bit of flavour.' She hesitated, then turned to our guard. 'Do you think your friends would like some scrambled eggs on toast?'

He too hesitated. Like Benedict he might have gone without breakfast. But duty prevailed: 'Better not, missus, we could be going any time now.'

They did too. They took off ten minutes later without a word of explanation, and not a shot fired.

'I suppose the army just didn't turn up,' Mother speculated now as Mrs Mulvogue listened fascinated. 'Thank God no one was hurt anyway.'

'Poor Kitty,' said Mrs Mulvogue, 'but do you see what I mean, Bernie? The devil makes work for idle hands. Now if those lads had a hobby to keep them occupied they wouldn't be running around terrorising decent people. It's the parents I blame.'

The wee woman nodded agreeably and passed La Mulvogue another whack of cake.

For safety's sake we were to go canvassing in groups of two or three. The parents were in the vanguard of the campaign. I followed them up to Mulvogue's one evening in the week before the election. We gathered in the hall for instructions and maps of the streets we were to cover.

'Keep together now,' warned Mr Mulvogue. 'Seamus and Noel will be driving round in the van, throughout the whole area.' He pointed out the window at a blue van mounted with giant posters of Mr Mulvogue. 'VOTE MULVOGUE ONE', it said, and 'VOTE MULVOGUE FOR PRO-GRESS'. 'And Paddy will be out in his car too. So if anything happens, or there's any problems, they'll be keeping their eye on you. Not that we expect any problems, but Sinn Fein, the SDLP and the Alliance Party will all be out there tonight. I know I can depend on you all to make sure the evening goes off without incident.'

I was paired off with a little bird-like woman called Josie Meeley. She was a great character, small, thin, haggard, kindly. A terrific laugh. If she had been born somewhere else and in more fortunate circumstances she would have been a lawyer, a businesswoman, a capable administrator. As it was she was a widow. She mentioned that two of her five sons were in Long Kesh.

'What for?' Mother asked as we filed out of the great house.

'Nothing.'

'But what did they charge them with?'

'Ballykinlar.'

'Oh aye, same as our Diarmuid,' said one woman.

'Same as half of the Falls!' said another.

Josie was an asthmatic and lived on a pension. Yet she brought her sons food parcels every week. An unmanly and unpolitic thing to eat prison fare.

'Mr Mulvogue's a saint,' she whispered as we watched the good man getting into his car and setting off for the Shaw's Road. 'He's always sending stuff up for the boys. I don't know what I'd do without him.'

We were trailing behind the others as we went out through the high gates in the stone wall when we heard a voice call weakly from the house: 'Wait for me!'

It was Mrs Mulvogue. She ran down the steps winding a long cashmere scarf around her head and neck.

'I forgot my gloves,' she said as she joined us. 'Where's Paddy Danagher? I was supposed to go up to Leenadoon with him and Brian.'

'I think they've gone already,' said Josie. 'They maybe thought you weren't coming.'

'But Brian knew I was to go! Honestly, that's just typical! He's so thoughtless, going off like that without me. Wait till I tell his father.'

'Sure he probably didn't realise . . .' Josie suggested diplomatically. 'Why don't you come with Annie and me? We're going up to Bloomfield Park and Dromona Gardens. It's all private houses and it's not far to walk.'

'Oh I don't mind the walking,' retorted the great woman, 'not a bit of me. I'm well used to walking.'

Josie looked as though she doubted this, but said nothing. I, of course, knew my place and didn't say a word. Mrs Mulvogue graciously agreed to accompany us, an enclave of privately owned houses being more secure territory than the sweeping plains of Housing Executivedom that made up most of Andersonstown. We set off up the hill towards Bloomfield Park. Josie decided that we should start on the left, work our way up to the Glen Road, then come back down on the right-hand side of the street.

'Whatever you think,' said I agreeably. There would be young men in houses on both sides of the street.

We walked confidently up the first garden path, rang the bell and waited. A boy of about twelve in his school uniform answered the door. 'Yes?' he asked.

'Hello,' began Josie, 'we've come about the election on Saturday. Could we see your mammy or daddy?'

Faintly disappointed, the boy disappeared back into the house, leaving us to sniff the aroma of stew that was issuing into the street. He came back almost immediately. 'M'mammy says we're at our dinner and she can't come out,' and he closed the door in our faces.

I felt foolish, Mrs Mulvogue looked uncomfortable, but Josie only looked the more determined. 'Apathy,' she muttered, leading us down the garden path, 'they'll not conquer Russia with that attitude,' and she led us next door.

'Yes?' At least it was a woman who opened the door this time.

'Hello, it was about the election. We're here on behalf of Liam Mulvogue, Independent Nationalist candidate for the Falls ward.'

'I'm sorry,' said the woman, 'we always vote for the SDLP.' She went to close the door.

'But do you know what Mr Mulvogue stands for?' asked Josie quickly. 'Have you seen his . . .'

'Look, I'm really not interested, I think the SDLP does great work.' The door closed quietly, with civility. Undeterred, Josie slipped a copy of the Mulvogue manifesto under the door. There was no answer at the third door. At the fourth house a Dobermann Pinscher sat up on the porch as we pushed open the gate. It began to growl.

'Holy God!' breathed Mrs Mulvogue, 'look at that animal. We'd better give this place a miss.'

'Are you sure?' asked Josie uncertainly, 'it might be all bark and no bite.'

'Liam said we weren't to take any risks.'

The matter was settled; we moved on. As we continued we noticed a rival party of campaigners coming down on the other side of the street. Sinn Fein, We Ourselves Alone, tonight out in force. There were more than half-a-dozen of them, covering two houses at a time. They looked over at us and called out: 'Who do you represent?'

'Liam Mulvogue.'

'Never heard of him,' they yelled back.

'You'll be hearing plenty of him in the future,' Josie threatened.

'Oh yeah? Well good luck, you'll need it.'

Ignoring the banter, Mrs Mulvogue turned in at the next gate. 'Maybe I should speak this time?' she suggested. She had winced each time Josie had gone into her spiel with her comfortable Belfast accent. 'Just for a change?'

'Certainly, have a go.'

I obligingly knocked on the door. It was a man this time. 'What can I do for you ladies?' he asked cheerily.

Mrs Mulvogue took heart. 'Actually we've come to canvass your vote for my husband, Liam Mulvogue, in the coming election. We were wondering . .'

'Mulvogue?' he interrupted, his brow clouding over.

'Yes, Independent Nationalist.'

'Like hell he's a Nationalist! Wasn't he in that People for Peace carry-on? He's not getting my bloody vote. Tell him from me we want peace with justice, the bastard.' The door banged, Mrs Mulvogue started. We led her white and trembling down the garden path.

'Some people's awful ignorant,' declared Josie in disgust. 'Take no notice of the likes of that, Mrs Mulvogue.' But she had taken close notice and was happy to let Josie do the talking for the rest of the evening.

The reference to the Peace Group had depressed me. We were still living with the fallout. Only the news that Niall French was kneecapped by the Provos for squealing to the soldiers had brightened the past year; Brendan spotted him one evening limping up the Glen Road. It was an unexpected but satisfying development. Paid in their own coin. But even the warming thought of Fuckface French being held down to have his kneecaps blown off at close range did nothing to cheer me now. There was no detectable groundswell of support for the Mulvogue campaign. I could not say with certainty that we had secured one vote. We had been abused, ignored, argued with, insulted, but we had probably had no effect on the outcome of the election, and not a single passable young man had come to the door.

It was well after nine. As we trudged along, growing more and more disheartened, we spied Paddy Danagher's car cruising round the corner, surmounted by the monstrous, double-sided billboards bearing the likeness of Liam Mulvogue. Mrs Mulvogue sighted the car and gave off an involuntary cry of relief. She bolted out into the road and stopped the car in its tracks.

'Jesus! Mrs Mulvogue, I was nearly over you there!' cried Paddy, 'you ran out that quick!'

'That's all right, Paddy, sure there's no harm done. I'm fine.'

'How's it going then?'

Josie made faces behind Mrs Mulvogue.

'It's not.'

'I was thinking I would go with you, Paddy,' said Mrs

Mulvogue suddenly. 'We don't really need three of us, and you're on your own . . .'

Paddy understood the situation immediately. 'Certainly,' he said, opening the car door, 'get in, Mrs Mulvogue. I could be doing with the company.'

As she was settling herself in the old Morris Minor, which wasn't what she was used to, a van pulled up beside us in the middle of the road. It was plastered with posters proclaiming the glories of Sinn Fein and their candidate Leonard Meehan, a man with plenty of teeth and a drooping moustache. There were half-a-dozen men crowded into the front. I noticed that Colum was driving.

'How's it going there, Annie?' he called out cheerfully.

'I don't know. Everybody's watching *The Magnificent Seven*.'

There were a few other pleasant remarks exchanged in a spirit of amicable rivalry. Josie knew Colum from her visits to Long Kesh, and Paddy and Colum were acquaintances through drink.

'We'd better get on here, Annie,' said Colum, 'we've got a whole lot of votes to win yet tonight.'

'You'll be lucky,' challenged Paddy hanging out of the car window, 'Mulvogue Number One!'

The Sinn Feinners drove off in peals of laughter. Paddy too dooted the horn and set off. Josie and I waved at Mrs Mulvogue, who was looking happier already.

Then we saw the billboards. Liam Mulvogue was gone, removed, obliterated. On top of his patrician features someone had pasted the purposeful glare of Leonard Meehan. Vote One for Sinn Fein and a New Ireland. The Sinn Feinners must have done it while we were chatting in the road. Not a bad move, the additional free advertising. Josie looked at me. Her mouth had dropped open. We looked after the car as it approached the Andersonstown Road. A group of young men on the corner saw the Sinn Fein posters and sent up a cheer as Paddy drove by. Mrs

Mulvogue smiled, and waved graciously to the crowd. She was making a difference already.

Dawn spluttered up over the Black Mountain: a magnificent day for an election, clear and dry, maybe even a smatter of bright sun. At seven we assembled purposefully at the Mulvogue mansion. Campaign headquarters. Thirty-five of us, good persons and true, intent on victory.

We knew rightly that Liam could not win. The point was to make a good showing. He greeted us warmly in the glowing hallway. Eithne appeared from time to time from the morning room, gracious, condescending, one eye on our feet, the other on her floor coverings. We gathered in the white drawing room. It ran the whole length of the house. Three fine bay windows and a stone hearth large enough to accommodate multiple pairs of bare feet. A scattering of Persian rugs on polished parquet.

We stood awkwardly amid the inlaid tables, the delicate statuary. The little streets upon the great. No one thought of sitting. We stood to receive orders before battle. Liam placed himself in the doorway, coughed for attention.

'Firstly, I'd like to thank you for turning up today and for the work you've put in, and for the support you've given us over the past few weeks. I couldn't have got this far without you. Now . . . we have to be realistic. You know what we're up against, and that the chances of winning are fairly slim. But your efforts have ensured that our chances have improved considerably, and that in itself is a victory. To win at the polls would be a bonus. But I'll be happy if I don't lose my deposit.' A titter ruffled dutifully through the assembly. 'To those of you acting as scrutineers, you can expect a lot of impersonation. But whatever you do, don't challenge anybody. Do you hear? Let me be quite clear on that. I don't want you to challenge any voters, under any circumstances, for obvious reasons. The scrutineers for the other candidates can do it if they wish, but I'd be very surprised if they did. Because it becomes a police matter, and the RUC will be in attendance at every polling station. Needless to say we don't want them involved. You are only there to observe, so no controversy please. Have you all arranged with Paddy and Seamus to pick you up at lunchtime and take you to cast your own vote?' A murmur of affirmation. 'Good. That's at least a dozen votes I'm guaranteed.'

I spent the morning purportedly acting as scrutineer at a polling booth down the Falls. Abuses were rampant. Certain faces were familiar by morning teatime, having been in to vote under several aliases. But the scrutineers were tolerant, or possibly terrified, and nothing was said. At lunch-hour my understudy came in to relieve me and Paddy Danagher called to take me to vote in Andersonstown. Josie was in the car too. She was to go with me and vote on Mother's behalf. A fully approved, wholly above-board impersonation. Mother was acting as scrutineer in St John's parish, and it had been impossible to find anyone to take over from her at lunch-hour. She was determined not to lose her vote, and Josie had offered to go in her place.

'I'll just pretend to be you,' Josie explained, 'nobody'll be any the wiser.'

'But it's illegal,' Mother said uncertainly.

'Ach me arse and that for a yarn,' retorted Josie, 'haven't the Unionists been gerrymandering the elections here for the past fifty years? Just let anybody try to stop me voting. Sure, Annie'll be with me, won't you, love?'

'Yes,' I agreed, 'it'll be fine.'

'And don't forget to call me Mammy.'

We arrived at the Holy Child school shortly after one. 'We'll not be long, Paddy,' Josie assured him as we got out of the car, 'for I'm starving hungry, and I'm not going back to that polling booth unless I get something to eat.'

We made our way across the school yard, up the steps

and past the RUC men at the entrance, and looked around for the 'Macs.

'Over there,' said Josie hurrying me along, 'come on now, I want to get to Hughes in time for the fresh baps.'

We joined a queue to our right and shuffled gradually towards the table. A slight little man with sandy hair and a red rosette in his lapel sat ruling voters' names off the computer listing. To each side of him sat nondescript, middle-aged citizens struggling to keep their mind on the proceedings. They sipped tea as their eyes wandered around the hall and the voters filed past. No danger of getting involved.

We edged closer. My heart constricted. There, at the other end of the table, was Margaret Marian. Huge, gross, unmistakable amid the folds of red flesh. She was a longtime acquaintance of the wee woman's, and sister of as well as scrutineer for the Alliance Party candidate. Jaysus, such luck. Anybody but her.

I decided not to say anything to Josie. I didn't want to throw her. She was giving a terrific impression of unconcerned rectitude. 'Over here, daughter,' she urged as I drew back behind the line of people.

Maybe Miss Marian would not notice. Unlikely. Eyes like a hawk and time for everybody else's business. Maybe she too was under orders not to challenge. She was nibbling away at a slice of sultana buttercake. That might keep her busy. We might get away with it. We were at the table. The man in front of Josie gave his name.

'MacEntaggart.'

'MacTaggart was it, son?' inquired the little man.

'No, MacEntaggart.'

At the edge of my vision I could see Miss Marian. She had spotted me. I kept my eyes carefully averted, looked unconcernedly around the room. A woman with a baby at the next table. That was handy. I could stare warmly at the child. But Miss Marian kept her eyes on me, prepared to smile when I turned in her direction, to ask after my mother as she had done other days at bus-stops, in the people's taxis, at school concerts. She thought me a nice wee girl, the spit out of my mother's mouth, a real Mohan, nose and all. She and Mother had laughed over my nose. 'By the help of God she'll grow out of it, Bernie.'

I couldn't take it in good heart.

She waited now for me to turn, to recognise, to smile politely, to briefly alleviate the monotony. I fixed my eyes on the computer listing. The official had found the name. 'Oh aye, here you are here. MacEntaggart, Joseph Thomas, 447 Tarnlough Gardens. There you are, sir, just over there.'

It was Josie's turn. She was enjoying herself, oblivious to the fat threat on her left. The little man looked up expectantly.

'Bernadette McPhelimy.'

'What was that, love?' Silly oul' bollocks, had to rub it well in.

'Bernadette McPhelimy.'

Miss Marian picked up on it the second time. Not alarmed at first, assuming it was someone with the same name.

'Address, love?'

Christ! This would do it. Our number was up.

'5 Craigavad Road.'

That was enough. Miss Marian heaved into action. She leaned up out of her chair, across the table and bellowed: 'That's not Bernie McPhelimy!' Her face was red as a boil, her neck pumping blood.

The official looked up, suddenly nervous, his neat little Protestant face consternated. Josie held her breath, weighed up the danger.

'I beg your pardon?' sez she cheekily to Marian.

'You're not Bernie McPhelimy,' Miss Marian challenged, very sure of herself.

Josie stood back, not a quiver, not a bother on her and observed her bulky assailant. 'I don't know what this woman's talking about,' she declared evenly. Totally convincing.

The official wetted his lips. 'You are Bernadette Mc . . . eh . . . McPhelimy of, eh . . . 5 Craigavad Road?'

'Of course.'

'I'm telling you she's not. I know Bernie McPhelimy well . . .

'Of course she's Bernadette McPhelimy,' said I, mildly, reasonably. 'She's my mother.'

She was momentarily stumped. She had forgotten me for the moment. Now she looked from Josie to me to the little man.

'She's not, I'm telling you she's not. That's her daughter all right, but that's not Bernie.'

'What?' said the official feebly. 'How could that be the daughter if this isn't the mother?' The listing in his hands was trembling with him. He had not anticipated a challenge to a voter – not in Andersonstown, cowboy country. He should by rights call in the police. The consequences crossed his mind. He feared for his life.

'I'm telling you, that woman is not who she says she is,'

'You're talking nonsense, missus, I should know who I am,' Josie insisted, boldly holding her ground.

'I insist that we call in the police.'

'Now there's no need for that kind of talk,' he choked out, 'we'll be able to settle this on our own. Now don't get excited, Miss Marian. Sit down there,' turning to Josie, 'can you prove you are who you say you are?' he inquired hopefully.

'Look, I'm her daughter and I can identify my own mother. I have my student concession card with me if you want to see it. Here.' I produced incontrovertible evidence.

But by now Miss Marian was standing up causing a commotion. She had the attention of the entire hall. The police standing in the doorway were beginning to take an interest. They had taken a step in our general direction and stood waiting to be summoned. This alarmed the little official more than anything. He couldn't possibly call in the peelers, not here.

'This seems to be in order,' he said to Miss Marian as he held out the card. 'You must be mistaken.'

'No I'm not. I told you that was the daughter, but that's not Bernie. I've known her for years. We went to the same school. We were in the Young Christian Workers together.'

Josie fixed her with an insolent glare. 'This woman doesn't know what she's talking about. Now I've come here to vote, here's my card. You're holding up the queue, mister.'

He made a bold decision. He crossed the names off the listing and handed us both a voting slip.

Miss Marian became apoplectic. She began to shriek. 'Help, police!' She waved an arm over the heads of the small crowd that had gathered.

'That's enough now,' said the little man sharply. 'You've obviously made a mistake.'

We voted in three seconds flat and turned to walk to the door. It seemed a long way off, so much ground to cover. The police were looking at us, coming towards us. Mildly interested. Probably eager for the diversion.

'Is there anything the matter, miss?' inquired a burly constable, approaching me, the harp surmounted by the crown glinting on his shoulder.

'No, nothing. One of the women on the counter thought my mother was someone else. But we had identity, so it's OK now,' – it wasn't. Miss Marian was still yelling in the background. 'I'm telling you, that's not Bernie McPhelimy.'

The constable looked towards the Macs. We moved on, Josie squeezing my arm: 'You're walking too fast, Annie. Just take your time, take it easy now.' A real brass neck.

The RUC man had moved towards the table. We could hear the official holding his own, poor wee man.

'But they had proof . . .'

We made it out the door, charged down the steep flight of stone steps and into the waiting car.

'Take off, Paddy, for Christ's sake. And go like the hammers of hell!' Hit and run. Immensely satisfying. We headed for Hughes' bakery and the sweetness of fresh baps.

23

Sewerage

Eileen's father raised mushrooms in his spare time in a yellow plastic basin under the kitchen sink. He worked at the sewerage farm at Ballymacracken. There were twenty-two Protestants employed there, two non-practising Jews and a Vietnamese refugee, the latter having presumably been misinformed as to prospects generally in the province. Mr Duffy was the token Catholic. He seemed to get on well with most of his workmates but he knew some of them to have connections in the UVF, UDA and among the hard-core Paisleyites.

It was a source of constant anguish to his family that his work place was so isolated, so well suited for an ambush. To get to work he had to take a slip-road off the motorway onto an empty dual carriageway flanked by high hedgerows on both sides. Then there was the big, flat parking area with unobstructed views into the glass offices where he worked; the perfect target for an indiscriminate sectarian killing.

Once or twice I stayed with the Duffys overnight. In the morning, as we lay in Eileen's room waiting for her brother to finish in the bathroom, we could hear Mrs Duffy seeing her husband off. A daily ritual of blessing, warning, threatening.

'Bless yerself with holy water, Sean. Now ring me as soon as ye get in, love. Just to set my mind at rest.'

'Sure I do it every day. Now give yerself peace, Josephine. I'll be all right.'

'Well don't say anything to get their backs up, and watch there's no cars following you.'

Mr Duffy would ring home at lunch-hour to assure his wife that he hadn't been assassinated and again before he left work at four o'clock, so that she would know when to expect him. He was an agreeable little man, slight, with layers of black wavy hair; he was witty, easy going and had a lovely singing voice. I couldn't imagine anyone wanting to drag him into a car, put a hood over his head and take him out to some quiet spot to put a bullet in him. He was entirely harmless and probably more frightened of the IRA than of the Protestant paramilitaries.

But things were very tense at the time; the time of the Shankill Butchers. The lunatic fringe had stepped in, selected Catholics at random, tortured and murdered them – hatchet in the head, rosary beads strung through the ribcage, breasts sliced off. All imaginative stuff, better than your average shoot and run job.

'It wouldn't be so bad if they just shot him from the distance,' Eileen would say, 'I mean it wouldn't be good, God forbid, but it would be a lot worse if they tortured him, if the Shankill Butchers got him.'

It was particularly tense coming up to July and the Remembrances of 1690; King Billy crossing the Boyne, God love him, and he anxious to be back in the Netherlands picking tulips. Or maybe with his finger in a dyke somewhere. Anywhere but bloody Ireland, that summer's day. I wish I wasn't in Carrickfergus. Then on to the blasted Boyne, old Rubicon of the Pale.

They fought on the first of July, James with his half-hearted Frenchmen – the mug swapped the bold Irish Brigade for this crowd – and Willie with the English, French Huguenots, Danes and Brandenburgs, and the blue Dutch Guard and the odd Ulster Protestant thrown in. The beginning of the end for us. July first, 1690. But the Protestants celebrate on the glorious twelfth of July. Just to be contrary.

This year things were warming up early. At work Mr Duffy was increasingly subjected to wee sly digs. Some

men became openly hostile. He began to feel uncomfortable. When the jibes and wee digs didn't blow over as usual
in a few days he began to panic in his own quiet way: they
were going to finger him. They were going to set him up
for the death squads. The entire family was sick with
worry. I sat in the kitchen with Eileen one Tuesday night
eating homemade apple-creams and we heard her parents
arguing through the wall.

'It's not worth it, Sean. For Christ's sake get out of there.'

'Talk sense, woman. Where else am I going to get work?
Sure look at how many's unemployed. And there's plenty
of younger men out of work I'd have to compete with.'

'I'd sooner have you unemployed than dead. Think of me
and the kids.'

'I'm not goin' to let the bastards put me out of my work.'

Eileen was crying, her sisters who were spooning apple
and piping cream into the little pastry cases were crying, I
was crying in sympathy. But that night I developed a plan.
·I decided that it must be carried out the next day.

On Wednesday morning I revealed the plan to Eileen in
the school assembly yard, between Spanish and English
Lit. She was impressed. It was simple but could work.

'But what if we're found out? I'll get massacred and
Daddy'll get the sack.'

'How would anyone ever know that it was us? Even if
the police guessed, they could never prove it. But we'll
take every precaution. We should do it from downtown. So
they won't be able to trace it. Well? Do we do it or not?'

'All right . . . we do it. But don't tell anyone, ever.'

'No fear. Now, how are we going to get out at lunch-
hour?'

St Catherine's, organised along the lines of a POW camp,
required that its students stay in the grounds at lunchtime,
unless they lived nearby and went home to lunch. But we
were seniors and seniors could get a pass to go to the sweet
shop next door to the school. We sometimes got a pass and
didn't come back in the afternoon. We would mich, go on

the beak, wandering through the graveyard which was just over the bog-meadows, in case we ran into an undesirable like a nun or teacher. That day we managed to get as far as the sweet shop with no trouble. We even managed to smuggle out our school bags wrapped up in our dexters; it would be suicide to go home without them. We waited for a crowd to gather at the shop counter and proceeded to edge our way to the door. I glanced up and down the street. Nobody about. Now! We slipped out the door, ducked over the road and turned the corner at Iveagh Drive. We would have to take the back streets; there would be too many teachers on the Falls Road buying chips and trying to pick up masters from the local boys' school.

We decided it would be better to walk all the way downtown, school bags and all. It took us the best part of an hour, but we had managed to stay out of sight. The centre of the city would be less of a problem, the numbers of Catholic passers-by being diluted by a generous Protestant element who most likely wouldn't care that we were miching school. We emerged at Castle Street, got through the security gates – a cursory frisk – and made our way up Royal Avenue. We were looking for a phone box, ideally in a discreet location. We passed half-a-dozen phone boxes along the street. They had all been vandalised.

'God,' Eileen ejaculated, 'where are we going to get a bloody phone that works?'

'They won't all be gutted,' I said confidently, 'besides, it's too exposed here. Just say the police or the army were tapping the lines, they could trace the call and be round here in a shot. No, it's better to do it from somewhere they can't access easily.'

'Like where?'

'Like upstairs in Woolworth's. They have public phones at the back of the cafeteria. We make our call from there and nip quickly down the escalators, go across the ground floor to the Ann Street exit and we're away. The whole area's cordoned off into a pedestrian precinct. We'd be miles away by the time they got there.'

'But those phones . . . they aren't in proper kiosks, they just have those plastic capsules you have to stick your head in. Someone using another phone could overhear us.'

'Then we'll bide our time and make damn sure there's no one else about. It'll only take us a few seconds and we'll be away like a shot.'

Furtively, with a grim sense of purpose, we made our way to Woolworth's; past the groceries and luggage, beyond the sewing machines and haberdashery, up the escalator, round by the light fittings and into the cafeteria. It had the unreal, soporific quality of an airport lounge. Rows of stuffed circular seats engulfed rows of brown formica-topped tables. Everything was a subdued orange: the vinyl seat covers, the wall lights, the salt and sauce sets, the menus . . . We stood at the entrance, examining the phones on our right. There were three of them. All three were in use.

'Have you got any money?'

'Why?'

'We have to look natural. We'd better get something to eat or drink.'

'I've got thirty-five pee.'

'I've got fifty pee, but it's supposed to be for tights.'

'You don't need tights, do you?'

I raised my skirt to reveal gaping, untighted distances just above the knees of both legs.

'I suppose I could go till Friday.'

'I'll see if I can get you a pair of our Marie's tights. She always has plenty.'

'No, you're OK. I can pinch a pair on my mother.'

We made our way to the counter and ordered tea and two buns. Maybe a last hearty tea-break. We sat down in an alcove not far from the phones. Two were now free.

'We should have no problems. The place is almost empty.'

'Shouldn't we try now?' Eileen urged nervously.

'No, we'll have to leave the minute we've done it and I'm not leaving this bun, I paid twenty-five pee for it.'

Eileen saw the sense in that. We ate and watched. The third caller finished and left. There was no one now at the back end of the cafeteria – the lull before afternoon tea. I braced myself and dug out the number.

'OK. Are you ready? Close your dexter and get your bag.'

'Right.'

We attempted to amble nonchalantly over to the phones, left our bags down and crammed our heads under one of the orange plastic capsules.

'Are you going to use a hanky?' asked Eileen fearful.

'What for?'

'You know . . . to muffle your voice.'

'No! I'll put on a really thick accent.'

'Right, away you go then.'

I cleared my throat, lifted the receiver and dialled. It was answered almost immediately.

'Hello, *Belfast Telegraph*. Can I help you?'

I took a deep breath and spoke in a low, harsh voice, 'Just shut up and listen,' I ordered. My voice sounded like someone else's.

'What? What did you say?' the switchboard operator was instantly alarmed. Maybe she thought it was a dirty phone call.

'Just listen and get it right.' Another deep breath. 'A dead body has been dumped at the Ballymacracken sewerage works. It's a regular dumping ground and there's a body there now. Tell the police.'

I dropped the phone and was out the door in a second, Eileen already flying down the back stairs in front of me. I grabbed the back of her coat, pulled her up sharp. 'Slow!' I ordered. We crossed the ground floor at a cautious, unre-markable pace, went out into Ann Street and walked quickly, but not suspiciously so, up to Royal Avenue. There we crossed the road, nipped into Anderson and

McAuley's and went straight to the book department. We paused to take a breath and to calm down. It was quiet here. Our presence would not obtrude.

'I shouldn't have said "dead",' I breathed, picking up a novel, pretending to skim through it.

'What?'

'I shouldn't have said "dead" body. Obviously a body is dead. It wouldn't be a body if it wasn't dead.'

'So what?'

'So someone who has truck with dead bodies wouldn't bother to say "dead". They would take that for granted.' I knew it probably wouldn't matter. It just detracted from my credibility as a desperate character.

'It doesn't matter. You were great. She'll have reported it and they'll be ringing the police now.'

'I hope so. I suppose they'll have to investigate it one way or the other, and with the police involved you're not likely to get the average murder gang hanging around the sewerage works for a while.'

'I hope you're right.'

'Now don't be telling your father.'

'No fear.'

'Not even if he guesses. And never, ever admit it to anyone. You know I won't. But then I'm a better liar than anyone I've ever met.'

'I swear to God I won't tell. What are we going to do now?'

'Do you want to go to Boots? They got in a whole new range of fruity face packs.'

'But they give you pimples . . .'

We made the six o'clock news on all channels, current affairs at seven, the local news again at nine, ten and midnight. Every hour on the half-hour. There were ructions at the sewerage plant. We heard it all from Mr Duffy. The police swept down like seagulls, the army with them, and combed the entire area. They thought they would find a score of corpses; the missing and the kidnapped. We didn't expect such a fuss. The workers were collected in the reception area and questioned one by one. One was taken to Castlereagh and held for questioning for two days. The buildings were taken apart, the lawn dug up. The sewerage pits were dredged. Of course no body was found. But Mr Duffy felt that the police were not satisfied. The day's operation seemed to have unnerved him even more than the everpresent threat of assassination. But Eileen and I were sure that when he calmed down he would appreciate the benefits. There was no doubt about it, we had saved his life.

At St Catherine's the following week I was summoned to the general office.

'Sister Bonaventure wants to see you.'

A pain in the arse, but there was nothing unusual in it. A clear summons could not be ignored. I walked through the long, empty corridors towards the heart of the school and knocked at the door of the general office. She was standing there with Sister Clare of the eternal bitchy smile, and Sister Anthony who, although old and decrepit, still had enough life in her to be a bad-hearted oul' cow.

'Ah, Annie, come in. I have a job for you.' Bonaventure gave me one of her half smiles.

I hated it when she gave me something to do. I was always so nervous in her presence I could never remember exactly what she said.

'I have guests in my office. I'd like you to go down to Mrs Mackey's room and collect a tray of tea things and bring them into my office. Is that clear?'

'Yes, sister.' I backed away as though from a high altar and went to Mrs Mackey's room.

Now Mrs Mackey really hated me. She was in charge of domestic science. Once, because I was class prefect, I had to visit her class for roll call. While she was counting the class I ate a few oul' bits of cake mixture. Just what would fit in the curl of a finger. But the effect on the daily production of sponge rings was disastrous. I was accused as though of a foul and heinous crime. That had been four years earlier, but I had been banished from Mrs Mackey's classroom from that day to this. I knew how pleased she would be to see me.

'Why did Sister Bonaventure send *you*?' she demanded to know, narrowing her mean wee eyes.

'I don't know, miss.' I tried to look harmless.

'You wouldn't know how to serve up a cup of tea, would you?'

I thought for a moment: 'I suppose you just pour it out, miss.'

'Huh. Just make sure you do, and I don't mean all over the visitors.'

'No, miss.'

'And don't let the tea slop on to the scones.'

'No, miss.'

'And don't be dropping the tray.'

'Right, miss.'

'And I want a full report. Do you hear me?'

'Yes, miss.'

I edged out of her room and set off up the corridor. She stood in the doorway scowling after me. I got great satisfaction out of cursing the oul' bitch under my breath. I reached the front hall outside Sister Bonaventure's office without mishap and nervously approached the office door. I balanced the tray on my left arm and opened the door with my right hand. I looked across at her desk. She wasn't there. I looked at the other side of the room. There sat three British army officers all in a row, like decorations under the window, their peaked caps on their knees. They rose ceremoniously as I entered. I could feel my face freeze. As my hostility rose up, a horrible suspicion was forming in my brain. Were the fuckers on to me? What was the penalty, I wondered, for making hoax calls. Who the hell did Bonaventure think she was, getting me to serve tea to the Brits? My anger calmed my nerves. I boldly went into the room, deposited the tray on the desk and turned to go. Damned if I would play Mother for them, I was thinking.

'Hello,' said one of the officers, in that ridiculous public school voice which never seemed real to me, 'aren't you Annie McPhelimy?'

My heart drummed in my chest, a Lambeg drumming. 'I am,' I replied curtly, staring at him.

He paused. I couldn't imagine what he wanted. He was blond and very handsome in an offensive way.

'Sister Bonaventure was telling us that you do a spot of acting.' I said nothing. It was obviously a trap. 'She tells us you are very good at doing different accents.'

I turned up the corners of my mouth with mock polite-ness and put my hand on the doorhandle.

'Eh, just before you go,' he said, 'we were wondering if you'd do an accent for us? You know, Scots or French or something.'

Sister Bonaventure was the end: Annie McPhelimy, performing flea.

'Would you then? Can you do Scots?'

I could see they were from a Scots regiment. I nodded, anybody could do Scots.

'Would you then?'

'No.' I was quite clear about that.

'Well, English then?'

That was it. He was determined to make me do accents. They would ask me to do a thick, low Belfast accent. Maybe they were concealing a tape recorder. I shook my head.

'Well what about Australian? We've just come back from Australia. Funny accent. They say if you can do Australian you can do anything.'

'I've never heard it,' I lied. I had seen *The Summer of the Seventeenth Doll*, *Skippy the Bush Kangaroo*. It sounded very like cockney to me.

'I have to go,' I said and whipped out of the office, closing the door behind me. I couldn't decide whether I should be more angry than scared. How could they possibly have found me out? We were so careful. Were they able to trace my voice from that one phone call? Impossible. The *Telegraph* couldn't tape every call. Why would they send all those officers for me? Unless they thought it was only one of my other crimes? Maybe they thought I knew about the bodies?

Eileen and I speculated nervously for the rest of the afternoon. But that night we were put out of our misery. The school was on the news.

'A large cache of arms and explosives was found today at St Catherine's girls secondary school on the Falls Road. The arms were hidden in the roof of one of the domestic science classrooms. An army spokesman said that more than twenty pounds of explosives were found in a dangerous condition. It is believed that information leading to the find was provided following recent arrests in the Ballymurphy area. The headmistress of St Catherine's was unavailable for comment.'

24

The Kesh

It was a typical Belfast summer day: very wet, very tense, very troubled. Mother had been down the road visiting her sister Kathleen, who was in a terrible state. Tony had been arrested the week before. Kathleen was left with Rosaleen and the six children. Mother had trouble getting home. The riots for the anniversary of internment kept the buses off the roads. The people's taxis were running, but the Falls was barricaded in places with burning buses and cars, and the going was slow and dangerous.

'Annie, you'll never guess who got lifted.'

'Aunt Kathleen.'

'Ach, don't be ridiculous!'

It wasn't at all ridiculous. She was a one-woman guerrilla campaign.

'Not Colum again?'

'No, Colum's keeping very quiet. You remember that good-looking big fella was up at our house with the Provos the day your father took bad?'

My heart constricted, but I paused, apparently for thought, and said vaguely: 'No, who?'

'Hugh O'Neill, his name was, very tall and good-looking.'

'Oh aye!' I said at last, 'I think I do. The one who kept looking out the window.'

'That's it! He was a lovely big fella. Anyway he's in Long Kesh with Tony. They're in the same cage. They lifted him last month, and Tony says he has nobody to visit him, you know, coming from Donegal. It's an awful long way for his mother and she's an invalid. And he has nobody else. His father's dead and his two sisters are living in America. I feel awful sorry for him. He was very good to your father that day.'

'God,' I said, 'that's awful. Wasn't he a medical student or something?' With Mother, doctors were just second to priests in being due respect and esteem.

'Aye, he's supposed to be very clever. I feel awful sorry for him.' She paused to poke the fire. I held my tongue. I said nothing, not for me to be making heady suggestions.

'Tony was wondering if you would be game to go up and see him.'

'Me?'

'Tony says he'd have to arrange a pass, but there shouldn't be any problem.'

'OK. I don't mind. I'll go and see him.'

'I'll tell Rosaleen then. Maybe you can go up next week.'

Naturally I knew what the wee woman was up to. I was no longer a child; and someday, sooner or later, I was bound to be thrown into the company of young men. She was bowing to the inevitable. But at least she would do her best to ensure that my love interest was out of reach. In prison would be ideal, preferably serving life. My ingrained sense of loyalty and honour would ensure that my fancy did not stray, and of course it would be a wholly platonic relationship. Hugh would be a captive suitor. He would become attracted to me, if only out of boredom and lack of choice. He would make me hand-tooled bags and wooden Celtic crosses. He would be an entirely suitable young man. He could, Mother would imagine, finish his medical degree through the Open University, BBC 2, and I would stay at home and dedicate myself to my career. There would be no physical contact, none of that nonsense, all cerebral interchanges. Still, he was gorgeous, and he wasn't an informer. He would do nicely to be going on with. I went up that Friday with Josie Meeley, who was going to visit her sons. We met outside the White Fort Inn, about a dozen women, a few children, one old man, each with a parcel of clothes, food, books. Hugh was also studying English Literature with the Open University, so I brought *Chaucer, the Compleat Works, Piers Ploughman* and Hobbes' *Leviathan*, light background reading, imagining he would have ample free time. It was freezing that morning, and now it started to rain.

'Thank God,' said Josie, 'the rain'll take the cold away.'

But it was horizontal rain, the sort of rain that, driven by the wind, came in at you under your umbrella, soaking your chest and thighs. We were reasonably wet by the time an old blue van pulled up in front of us. It was just after ten. The driver got out, stomping his feet on the ground, blowing on his hands.

'Here's Declan now,' said the old man. 'About time too.'

Declan opened the back doors of the van. 'Pile in now, girls,' he invited, 'and you'd better huddle up together. The heater's not great in this oul' yoke.'

We piled in and sat on the padded benches down each side. The children sat on the floor.

'Is that everybody?' asked Declan from the driver's seat.

'Hold on a wee minute,' Josie commanded, 'Big Angela's not here yet, but she's definitely going up today.'

'Holy God!' Declan ejaculated. 'That one's always late. I might have guessed.'

'Here she is now,' said the oul' fella, pointing out the hefty figure just then rounding the corner at top speed. Declan was already revving up the engine when she climbed breathless into the back.

'I was nearly away without you there, Angela,' Declan teased.

'Ach you were not, God forgive ye. You wouldn't have left me behind and me hasn't seen my man for a week,' she retorted cheekily.

'Sure I'd come round and visit if you're lonely,' said the dirty oul' man.

'God forgive you, Fitzy,' Angela admonished, 'but at your

time of life you should be praying for a happy death instead
of keeping after the women.'

We set off in high spirits, with oul' Fitzy joking about
how much he fancied redheads and Angela threatening to
have him shot for harassing a prisoner's poor wife. It was
freezing in the van. My coat was wet from the sleeting
rain, and now the cold dampness of the wool was working
its way through my pullover and blouse and into my chest.
I could feel the frogs gathering in my throat. My nose gets
bright red when the temperature drops to a certain level.
As a child the kids in the street called me Rudolph the
Red-nosed Reindeer. Well the nose was beginning to colour
now, a light pink at this stage. I would look a sight by the
time I got to see Hugh.

I folded my arms tightly across my chest and moved
closer to Josie. It might have been the numbing cold, or the
thought of Long Kesh getting closer, but we grew silent as
we neared Lisburn and turned off for the camp. I had seen
it many times from the motorway, a sprawling expanse of
grey wall, crowned all along the perimeter with floodlights
and watchtowers and endless lengths of barbed wire. It had
been built on a flat, ugly patch of land, a former RAF
airfield. It seemed to go on for miles. At night the super-
structure of searchlights and floodlights lit up the sky for a
great distance, an eerie glow in the night. Today it seemed
menacing. As we pulled into the forecourt the size of the
place became depressingly apparent. The walls were much
higher than they looked from the motorway. They
stretched forever on each side of the immense grey iron
gates. We sat, cold and silent in their shadow, and waited.

We waited for twenty minutes while Declan cleared our
passes. Then we got out of the van and went through the
turnstile at the side of the gates. We passed into a portakabin checkpoint, got frisked and bag-searched and were
directed onto another bus. We sat for a further fifteen
minutes while the bus got clearance. I could see nothing
but the grey clinker blocks of the walls, and the tarmac of

the road. At last the bus rumbled into slow motion, taking us nearer the heart of the camp. We could hear the dogs barking somewhere behind the walls. It went on incessantly, pure Auschwitz. We passed through another set of high gates and the bus drew up outside another portakabin.

I was glad to get inside; by now my nose was glowing a deep red, and it had begun to drip.

Josie, who was made of tougher stuff, hustled me inside. 'Come on, get in quick,' she urged, 'and try to get a seat near the heater.'

Of course I wasn't quick enough, and we ended up at the colder side of the room. It was a big, rectangular space, empty but for a row of orange plastic chairs around the walls, and a large but ineffectual paraffin heater. There was a small servery at the top of the room.

'That's the wee kitchen,' Josie explained. 'It's run by the Quakers, God love them, they're awful good. It'll be opened in a minute, and we'll get a wee cup of tea.'

We got a wee cup of tea and I slowly began to thaw out. But the fumes from the paraffin were beginning to catch in my chest. I began to cough. I knew how I must look, my eyes watery and red, my clothes damp and wrinkled, my nose a beacon. I crossed my eyes and looked down my nose. There it was, glowing away. And the skin around it would be raw and flaking from the constant application of tissues to stop the drips. I was feeling miserable, and guilty because I was feeling miserable. Unlike the other women here I had no father or husband or brother or son behind the grey walls, and I hadn't been trekking up to this hole twice weekly for years. I would try to look cheerful. I didn't want to depress the inmates. I tried to cough discreetly into a tissue.

'Right, this is us,' Josie announced some time later, 'we're in the next batch.'

The next batch was herded out the door and back onto the bus.

'We're going to the visiting area now,' Angela explained.

'Only we have to get searched first,' Josie added.

'Didn't we get searched at the entrance?' I inquired naively.

The others burst out laughing but wouldn't enlighten me. We drove again through corridors of grey concrete and alighted in front of yet another portakabin. Inside, at the top of the room, was a counter manned by women warders. We had to leave our parcels with them for distribution to the prisoners later. The lower half of the room was curtained off into cubicles.

'That's where we get searched,' whispered Josie, 'now don't be giving them any lip. I told your mother I'd look after you.' I had no intention of giving them any lip. I had no intention of opening my mouth.

'Is it women warders search you?' I asked.

'Aye, but you call them screws.' I made a mental note.

We shuffled into the search queue and waited our turn. Two women were searched at once, one in each cubicle. Josie went in just in front of me. I had nothing to hide, but I felt sick with nerves as I went behind the curtain.

There were two women there, one tall and angular, the other wee and wiry. The wee one smiled.

'Who are you visiting?' she asked.

'Hugh O'Neill.' She wrote something on a clipboard.

'Put your bag down there and take off your coat and gloves please, love.' I did as I was bid. The other woman emptied out the entire contents of my bag and began to go through my things.

'Take off your boots please,' said the little screw. I must have looked at her in disbelief. I wondered what else I might have to take off.

'Your boots,' she repeated sternly. I took off my boots. My woollen tights were wet. I stood with my toes steaming as she gave me a full body-search. She made me take the slide out of my hair and felt around my scalp. Then she felt all down my arms, across my shoulders and down my chest. She felt under my bra.

'Not much there,' she quipped. I smiled idiotically.

She felt around my vagina. I couldn't imagine what she was looking for. It had never occurred to me that women could be driven to hiding things up there. I never imagined they could even get much up there. I was praying that her hands were clean. Finally she felt all down my legs.

'OK, love, you can get dressed again,' she said. 'Is it any warmer out now?' she added pleasantly.

I couldn't believe she had switched to casual blethers. I don't know if I managed an answer as I struggled into my boots and outer garments. I couldn't get my hair back into the slide.

'I'll have to keep these,' said the tall screw, indicating three or four pens, a pair of nail scissors, a notepad, a couple of letters, and a chapstick. 'You can pick them up on the way back. You go out this way, over the yard and wait on the steps. Don't go in until they tell you.'

I followed her directions and found myself on a short set of wooden steps leading up to an enormous portakabin. There was no one else about, no sign of Josie. It was raining again. I stood, coughing frequently, waiting for someone to appear. I remembered the time a whole crowd of us went to visit Terry in Mountjoy jail. He had gone down to Dublin for the Easter parade and had been detained by the Gardai on a charge of joyriding. He had always been fond of cars. And now here he was, only sixteen, and doing six months in Mountjoy. It was raining the day we visited him, lashing out of the heavens. He sat on the other side of a rickety counter with his ginger hair all cut away to nothing. You could see the scar left on the side of his head from the bottle of the boing. A giant of a warder stood right behind him, listening to everything we said. We could see that Terry was afraid of him. Aunt Minnie was crying.

'You didn't write all last week, son,' she sobbed.

'The pen burst. It was the only one I had,' Terry explained. He had been subdued, not a bit like himself.

'Here, I have a pen here.' Father searched in his pockets

and produced a biro and a handful of Marie biscuit crumbs. 'Take this, Terry.'

But the monster warder had leaned down and snapped: 'Don't touch it, McVeigh.'

We all automatically recoiled, leaving the pen on the counter.

'Visitors are not allowed to pass anything to the prisoner,' chanted the warder.

'But it's only a pen . . . so that he can write home . . .' began Alex, reasonably.

'It's not allowed. You can leave it at reception if you like.'

'But will he get it?'

'It's not up to me to decide.'

Later we had crossed the prison yard in the teeming rain. Terry had cried when we left him. Aunt Minnie hadn't stopped crying all day, and now Mother and Kitty and Benedict had started.

'Did you see the way they've had all his lovely ginger hair cut, girl?' Minnie asked the wee woman.

'Sure it'll grow back thicker, Minnie,' Mother soothed.

In the minibus on the way back to Belfast, Father and Alex sang 'Kevin Barry'.

> In Mountjoy jail, one Sunday morning,
> High upon a gallows tree,
> Kevin Barry gave his young life
> For the cause of liberty.
> Just a lad of eighteen summers
> But no one can deny
> As he walked to death that morning
> He proudly held his head up high.

But the women weren't consoled, they wailed all the louder the whole way home.

I felt like crying now, with cold and misery. I was beginning to think no man was worth it. At last a male screw came out onto the top of the steps.

'Right, you can come up now, love,' he called down. I followed him inside. We were in a dim, narrow corridor. The passage cut the cabin in half, on each side there was a row of cubicles, the walls half-glassed, and with no doors. I could see the prisoners behind the small tables in the cubicles, their visitors sitting opposite.

'Down here, please,' the screw directed me into an empty cubicle and told me to sit down. He left. I suddenly remembered why I had come and something of the excitement I had felt about the visit returned. It would all be worth it, and if I came up again I would know what to expect.

'Hands on the table, please,' a great voice commanded. I quickly took my hands out of my pockets where I'd been trying to warm them and placed them on the table. I looked round, I could see the big screw at the other side of the passage.

'I won't tell you again,' he admonished. He hadn't meant me. Still, it felt like being called to Sister Bonaventure's office; it felt like being in trouble. I became very conscious of the screws walking up and down, glancing into the cubicle. I realised I must have been waiting fifteen minutes. Josie had said we would only get half-an-hour. There wouldn't be much time left. Another screw came into the cubicle.

'Are you waiting for Hugh O'Neill, miss?' he inquired.

'Yes,' I responded hoarsely.

'I'm sorry to have to tell you that the visit has been called off. I'm afraid you've had a wasted journey.'

I hesitated. 'Is he not well?' It was all I could think to ask.

'Nothing like that. The visit has just been postponed. You'll get another pass shortly.' They bundled me out of the visiting area, and I made my way back to the search room. Josie thought it was very odd.

'That's very odd, isn't it, Fitzy?' she commented as we

travelled back to Belfast, 'I've never known that to happen before, have you?'

'Not unless the man was sick or something. It's queer all right.'

No one felt like talking. The visits had depressed everyone, Josie said they always did.

'It breaks my heart to see them,' she said, serious for once, 'looking so thin and pale. You wonder if they get enough to eat. And you know maybe they'll get a hiding after the visit, you know, if they find anything on them. So will you go up again?'

'I suppose so, if I get a pass.'

But there were to be no more passes. Rosaleen found out the truth when she visited Tony the next day. Apparently O'Neill had been extradited to London, without warning, to face charges of sending letter bombs to British MPs. He was found guilty and sentenced to fifteen years imprisonment. As far as I know he is still there.

25

The Funeral Trousers

It was late August, a lovely Belfast summer evening, only slightly wet. The eve of Marie Duffy's wedding. I was seventeen; it would be the first wedding I ever attended in the adult capacity. In my excitement, in my eagerness to look well, I had made the mistake of having my hair coiffed. I had been in Aunt Minnie's that morning and her younger daughter Mamie had encouraged me. She brought me to her friend's hairdressing shop down the Grosvenor Road. I had put myself in their hands and now I looked ridiculous; they had made my hair into a 'beehive', piling it high on top of my head, placing a black velvet bow in it part way down the structure; then when they got it in place they sprayed it with lacquer, till it held firm as a high-rise building. I didn't say anything to Mamie and her friend, but was relieved that it was raining when I left the shop. I would be able to hide under the umbrella. I complained bitterly to Mother.

'It's not that bad,' she consoled, 'at least it's groomed-looking. It's a beehive, isn't it?'

'It's more like a haystack. And nobody puts their hair in beehives nowadays.'

'They did when Mamie was a girl.'

'Mamie's thirty-five!'

'Well it's not that bad, love, honestly.'

After tea I went into the privacy of the sitting room to work on the beehive. It would be hard to demolish, so thickly was it varnished in lacquer. I started trying to dislodge the velvet bow. That's when I heard the first shots. They seemed to be coming from the motorway. I opened the door into the hall. The family were in the living room. The door closed and the TV blasting – Clint Eastwood making their day. They wouldn't have heard the shots. I opened the front door and heard a second round of firing, three or four. They came from the motorway roundabout at the bottom of the street. I ran out onto the path. There were two women running up Kennedy Way and behind them a young man, running at first, then stumbling, falling. Behind him again, another young man, with a gun, and close by a waiting car, the front passenger seat wide open.

Now I understood – the second young man had just shot the first young man. Good to get that cleared up. But why would he be shooting anyone at seven o'clock on a lovely Friday evening? Jaysus! He was actually shooting at live human beings. I took off at top speed, my knees coming up almost to my chest, heels thumping my buttocks. I was running towards the roundabout, to where the young man was trying to crawl away from his assailant. It was no more than fifty yards from the house, but it took a long time to get there. I heard my shoes pinging on the tarmac, I saw the road cracked and broken in places. Now I was running on top of the big, white, spray-painted letters: YOU ARE NOW ENTERING FREE BELFAST. I was reading them up the wrong way but I could see that the lettering had faded with the rain. It would need a touch-up. I kept running, taking deep breaths through my nose and mouth. The sewerage farm on Kennedy Way was stinking that night. I caught the stench at the back of my throat, as though I had swallowed rather than smelled it.

I was very close now. So was the gunman. He had reached the fallen figure. He stood over the victim and paused for a second. Then he raised the gun, something sleek and automatic. He pointed it at the victim's back. I heard a voice shouting: 'No! Don't shoot!'

It was my own voice. But strange. Strangled and disem-

bodied. But the gunman hardly glanced at me. He pulled
the trigger and fired again.

Behind me the two women screamed: 'Jimmy! Jimmy!'

Jimmy was now lying quite still at the side of the road.
But again the gunman stooped to fire, emptying the gun
into his back. I was still yelling, pointlessly, 'Don't shoot!'
But there was no talking to him.

By now I had almost reached the gunman. He straightened and looked directly at me. He seemed completely
calm, unfazed. We stared at each other as we stood on
opposite sides of the body. I knew there was no danger that
he would shoot me or the two women. He might have been
a murderer, but he knew how to treat a lady.

> Sir knight, I fear me not the least alarm,
> No son of Eireann would offer me harm,
> For though they love riches and golden store,
> Sir knight, they love honour and virtue more.

Only he almost certainly wasn't a son of Eireann. More
likely a stalwart Ulsterman. Not in the ancient provincial
sense, but in the modern, Loyalist, no surrender sense.

He watched me for a second, expressionless. I did not
concern him. Thinking back, it seems strange that I said
and did nothing. But nothing occurred to me at the time.
Nothing appropriate. I just stood there, disbelieving, impo-
tent. He could not have been more than eighteen. His long,
fair hair fell over his face as he bent over the fallen figure;
round, narrow shoulders, jeans bleached white with use.
He held the gun casually at his thigh. Then he straightened,
calmly turned away and got into a car parked at the
entrance to the slip-road. The driver barely waited for him
to pull the door closed before he started up and headed off
down the motorway. They were out of sight in a matter of
seconds. The whole encounter lasted less than half a
minute. The longest possible half a minute.

The instant I looked at Jimmy Carson I knew he was

dead. I could see no blood at first, but he was quite grey. I sensed that he had given up the ghost. The women came over to where he lay, his wife, obviously pregnant, and his mother-in-law. The young wife stood in disbelief over the body. I noticed that she did not bend or try to touch him.

'He's not dead is he?' she asked fearfully.

I could not answer her. But her mother, a very ample and able woman by the cut of her, was yelling at the top of her lungs. A lament presumably calculated to waken the dead.

'In the name of Jesus,' she bawled, 'is there nobody to help us?'

Her roars must have ripped through the nearby houses for the neighbours began appearing at their doors. I could see Father rushing towards us. He quickly took control of the situation. He stopped cars, organised a blockade of the motorway roundabout, in case, as sometimes happens, there is a second car with gunman and other accessories. I was sent back over to the house with the weeping wife and the hysterical old woman in my unlikely charge.

'He isn't dead is he?' begged the wife, 'don't tell me he's dead.'

'He'll be all right,' I replied idiotically, knowing she knew perfectly well that he had died instantly.

I noticed that she was wringing her hands. A clichéd expression of anguish. All I could think of was the Valium. We'd have to give her a few Valium. I couldn't get her in the door. She kept hanging back on the path, looking over at the roundabout now crowded with people. As I half-forced her into the house I could hear the pointless blare of an ambulance siren in the distance and see Father bending over the body. He would be saying the Act of Contrition into dead ears. Mother received the two women with open arms.

'Get my tablets,' she mouthed urgently over the girl's head as she led her into the little living room.

I hastily complied with orders and was back in a minute. Sinead had been directed to put on the kettle. Together we dispensed Valium and tea. The wife's name was Josephine. Josephine of the long, black hair and small, comely features. They had been married less than a year. She didn't want to take the tablets because of the baby.

'But, love, it's not good for the baby you being so upset. Now take just this one,' Mother coaxed.

Her mother, Mrs Curry, took four thankfully. She seemed to be doing her best to control herself.

'But he's not in anything, our Jimmy,' she sobbed, 'I swear to God, missus, he's never been interested in any organisations. Just Josephine and the baby comin' . . .'

'I know, I know,' soothed Mother, 'now don't upset yourself, Mrs Curry, your daughter needs you.'

Josephine was silent for a time. She sat staring at the floor, rocking back and forward, gripping a cushion on her lap.

'I know he's dead,' she broke out at last with a painful, choking sob. 'Oh Jimmy! Oh my Jimmy!'

Sinead handed me a Valium. I gulped it down gratefully. My beehive was still bobbing stiffly at the top of my head.

The Special Branch men were patient and kindly, although not clad in Aran jumpers. By the time they arrived to question me I was in almost as bad a condition as Mrs Curry. A fine sight. My face swells horribly when I cry. Not of course when I employ the minor cathartic slow drip, the quiet trickle down the melancholy cheek. Such as when Lassie goes home, or at the beach scene in *Ryan's Daughter*, or when someone sings 'The Old Bog Road'. But where grand emotional traumas are concerned I puff up like a well-boiled side of beef, just as shiny, just as red. My eyes turn luminous green, so swamped are they in moisture, and gradually disappear behind bloated lids. My tears don't come evenly or silently. Instead they gush forth in conjunction with great gasping sobs and heaves of the chest. It is no wonder that crying gives me hiccoughs.

I was somewhere between the sob and the hiccough stage when the two detectives arrived. It was about nine o'clock. I probably helped little with their inquiries. It was hard to focus on their questions, what with the shooting, and the Valium, and the fuss made by neighbours and family, and that cursed high-rise beehive, which had at last been unseated from its lofty perch and begun to sag and droop down the right side of my head. A more precarious version of the leaning tower of Pisa.

'Could you describe the gunman?' one of the Special Branch men asked gently.

I gulped. 'Yes, I think so.'

'Well? What did he look like?'

'He was very young (sob) and scrawny (double sob) with long blond hair (sniff) and acne,' – tearful outburst.

'There, you're all right, love,' he said, 'you're doing fine. Just take your time now.'

I took my time. It took them an hour to get it all out of me. Every now and again my mind would wander.

'Mammy, I don't want to go to Marie's wedding.'

'Ach don't say that, love. You'll feel better in the morning.'

'No I won't.' I felt life would never be normal again.

'Of course you will. It'll do you good. It'll take your mind off it. And Eileen's depending on you to be there.'

'Are you sure the car was two-toned, Annie?'

'Yes, the roof was lighter than the body . . . I'll have to take this down,' I blushed senselessly.

'Take what down?'

'This stupid hair.'

The detective paused, waited for me to collect my thoughts and hairpins. I was now yawning profoundly.

'Annie, would you be able to identify the gunman if you saw him?'

'Identify him?'

'Yes, pick him out of a line-up or recognise him from photos.'

'No, no, I'm sure I wouldn't.'

'But you've given us a very good description of the man. You seem to have got a good look at him.'

'Yes, I remember all the different bits clearly enough, I just haven't got a very good picture of how it all fitted together.'

The detectives exchanged glances.

'I think that'll be enough for tonight, Annie. Thanks very much for that. We'll be back at some stage to clarify a few points. If you think of anything else in the meantime you can give us a ring.'

They were lovely men. But we never saw them again. I presume the case didn't warrant much manpower. There was, after all, nothing to it. A perfectly executed, perfectly average, indiscriminate sectarian killing. The victim a Ballymurphy man. No harm done there. No shortage of men in Ballymurphy, and the half of them on the boru anyway.

Father locked the door behind them, erected the usual boobytraps around the house, mechanical and electronic. Forty thousand volts for anyone foolish enough to come to the back door. I went to bed, but could not sleep. Father sat up most of the night, listening to the police messages on his squadron of radios, all lined up along the dressing table, Mother's perfumes and jewellery box and holy pictures and knick-knacks shoved off the one side. About two o'clock there was a brief exchange between a mobile unit and the Lisburn Road barracks. A vehicle answering the description of the getaway car had been stopped on the Donegal Road. The two male occupants were held for some time and then released.

'The fools, the fools, the fools!' said Father quoting from Padraig Pearse's oration over the grave of O'Donovan Rossa, 'they have left us our Fenian dead. And while Ireland holds these graves, Ireland unfree shall never be at peace!'

'Shush,' said I, 'do you want Mammy to hear you?' It wouldn't remind Mother of Pearse of the skelly eye, but of

Mrs French ranting at the Brits. We never spoke now of Mrs French, or of Bunbeg or of the Peace Group.

The following day we heard that Jimmy Carson's father, on being told of his son's death, suffered a massive heart-attack. He died in the Royal that afternoon. After that his doubly bereaved wife Martha had a nervous breakdown and was ill for many months.

Some months later I received word that I would be expected to give evidence at the murder inquest. At the time I thought it might be quite interesting. All wigs and gowns, depositions and cross-examinations. If they tried to do a whitewash I could, in the classic Republican tradition, refuse to recognise the court. I refuse to recognise the court. I fail to recognise the court. I fail to recognise the jurisdiction of this court on the sovereign soil of Ireland. But then Mother would massacre me. We'd all be under suspicion. Father and Thomas and Brendan would be lifted, maybe beaten up. Thomas would blame me if he lost any teeth. Brendan's head was always splitting open. He couldn't afford to have it split open again. The three of them might even be interned. The boys wouldn't be able to finish their education, which would be even worse than their having their mouths and heads kicked in. They would end up in Long Kesh, making Celtic crosses and tooled leather wallets. We would have to bring up food parcels every week and endure intimate searches. But Father couldn't eat Long Kesh food even if it were politically acceptable; his ulcer would burst in H-block. He would die on the way to the Royal. They would not release his body for burial. And it would all be my fault. Maybe I would at least pretend to recognise the court.

But my parents worried that the inquest might have a very unsettling effect on me, coming as it would shortly before my A-level exams. They were even more disturbed when we received a message via a friend to say that Jimmy Carson's mother wanted to meet me before the inquest. It appeared the poor woman wanted to see me because I was with her son in his dying moments.

'She wants to thank you,' said Mrs Magee, a mutual acquaintance.

'But I didn't do anything. I couldn't.'

'But you ran out to him. Nobody else did.'

'Nobody else heard the shooting.'

'But you were with him when he died.'

'Yeah, but he didn't know that. Fat lot of good I did him.'

'You were there.'

Father's presence was also requested. He had said the Act of Contrition in the absence of a priest. A sacred duty fulfilled. Jimmy's place in heaven had therefore been guaranteed. Father would have to come with me. And Mother. She had been so good to wee Josephine and her mother. I thought it wouldn't be so bad. Anyway it would be a break from study. Mother took it more seriously. We would all have to look presentable, she decided. It would be just like visiting a dead house. Father must wear his funeral suit, it was by far his best outfit. He did not, however, seem keen to don the sober black number. By the time he had struggled into it on the appointed evening he remembered why he never wore it – the zip of the trousers kept coming undone. He kept forgetting to ask Mother to fix it.

'I can't go,' he announced with satisfaction, 'I'll drive the two of you and wait in the car, or come back maybe.'

'Oh no! Not a bit of you! You're going in with us. That poor wee woman wants to meet you. Now come over here with that zip. I'll soon get it closed.' She was as good as her word. 'Now don't be going to the toilet and you'll be all right. Don't drink too much tea.'

'Jaysus!' Father blasphemed, rolling his eyes. 'This is going to be a night and a half!' Muttering foul language and other curses he got into the car and we headed for Ballymurphy.

Slieveban Crescent was alive with children and bicycles and mongrels. The pitted road was splashed with paint-bombs and scattered with broken glass, the leavings of spent petrol-bombs. The house was the usual white pebble-dash, semi-detached with an unkempt front garden and ugly concrete porch. The front door was open and from the commotion inside we could tell that the house was full. We had heard that Mrs Carson was in such a bad way she could not be left alone for any length of time. So the neighbours rallied round and the place tended to be like a halfway house.

Mother set foot in the hallway and cried out, 'Anybody in?'

Father was busy checking his zip.

We were led into the living room by a pleasant, fat-faced woman who introduced herself as Nancy-over-the-road. The room was packed, as if for a party. Mrs Carson sat by the fire at the centre of the collective concern, her neighbours, friends and relatives grouped about her in support. She looked thoroughly worn and haggard. She had obviously 'let herself go'. Her grey hair hung long and dragged around the small wizened face. She was not fit to stand up, but she looked eagerly across the room and focused on me. She motioned me to come over to her and put her feeble arms out to hug me. I bent down awkwardly and allowed her to clasp me to her as she rocked back and forth in greeting.

'God love you, daughter. God love you for you're a good wee girl.' She was moaning and sobbing. I didn't know whether to feel more touched or embarrassed by the display. It struck me as unfortunate. I wished she'd stop. A swift glance at Father told me that he shared my discomfort. He had been settled on the big sofa between two garrulous, wide-hipped women who had decided to entertain him. Mother meanwhile nodded encouragement at

me. It was Big Nancy who finally came to the rescue. She
took me by the arm and led me to a chair at the other side
of the fire. Mrs Carson was still sobbing in anguish. It was
a bloody awful scene. Everyone was trying to quieten her.
They had all been through this before. All except us and
we were failing to warm to the situation.

'Maybe it's better to let her get it all out of her system,'
Mother suggested more tentatively.

This was more than one little woman could bear. 'Look,
missus, she's been like this every night for months and she
still hasn't got it out of her system. We daren't leave her
on her own, not for a minute, for fear of what she'd do to
herself. Sure, she hasn't slept in weeks. She's on four
different colours of sedatives. God love her. Her heart's
broke.'

Mrs Carson finally managed to compose herself enough
for the bawling to drop to the level of a low whine. The
conversation took a more banal turn. Unemployment, the
rent strike, the cost of electricity, the price of coal, and
weren't the army bastards? Eventually some soul asked
about my schooling. Mother was delighted to explain. She
launched into a catalogue of my incredible achievements.
Everything and more. Cups I had won, nice things people
had said about me, debates where I had dazzled with my
wit and knowledge, exams I had excelled at, awards I had
won ... Mother's memory was surpassed only by her
imagination. I was concentrating on picking the balls off
my school jumper, but I could not totally shut out the
litany.

'Oh she was marvellous that night ... the youngest ever
in Northern Ireland ... he said she wiped the floor with
the other girls ... the nuns were thrilled ...'

Father was staring at the ceiling, his head set at the angle
of a martyred saint I recalled from a holy picture in Clonard
vestry: St Sebastian, patron saint of archers or something.
Father clandestinely checked his watch. He would have
been thinking that he had just missed the nine o'clock

news. By the time Mother paused for a quick breath I knew that everyone in the room was sick hearing about me. I kept my head down and lined the brown woollen balls along the arm of the chair.

Happily Nancy saw her chance and broke in. 'Would yez take a wee cup of tea, Mrs McPhelimy?'

'Of course they would,' said our hostess, 'don't even ask.' Tea was served.

But even as the scones and ham sandwiches and Marie biscuits were passed around Mrs Carson started up again.

'It's the wee things that get her going, love,' whispered Nancy by way of explanation.

Mrs Carson was remembering the night of Jimmy's murder. She spoke softly, her voice broken with sobs. Jimmy and his wife lived in a house a few doors down from Mr and Mrs Carson. That night they had gone to visit Josephine's sister at Musgrave Park hospital. She had just had a baby. Mrs Drain went with them. They were expected home about eight o'clock. When they had not returned at ten the Carsons became anxious. At that time it was inadvisable to wander around Belfast in the evenings. Things have not improved greatly on that score.

'There isn't a light on in the house,' Mr Carson had commented. 'Where can they be at this time?'

He had put on his coat and walked up to the bus terminus at the Whiterock Road. There was no sign of them. He returned to the house and it was shortly after that they heard the news flash. A shooting incident at the Craigavad Road roundabout. Police were treating it as a random sectarian shooting. One man was believed to be dead.

'We knew immediately,' Mrs Carson insisted, 'I swear to God we just knew. We knew it was Jimmy.'

I didn't doubt her for a minute. She had broken down again. Nancy gave her a sedative and poured out a fresh cup of tea. But already Mrs Carson was wiping her eyes and taking up the story again, going over and over the same sad details.

'His father just crumpled up and said, "Oh my God, it's our Jimmy." I said to him, "God forgive you, you don't know that." I was only trying to calm him. But he knew bloody rightly. I sensed it. I'd been that worried all night. There was no lights on at Jimmy's and he always left a light on when they went out. In case they'd get broken into.'

By now most of the women in the room were nattering among themselves. One or two tried to change the subject, but the poor little weed of a woman went on endlessly as the rest of us drank tea or crunched the fig-rolls forced on us by Big Nancy. I wanted to get out of there, to go home. I glanced at Mother. She was dutifully, painfully following Mrs Carson's narrative. I looked over at Father. He, goat-like, was reaching the end of a rather frayed tether.

The only man in the house that night, he had made a great impression on the women. They were falling over one another to warm up his tea and fill his plate. He made eyes towards the door, but we both knew it was up to Mother to make the first move. Her prerogative as woman of the house. We neither of us would have the authority to lead the escape.

At that point Mrs Carson became agitated. She was suddenly struggling to get out of her chair and yelling at me, 'You were the only one, love. The only one came near him when he was lying dying. You did what you could for him, God love you. You're a good wee girl. Christ help my poor Jimmy, he never done nobody any harm. God love him, he was a good child. You should have seen him in his Confirmation suit. It'd break your heart. And the bastards killed him. God forgive them, for I can't.' She had managed to get to her feet and was making for my chair. It was very odd, but I found myself trembling. The women were trying to hold her back, but she pushed them away and rushed over to me. She threw herself down on her knees in front of me and began rocking to and fro, crying and bawling the whole time, 'He was only twenty-two, not even a year married. He never even saw his own baby. And his wife never comes to see me now. They said I upset her. They won't let her come to see me at all.'

I was trying to control the rush of feeling that swamped me. My head suddenly felt hot and sore. My eyes were filling up. The tears would have to come out, there was already too much pressure on the sinus cavities. I realised I was holding the little woman fast against me. As if she were a child. I was feebly patting her head as the tears burst their banks and coursed stingingly down my cheeks, over my Mohan chin and down the front of my neck. I was sobbing hard now, my chest and shoulders jerking painfully with each sob. I was mortified to hear myself crying out loud.

It was at that point, as I raised my grotesquely swollen face over the head of the hysterical woman, that I caught sight of Father at the pinnacle of his discomfort. He was perched unnaturally on the edge of his cushion, rather squashed because of the two women flanking him. They appeared to have spread sideways in the course of the evening. He was trying to balance a china cup full of tea in one of his big hands. With the other he was trying to use his plate to mask the fact that the zip of his funeral trousers had finally given way, exposing the stark white of his Y-fronts against the background of black gabardine.

He caught my eye as he made discreet efforts to juggle cup, crumb-covered plate and zip. His despair was mild compared to my own at that moment, but he quickly realised that I had noted his predicament. A wry, hopeless smile twisted his mouth as he fiercely sucked in his cheeks to keep from laughing outright. I felt the tension leaving me. We would be going soon. I would have to position myself in front of Father so that we might escape with some shreds of decency and without mortifying Mother. I eased Mrs Carson back into her seat and tried to focus on

Father's dilemma. I knew Jimmy would hardly mind. We effected our exit with relative decorum.

I never saw Mrs Carson after that night. She was not well enough to attend the inquest. The coroner wasted little time and returned an open verdict. Some time later I heard that Mrs Carson had partially recovered and was well enough to resume her job at the holy shop next to St Peter's. I thought of her only rarely then.

The night before my wedding, in the midst of the turmoil of uncooperative hair and drooping petticoats, a friend brought me a present from Martha Carson: a set of mother-of-pearl rosary beads. I had given up saying the decades of the rosary at the age of fifteen. By that time I had accumulated over two thousand years of plenary indulgence, enough to do me my day. So much for Martin Luther. And I estimated that I could sin safely for the greater part of my adult life and still do only a brief stint in Purgatory. But a rosary is a lovely thing to have, to dangle and to finger. A lovely thing to have.

26

Bogged

(handwritten: -no change, progress - cycle of viol continues)

(handwritten: -2 real events)

My life is now nearing its autumn beauty, and still the pangs of Ulster rage. The BBC reports:

'Today two British soldiers were murdered in horrific scenes of mob violence. The soldiers were killed during the funeral of one of the three people shot dead in the Milltown cemetery last Wednesday. We should warn you that certain scenes in our report may cause distress to some viewers.'

Andytown Road. Hales fruit shop, the Gem, the Spar supermarket. Just up from Deveny's. I thought of Mr Deveny at the window, behind his standard roses.

'The confrontation resulted when the soldiers, who were in civilian clothes, mistakenly drove into the funeral cortège.'

The funeral march, a decent turnout, advancing with dignity. Off in the background something develops. Young men break away from the cortège, alerted by some indiscreet movement of the soldiers', who stick out an Irish mile with their close haircuts and foreign faces. They move quickly towards the car stopped in the service road outside the Spar. The camera zooms in anticipation. The two men in the car are already alarmed.

'About two thousand mourners scattered in terror, fearing another Protestant attack, such as that which took place at Milltown cemetery just a few days ago, when the soldiers' blue Volkswagen sped towards them.'

The driver checks behind, shifts gear and reverses at high speed, scattering all in rear of him, out onto the main road. He swerves, drives forwards, towards the funeral party.

The mourners tense, but the car backs away at speed down the Andersonstown Road, in front of Casement Park. But the centre of the road is quickly blocked by a black taxi. The Volkswagen brakes, skids a bit. The driver regains control, looks around. Still remarkable presence of mind. We see him thinking. A quick U-turn, escape between the taxi and the park railings. The car moves forward. But another taxi drives up blocking the way, and yet another cuts off the escape route on the left. Boxed in, banjaxed. The taxi driver directly in front leisurely descends from his vehicle. Draws on a cigarette, strolls towards the Volkswagen.

Behind him a group of young fellas are charging down the road. They've almost reached the Volkswagen. The driver hesitates, opens the door and produces a gun. A fatal mistake. He shoots once, maybe a warning. He's leaning on the open door, aiming the gun, threatening, uncertain. Another Milltown.

Another camera angle. From the other side of the road, behind the soldier. We see what he sees. The hordes advancing. We feel what he feels. The obscenity of fear. The surety that there will be no way out this time. As he levels the gun someone jumps, disarming him from behind, forcing him down between the car and the open door, battering vigorously. The assailant blocks our view.

'Sources said the soldiers apparently panicked when they were challenged by Sinn Fein stewards supervising the funeral and tried to drive away. Their bodies were found later on waste ground behind a supermarket. They had been stripped, badly beaten and shot in the head. Statements deploring the murders have come from all sections of the community. Mrs Thatcher says she will not rest until the perpetrators of this horrific deed have been brought to justice.'

*

The BBC had scooped the story again – the traitorous extradition of an IRA man from the Free State into the hands of the RUC.

'Once again riots broke out in Northern Ireland today as prison escapee and leading Republican Francis Fallon was extradited across the border by the government of the Irish Republic.

'Fallon was handed over to the Royal Ulster Constabulary and the British army at dawn in an effort to outwit Republican sympathisers who were planning demonstrations at all main border crossings.'

There follows an on-the-scene report from our man in Armagh. An Irish hillside at dawn. RUC men, soldiers and purposeful men in parkas mill around, grim with tension. The reporter is all but swept off his feet by the high winds, and behind him, on the crest of the hill, a British army helicopter drowns out his words. A car pulls up, not far from the helicopter and a skirmish breaks out as several big Free Staters attempt to remove Fallon from the car and hand him over to his British jailers. But Fallon, whose sandy head can be seen thrashing from side to side amid the humps of blue and bottle green parka, will not go gently into that dark dawn. If he can't escape he will at least ensure top-quality news coverage of the outrage. He is yelling, 'Free State traitors!' as they grab him, limb by limb, and lift him out of the car. But he will not make it easy for them. With a great arching jerk of his back he wrests his legs free and kicks out, deftly sinking the boot in one man's side. The pair in charge of his arms struggle to hold him. And now the northerners advance, to take him into custody. 'No.' He defies them as they approach sideways. He lashes out, seemingly with all four limbs at once. The joint forces of the Garda Siochana and the Royal Ulster Constabulary are hard put to contain Mr Fallon. And they do not subdue him. The cameraman has got directly in front of him now as they begin to half-trail, half-carry him backwards into the helicopter. Even as he writhes and thrashes Fallon looks full into the camera, breaks the Thatcher ban on IRA interviews.

'Up the IRA!' he yells with gusto, not ceasing in his struggles with the men now dragging him along the ground. They have pulled his jumper up over his head. He digs his heels into the soft green turf. '*Tiocfidh ar la*!' he declares, getting his head free, 'Our day will come!' he translates obligingly.

A huge plainclothes policeman tries to silence him by clapping a thick, Protestant hand over his mouth. But Fallon twists and bites the hand that holds him, shouting even louder, '*Tiocfidh ar la*! Up the IRA! Brits out!'

In the end the combined forces of North, South and the empire are too much for one slight man. They lift him kicking into the helicopter, uniformed arms reach down to grab him. His legs are still flailing wildly as they disappear into the cabin. The helicopter takes off immediately. Yet even over the drone of its engines, the whirr of the propellers, the howl of the wind, we can hear Fallon screaming in defiance, '*Tiocfidh ar la*! Our day will come!'

Today I saw the photo in the paper. One dead soldier and Father Regan. They are flanked on the page by El General Pinochet, and Fergie in a pink ski-suit. A killing image. He's lying sprawled and bloody like a crucifixion, his chest red with blood, and more blood pouring from the head wound, running into surrounding puddles. A bit of Andersonstown that will be forever England.

He's wearing only trunks and a pair of short white socks. The sock-soles are black with muck and oil and rain. Footshape stained, a final imprint, his last stocking-soled stand. A bad place to die, the mucky, patchy tarmac of the waste ground, a mundane spot behind the Spar supermarket, Hales Choice Fruits, the Golden Grove fish and chips, beside the ex-servicemen's club where I would go with Hilda to sit on orange boxes and torn plastic chairs, waiting for someone to ask us to dance. It never happened. And now here's that grim patch of ground starring in award-winning photographs of dead bodies and ministering priests. — Sarcastic, ironic

It's Father Regan, who didn't mind my marrying a heathen, didn't insist that the children be brought up Catholics. He is kneeling in the wet, anointing dead eyes, the chrism kept handy for murders and other sudden deaths. He would have whispered the Act of Contrition, all the comfort he could give. Oh my God, I am very sorry for having sinned against you, because you are so good; and with the help of your grace I will never sin again. No way.

Some woman, somewhere, as the wee woman would say, will be breaking her heart for him tonight. A wife or mother or sister, or all three, empty at the loss of his sweetness, heartsick at the thought of him dying in fear among strangers, destroyed at the idea of them laying hands on him, of them tearing him apart, a mindless mob, hardly human the half of them. And on the other side of the Irish Sea a thousand Irish mothers will be lying staring into the dark, mouthing the memorare: Remember oh most compassionate Virgin Mary ... Thinking of their bright, handsome sons riddled to bits under Ulster skies; in bleak, discorded slums, or on empty country roads.

And Jimmy Carson's demented mother will be mourning still, and faceless, eyeless Mrs Nolan, and young Lionel Thurston, the cockney with the red hole in his belly, will be suffering the fleshy consequences of an acceptable level of violence. The damaged and those who love them, heartsick and helpless. Always the women that suffer. The ancient pangs of Ulster visited and revisited upon them. No generation escapes.

'Somebody loves him,' she would say, for Provo, or Stickie, or soldier, or RUC man, 'the mother that bore him. Nothing's worth a life. When I think of the trouble and suffering that goes into bearing them and rearing them. The worry and the heartbreak ... Brendan was ten pounds

ten ounces. He was almost three weeks overdue. I was near
dead.'

Her rambling, and the rest of us egging them on. For the
cause, for queen and country, for peace, with justice or at
any price. For there will be no surrender, fuck pope and
queen both the same. Sons, sisters, fathers, daughters,
husbands and brothers will not be grudged, though they go
out to break their strength and die. We will not give an
inch and shall not be moved, till the last drops of blood,
orange and green, run down the street, through our four
green fields, one of them in bondage, to mingle with the
rivers of ceaseless rain, seep into the brown sucking bog,
and piss, peacefully at last, out into Belfast Lough, in the
wake of the Titanic.

- N.I. - like
- doomed society/culture
  - 1 way voyage to bottom
- Costello - left Titanic

Glossary of Irish Terms

All her orders	Everything she could possibly want.
Banjaxed	In a fix.
Baste	Literally 'beast'; a 'bad baste' is a villain.
Bean Sidhe	Banshee, a wailing ghost.
Boru	The dole (possibly a Belfast pronunciation of 'bureau', from 'unemployment bureau').
Chassis	Chaos.
Comeallyez	Traditional ballad or rebel song.
Dulse and yellowman	Edible seaweed, sold in paper bags, and yellow candy. Both are sold at the annual Lammas Fair in Ballycastle.
Free State	Former name of the Republic of Ireland.
The goes of	The antics of.
Hoak	To search and poke around for something.
Hold your wisht	Be quiet, shut up.
Not that he licks it off the grass	It's not an acquired trait, but something he was born with.
Quare	'Odd', 'great', 'unique' or 'very'.
Seanachie	Travelling storyteller.
Shebeens	Illegal drinking establishments.
Stumer	Fool, idiot.
Targe	A nagging woman.
Throughother	Slatternly, slovenly.